The Spectacle of Intimacy

_____

LITERATURE IN HISTORY

SERIES EDITORS

David Bromwich, James Chandler, and Lionel Gossman

The books in this series study literary works in the context of the
intellectual conditions, social movements, and patterns
of action in which they took shape.

Other books in the series:

Lawrence Rothfield, *Vital Signs: Medical Realism
in Nineteenth-Century Fiction*

David Quint, *Epic and Empire: Politics and Generic
Form from Virgil to Milton*

Alexander Welsh, *The Hero of the Waverly Novels*

Susan Dunn, *The Deaths of Louis XVI: Regicide and
the French Political Imagination*

Sharon Achinstein, *Milton and the Revolutionary Reader*

Esther Schor, *Bearing the Dead: The British Culture of Mourning
from the Enlightenment to Victoria*

Elizabeth K. Helsinger, *Rural Scenes and National Representation:
Britain, 1815–1850*

Katie Trumpener, *Bardic Nationalism: The Romantic Novel
and the British Empire*

The Spectacle of Intimacy

A PUBLIC LIFE FOR THE VICTORIAN FAMILY

Karen Chase and Michael Levenson

PRINCETON UNIVERSITY PRESS

PRINCETON AND OXFORD

Library of Congress Cataloging-in-Publication Data

Chase, Karen, 1952-
The spectacle of intimacy: a public life for the Victorian family /
Karen Chase and Michael Levenson.
p.   cm.   (Literature in history)
Includes bibliographical references and index.
ISBN 0-691-00668-7 (cloth: alk. paper)
1. English literature—19th century—History and criticism. 2. Home in literature.
3. Literature and history—Great Britain—History—19th century. 4. Public opinion—
Great Britain—History—19th century. 5. Privacy—Great Britain—History—19th century.
6. Family—Great Britain—History—19th century. 7. Great Britain—History—Victoria,
1837–1901. 8. Family in literature. I. Levenson, Michael H. (Michael Harry), 1951- II.
Title. III. Literature in history (Princeton, N.J.)
PR468.H63 C48 2000
823′.809355—dc21   99-058479

This book has been composed in Times Roman

The paper used in this publication meets the minimum requirements
of ANSI/NISO Z39.48-1992 (R1997) (*Permanence of Paper*)

www.pup.princeton.edu

Printed in the United States of America

1 3 5 7 9 10 8 6 4 2

For Alex and Sarah

Two More Chase-Levensons

CONTENTS

PART FIVE: *The Sensations of Respectability*

ILLUSTRATIONS

ACKNOWLEDGMENTS

MUCH OF THE RESEARCH for *The Spectacle of Intimacy* involved peering into small cracks and looking beneath heavy stones. We would have been lost in the shadows, were it not for marvelous help from archivists, curators, and librarians at the British Library, the Institute for Historical Research, King's College Archive, the Public Record Office, the Guildhall Hall Library, the Florence Nightingale Museum, the library of the Royal Institute of British Architecture, and the local libraries in Camden and Westminster. Our graduate students at the University of Virginia were the first to hear these ideas, and to their everlasting credit they didn't sit still. They tested and queried, teased and pondered; *The Spectacle of Intimacy* would not have happened without them. David Bromwich and James Chandler gave stimulus and resolve to our writing, offering encouragement and advice when we needed to hear them. Margaret Homans and Adrienne Munich provided a hospitable early home for our work on Queen Victoria, which first appeared in their coedited volume *Remaking Queen Victoria*. Herbert Tucker, who always widens the nineteenth-century horizon, was a canny editor for our study of Victorian walls, an initial version of which appeared in his *Companion to Victorian Literature and Culture*. Here at the University of Virginia, we chatter amiably with many people who stir us into new thought, among them Stephen Cushman, Jessica Feldman, and Mark Edmundson; Jerome McGann, Jahan Ramazani, and Caroline Rody; Patricia Spacks and Anthony Winner. Gordon Braden has been a great and understanding department chair, but he is an even better friend. Barbara Smith, the indispensable, has seen us through tight places. James Eli Adams and Robert Polhemus were wonderful readers of the typescript, keen and attentive, offering the insight that can only come from generosity. We thank the University of Virginia for the sabbatical leave that made this book possible.

The Spectacle of Intimacy

THE TROUBLE WITH FAMILIES

1

I cannot take leave of the subject without a remark on English
dwelling-houses, which stand in close connection with that
long-cherished principle of separation and retirement, lying at
the very foundation of the national character. It appears to me,
to be this principle which has given to the people that fixity
of national character, and strict adherence to the historical
usages of their country, by which they are so much distinguished;
and up to the present moment, the Englishman still perseveres in
striving after a certain individuality and personal independence, a
certain separation of himself from others, which constitutes
the foundation of his freedom. . . . [It] is this that gives the
Englishman that proud feeling of personal independence, which
is stereotyped in the phrase, "Every man's house is his castle."
This is a feeling which cannot be entertained, and an expression
which cannot be used in Germany or France, where ten or fifteen
families often live in the same large house. . . . In England,
every man is master of his hall, stairs, and chambers—whilst
we are obliged to use the two first in common with others,
and are scarcely able to secure ourselves the privacy of our own
chamber, if we are not fortunate to be able to obtain a secure
and convenient house for ourselves alone.[1]

The preceding, written by the physician to the king of Saxony, Dr. Carus,
appears at still greater length in the introductory pages to the census report of
1851, where the voice of rotund officialdom delivered its views on the Victorian family. Carus's entirely conventional opinions could not have been more
reassuring, or their Saxon origins more agreeable. For under the bland tones
of the report can be detected an eager desire for domesticity and nationality to
cleave together—and then what could be more pleasant than to have the proud
native character confirmed through the testimony of the Saxon foreigner? The
tribute seems to have roused the rhetorical passions of the registrar-general,
who will immediately affirm in his own voice that "the possession of an entire
house is, it is true, strongly desired by every Englishman; for it throws a sharp,

well-defined circle round his family and hearth—the shrine of his sorrows, joys, and meditations."[2]

The ambitions of the statistical harvest of the 1851 census were great: here was to be an enumeration that in its detail, its precision, and its scope corresponded to the fast-arriving modernity of the epoch. We now accept this census as the beginning of a new, more advanced form of inquiry; everywhere in the documents themselves are signs of a strongly willed historical maturity.[3] In the proud consciousness of achievement, the expository passages take on the slow, heavy tones of discursive authority. Nowhere is this more evident than in the discourse on "Families and Houses." Because the charge of the 1851 census was to count not only people but people in households, everything turned on the studious labor of definition. The controlling insight, plausible only on its face, was that a family was at once a spatial and a social unit, according to the principle that it is "so much in the order of nature that a family should live in a separate house that 'house' is often used for family in many languages" (*Census*, xxxv). Here, as elsewhere, what is true in general is considered even truer in England. But what was a family? What was a house? As the report frankly indicated, these were not easy, idle, or theoretical questions: upon their answer hung decisions on such fundamental matters as taxes and voting rights. Then, beyond the legal urgency, there stood the axiomatics of collective life, according to which

> The first, most intimate, and perhaps most important community, is the FAMILY, not considered as the children of one parent, but as the persons under one head; who is the occupier of the house, the householder, master, husband, or father; while the other members of the family are the wife, children, servants, relatives, visitors, and persons constantly or accidentally in the house. The head of the family supports and rules the family, —occupies the house. "Family," in the sense which it has acquired in England, may be considered the *social unit* of which parishes, towns, counties, and the nation, are composed. (xxxiv)

This picture of the household as social pyramid—a complex of relations, by no means all biological, that receive their coherence only from the form-giving power of "householder, master, husband, or father"—is not merely a concise sketch of patriarchal domesticity; it is also a rule of methodology. The great count on that Sunday in March required the army of enumerators to go in search of households constituted by the formal sovereignty of the master. The exemplary image was that of a father, as owner or rent payer, presiding over kin, servants, lodgers, and visitors, and enjoying "the exclusive command of the entrance-hall and stairs—and the possession of the free space between the ground and sky" (xxxvii). This titular head of household, whatever else he might achieve, creates the longed-for statistical epitome: the countable community.

What the report identifies as the desire of every Englishman—that "sharp, well-defined circle round his family and hearth"—was clearly a desire of its own. But what makes the census of 1851 anything but dry and wooden is that, even as it shares the dreams of the circumambient culture, with all the talk of "shrines" and "command" and "Englishness," it understands the presence of anomalies that will not be thought away. Immediately after affirming the normative character of the male-headed domestic circle, which may include servants and visitors around the biological nucleus, the report concedes that not every family fits this "essential sense" of the term: a family, after all, "may consist only of a widower, children, and servants, or a bachelor and servants; or finally, of a single woman occupying a small cottage" (xxxiv). But in the act of making this concession, the registrar-general comes to the verge of a metaphysical, or at least terminological, abyss: "Can a single person constitute a family, and thus 'be head and members at once'?" This question incites others: "Can a single family constitute a 'town'?" and "Can a single town constitute a state?" (xxxv). Here, where confusion beckons, the census can only doggedly repeat what the enabling act of Parliament prescribed: that the concept of the family has been absorbed in the concept of "occupier." Any resident owner, or any rent payer, including a single lodger, qualifies as occupier, and if this leads to the awkwardness of identifying a lone bachelor or widow "as the representative and equivalent of a distinct family," one can only mutter and carry on. The registrar-general grumbles audibly but tallies his figures.

The anxiety of definition emanates from a social instability. That resonant image, in which the "head of the family supports and rules the family, — occupies the house," had become a much-voiced standard, but no one, least of all the enumerators of the census, could doubt that violations of the rule abounded. Apart from the single woman in her cottage, there were the urban poor, especially the Irish, crowding fifty or sixty at a time into rooms no larger than 22 by 16 feet. Then there were the Scots. Living in flats, the typical city dweller in Scotland had all the advantages of the English householder, except for that exclusive control of entrance hall and stairs. But officialdom determined to treat self-contained Scottish flats like English rooms and chambers, an adjustment made "in order to secure uniformity in the returns" (xxxviii). Even so, the registrar-general admits that uniformity was an unrealized methodological ideal, if only because the intractable diversity often baffled the efforts of the enumerators and because any attempt to correct the many discrepancies "would be futile" (xxxv).

We begin with the struggles of the 1851 census to fix a definition of "families and houses" because this muffled disturbance is not only revealing in its own terms; it also serves as a figure for the social wound that brings our study into being: the public extension of a normative domesticity that then confronts, and indeed generates, trouble in paradise. No one can disagree with John

Burnett's assertion that the mid-Victorians were the most "family-conscious and home-centred" society in English history.[4] But the home centrality of the period was in every aspect shadowed by contradiction, resistance, refusal, and bewilderment.

Partly, the problem was that of an ambitious ideology that aspired to a universality or, in the terms of the census, a "uniformity," which was beyond its historical reach. We know that the domestic ideal was the special moral mission of the middle classes, who were in a position to circulate the good news, without being able to secure its acceptance. The failure of the working classes and the poor to heed the lesson was one consuming preoccupation; the indifference of the gentry and aristocracy was another. The middle-class ability to promulgate a credo was frustrated by failures to recruit other classes to its banner.

Quite as important, however, are the difficulties that the emergent ideal makes for itself—or, rather, makes for its living partisans. Here it is not a matter of an ideological reach that exceeds a social grasp; it is matter of internal tensions, self-contradictions, and new contingencies, which reveal the "essential sense" as a rigidity overlaying a moving ground. To see the mottoes of midcentury family life as expressing a stable orthodoxy is to surrender to a mystification.

Our work is a discontinuous history, and this because the public life of Victorian domesticity unfolded as a series of interruptions. The period of our concern, the three decades between 1835 and 1865, makes a fairly short span, but it witnessed rapid change that unsettled every attempt to fix the essence of family. Politics, law, war, and sexuality, these and other pressures deranged the settlement of home. Through close engagement with separate episodes we mean to respect their cultural density, in the attempt to show how Victorian private life came to know itself in the stress of popular sensation.

2

Ambitious and influential accounts by Jürgen Habermas and Richard Sennett have narrated the robust emergence of a public sphere by the end of the eighteenth century.[5] For Habermas, the development of the bourgeoisie, the new opportunities for assembly and intellectual expression, the rise of self-consciously constituted social networks and groups, the establishment of a vigorous press, and the growth of freely shared spaces (parks, squares, coffeehouses) all led toward the creation of a "reasoning public," a realm of civil society distinct from the state.[6] Sennett emphasizes the importance of the urban metropolis, which not only increased economic exchange but also incited individuals to adopt modes of public performance as a way of giving order and ceremony to their complex condition. Crucially, both thinkers connect the rise of a self-conscious public sphere with the excavation of a more circumscribed and defined realm of privacy. To invent the open space of visible civic life was at the same time to forge its invisible, personal contrary. Habermas notes that by the end of the eighteenth century feudal authority "had broken apart into private elements on the one hand, and into public on the other." Sennett speaks of the emergent "balance of public and private geography."[7]

Our study encounters the undoing of that balance.[8] The nineteenth century saw both an enlarged zone of publicity and an intensifying of the private domain.[9] In the words of Georg Simmel, "what is public becomes ever more public, and what is private becomes ever more private," and Alexander Welsh, who cites that phrase, notes that "the conditions that have produced greater publicity have created the issue of privacy."[10] Welsh has offered a detailed account of the growth of information in the first half of the nineteenth century, showing how, in the midst of unrelenting publicity, secrets become precious commodities. The very distance between the two domains heightens the stakes when the boundary is crossed and a highly valued private life is exposed to furious public churning.

Within this context, the Victorian investment in family life unfolds in the awareness that at any moment it can turn into the antifamily of popular sensation. The great domestic epoch was at the same time the first great age of information. The flotilla of newspapers with the flagship *Times* brought the early conditions of a mediated society: the rapid circulation of event and opinion, and the competitive pursuit of knowledge as a commodity in the struggle between the barons of information. But while the domain of newspapers was visible and decisive, it was by no means the only agency of public opinion. From broadsides sold on the street to the eminent quarterly reviews, from pamphlets to parliamentary reporting, in poems, in novels, and on the stage, through paintings and cartoons, the age was awash in text, imagery, and insinuation.

In one respect the apparatus of publicity appeared as a surging outer world that threatened the peace of home. In the endless search for stories, the information producers plucked at the secrets of domesticity. Scandal was a perpetual resource, but so too were the ordinary incidents of daily housekeeping. A middle-class family secluding itself behind garden walls was exposed to tales of other seclusions behind adjacent walls. One of the abiding activities of midcentury life was the production of family tableaus, the ceaseless manufacture in text and image of scenes of home life, the publication of a privacy.

But to see the "public opinion of privacy" as only an invasion is to miss one of the leading features of the age: the extent to which domestic life itself was impelled toward acts of exposure and display. As in those moments of rhetorical quickening within the 1851 census, a pride in domestic achievement drove toward overt expression. So estimable, so complimentary to national character, the virtues of an English home should not hide their light in the parlor. The inspiring motives of early Dickens, especially the motives of the Christmas books of the early forties, were often to encourage national celebration of the triumphs of privacy. The congregation of families in their sacred separate spaces was identified as the paradoxical foundation of sociality. The delight in being happily apart offered itself as the basis of community.

3

In that same 1851, which is the midpoint in both the century and our study, the census year and the year of the Crystal Palace, there appeared several more homely contributions to the rhetoric of pleasure and pride: pamphlets, manuals, and small fictions, which accumulated in parlors and kitchens, leaving their own impress. In the sentimental novel *Home Is Home: A Domestic Tale* (1851), one Mr. Dalton comes to the end of his hardworking day.

> He opened the door which led from the shop, and closing it behind him, found himself in his most snug and comfortable of sitting rooms, where his pretty wife and fine curly headed boy of some three years old hailed his entrance with delight. A bright fire, tea ready, and the kettle sending forth its full puffs of steam, all announced that he had been for some time expected; and now his boy is on his knee; his wife prepares his toast, and he draws from his pocket the new number of Dickens' last work which is just come in: this is a charming surprise to Mrs. Dalton, she calls him a "dear good man," and they prepare for an hour of unmixed enjoyment, after a day of industry and careful attention to their respective duties.[11]

The picture is characteristic in every respect, its derivation from Dickens openly acknowledged. Yet, in important ways, the "derived" aspect of such texts is a decisive cultural index. Far from seeking novelty or obliquity, work after work looks to align itself with the familiar, the already read. Readers often met, and must have enjoyed, an aggressive pursuit of cliché, as if the delights of home depended precisely on the refusal of novelty. Even in Dickens's own reliance on recurrent tropes and formulae there can be seen the ritual of repetition that offers readers the eternal return of the same cozy topos in the same rhythms. It is scarcely too much to speak of a nirvana principle that beckons in the midst of industrial modernity and social dislocation. Only come home, home to tea and fire and baby, home to Dickens, and there will be the reduction of tension, the achievement of balance, the security of enclosure, all part of the connotative reach of "comfort."

In *David Copperfield*, which also belongs to this midcentury moment, there occurs a scene that might serve as a paradigm for this fantasy of household peace. David, having arrived at Yarmouth, joins the family circle of his old servant Peggotty in their house constructed out of a boat pitched along the shore. Peggotty is holding her old workbox with Saint Paul's on the cover and the same old wax candle for the winding of her thread.

To hear the wind getting up out at sea, to know that the fog was creeping over the desolate flat outside, and to look at the fire, and think that there was no house near but this one, and this one a boat, was like enchantment. Little Em'ly had overcome her shyness and was sitting by my side upon the lowest and least of the lockers, which was just large enough for us two, and just fitted into the chimney-corner. Mrs. Peggotty with the white apron, was knitting on the opposite side of the fire. Peggotty at her needlework, was as much at home with Saint Paul's and the bit of wax-candle, as if they had never known any other roof. Ham, who had been giving me my first lesson in all-fours, was trying to recollect a scheme of telling fortunes with the dirty cards, and was printing off fishy impressions of his thumb on all the cards he turned. Mr. Peggotty was smoking his pipe. I felt it was time for conversation and confidence.[12]

The passage is rich with imaginative investments that arrange themselves in the Dickensian domestic idyll: the image of a perfect civility at close quarters, of a single room, a continuous social zone in which servants and masters, parents and children, males and females gather, and where the many bodies and objects meet in a perfectly tidy, perfectly snug equilibrium. Here is the middle-class boy David at home in his servant's family circle—the barriers of class and sex disappearing within the snug confines of the cozy room—where no one infringes upon the dispositions of another. "Conversation and confidence" become signifiers of the utopic community, built on reciprocity, acknowledgment of difference, and free expression in a climate of trust. The description evokes the mystery of space: that we inhabit it together, that we share air, and that many bodies, each with a mind of its own, can pursue separate pursuits within the same walls. This is Dickens's Elysium of liberalism founded on the serenity of domestic comfort. Home is at once the good community protected from the wind of social change and also the figure for social redemption.

What Dickens often allows himself to imagine as a magical interior, where emotions and objects distribute themselves in a perfect poise, appears in many other texts as the hard-won achievement of a robustly laboring age. But neither he nor the author of *Home Is Home*, neither the physician to the king of Saxony nor the registrar-general, could disguise the fact that alongside private pleasure and national pride stood less confirming emotions such as fear, frustration, anger, and envy. In another work of 1851, *Home Truths for Home Peace, or "Muddle" Defeated* by M.B.H., the trial of modernity is depicted as a struggle between the beckoning promise of comfort and the eruption of household anarchy. By all rights, insists M.B.H., her readers should be living in the epoch of family bliss. Aglow with the light of the Crystal Palace in Hyde Park, the author depicts the midcentury moment as a triumph for domestic economy, which once struggled with scarcity but now can finally enjoy the abundance of mass production. The "great characteristic of the present age is the constant endeavour to improve and to increase the conveniences and amenities of daily life, and to bring them within the reach of classes and individuals, who, a century ago, were expected to rest satisfied with the bare necessities of existence." As soon as a need presses or a desire quickens, "art and science hold counsel on the subject of remedy and supply" and then "some mitigation or invention is immediately produced, and 'COMFORTS' appear in the windows of the smallest village-shop, or surround the hearth of the humblest cottage, of which palaces and castles were but lately destitute."[13] Once there was constraint; now there is plenitude. And yet this rich offering of technological modernity has failed to transform the family—a failure of human will beyond the reach of science. Despite the promise of abundance, all around us are signs of the old muddle, threatening to return the world to its ancient chaos. So M.B.H. conjures a scene of domestic catastrophe, found

> in houses and in families where all the labour and sorrow, —the getting up and washing up, —the mending and making, the cooking and baking, —the sweeping and rubbing, the cleaning and scrubbing, —the folding and scolding, the blacking and clacking, —the smashing and crashing, —the petting and fretting, —the sighing and crying, —the calling and bawling, —the falling and squalling, —were going on from morning till night; and, notwithstanding the united efforts of mistress, maids and children, thus indefatigably employed, nothing was clean, nothing was mended, nothing was made, nothing was ready; but everything was left in more dirt and disorder at the end of the day. (4)

The obsessive attention given to the participial nightmare becomes as familiar a scene of writing as the rendition of life before a teakettle. With such contrasting images of private life, readers were invited to ask, Which family is mine? The disjunction between visible norms and one's own invisible private life became a chronic source of worry. When Dickens in *A Tale of Two Cities* evokes "a great city by night" and solemnly considers "that every one of those darkly clustered houses encloses its own secret," he points toward the gap between the secrecy behind household walls and the domain of incessant published discussion, where, after all, his own novel belongs.[14] How to make private life worthy of the public discourse?—evidence is ample that this question was one of the consuming facts of Victorian family life.

The census itself should have a new category for "comfortable persons"— so holds M.B.H. in a satiric moment within her study of Muddle. Among all the other subdivisions in the count of the population, she proposes a category for those who have triumphed over domestic chaos. In *their* homes the fire blazes, the grates draw, the fenders are just the right height, and "One remarkable characteristic in the apartments of comfortable people is, that they always appear larger in proportion to their actual dimensions. . . . Somehow or other, the furniture of comfortable people always takes the least possible space and affords the greatest possible convenience" (Home Truths, 166). This "somehow" marks the domestic mysticism that floats through so much published writing at midcentury, including the work of Dickens: the rapt absorption in the uncanny household idyll. When M.B.H. tries to expound the mysticism and to teach why some homes thrive and others decay, she invokes Dickens as her guide, as the one who has shown that the dispositions of a family, even their "words and thoughts," have the power "to impress their character on the inanimate objects by which they are surrounded; so that possessions gradually acquire a sympathetic likeness to their possessors" (15). Why is it that in the age of modernity, when her readers can choose among the "endless varieties" for securing convenience, they are so often unhappy and overwrought? Her Dickensian answer is straightforward: "It is from *persons*, and not from *things*, that the *feeling* of comfort must arise" (159).

Here is the household idealism, the domestic voluntarism, that becomes such a leading trait of midcentury ideology. Amid the new material plenitude—the apparatus of comfort and convenience vividly displayed at the Great Exhibition—an instinctive response was to moralize every act of domestic agency. The new abundance must be met by the defiant moral assertion of families: home in relation to the commercial economy stood as the soul within the thoughtless body, and if the home/head could become a judiciously arranged interior, then it would never be defiled by dirty commerce. Persons would always triumph over things.

But the effect of this apotheosis of domestic personhood, performed so often in the 1850s and 1860s, was to bestow limitless responsibilities on home dwellers, especially on the wife-mother, who was expected to be the mistress of household matter. Could she really be that sweet enchantress? Who would teach her? The answer, of course, is that any number of self-assigned mentors offered instruction, promising that enchantment was only three chapters away. Apart from the taboos of the parental bedroom, nothing seemed beyond the reach of instruction. For instance, in the sketch "A Home Picture," the newly-wed Rosina sits by the fireside on the first night of her wedded bliss and turns to her husband George, "You must tell me when I do [wrong], for it is one of the duties of husbands and wives to be faithful to each other's faults. I do not mean that we should sit in judgment on each other's conduct, and act the censor, but endeavor, by all means, to improve each other's character, so that our mutual influence may be refining and elevating."[15] Rosina is the figure of the ideal citizen of the domestic republic, one who submits to the endlessness of instruction, convinced that the self can never see its most glaring errors, and yearning for the glories of personal improvement.

Under the pressure of the instructionist ideal, the experience of the day breaks into a succession of component actions—managing, visiting, hosting, educating, charming—each of which stands open to the eye of the self-assigned domestic professional, gleaming with criticism. But if the manuals eagerly evoke images of disaster (the kitchen unswept, the children untaught), the promise of instruction is that once its lessons are duly heeded, then it will be possible to skirt the precipice on the way to earthly paradise. The guiding assumption of the advice discourse is that the achievement of the comfortable home is available to all genteel readers willing to follow the how-to directives of the text.

4

What if one failed? What if comfort eluded the yearning wife? What if the husband trampled on the cozy bloom, the children shrieked, and the fire smoked? The *Saturday Review* was more frank than most when it acknowledged that, "We cannot at once keep alive family love and escape family troubles."[16] The history that we are tracing is a history of love and trouble, of the links between broad norms and conspicuous exceptions. During the thirty years of the middle century, a vast machinery—textual, visual, political, personal—installed standards of household behavior that became proud weapons of the middle classes in their struggle against those on either social flank. And yet persistently the standards were flouted. Adultery, divorce, bigamy, the cruelty of husbands, the flight of wives—these sensational anomalies were stitched into the fabric of authority. The norm needed and cultivated the disturbance. An eagerness to display home virtue fed an appetite for domestic failure. Sarah Ellis solemnly intoned a warning: "There are private histories belonging to every family, which, though they operate powerfully upon individual happiness, ought never to be named beyond the home-circle."[17] Yet the naming of private histories became one of the avocations of the age, and it gives us our subject: the spectacle of intimacy.

The concern of this study is with the thrusting outward of an inward turning, the eruption of family life into the light of unrelenting public discussion. Without doubt, this discussion was an energetic reaction to domestic failure; but part of what we mean to show is that even the complacency of self-delight participated in the spectacle. The pervasive cultural compulsion to publicize the virtues of the family, to stipulate the criteria of pleasure, to determine standards for private expenditure, for relations with servants and for the design of houses, meant that even the minutiae of daily life were swept into the public theater. After all, when Sarah Ellis warns against the mention of private secrets, she immediately stirs prurient curiosity.

In one of her early sketches for *The Court* magazine under the heading "Curious Customs in the County of Middlesex," Caroline Norton wrote a light satire on "Public Prints and Private Characters." Seen in the context of her after-history, it is an eerily prophetic little text. The newspapers' invasion of privacy is her subject: like Ellis she regrets the loss of the "delicacy that would conceal names—the indulgence that would spare feelings."[18] She could not have known her fate when, in reflecting on "newspaper oppression," she wrote that "Home is no longer a sanctuary, nor a private existence in a man's own power; the character of the mother of a family is about as safe as the life of a brooding dove from a hungry hawk who has spied her; the name of her child may be bandied about coupled with a coarse jest or a lying report" (204–5). When Norton's husband accused her of "criminal conversation" with Lord Melbourne, prime minister of Great Britain, she became the wretched proof of her breezy satire.

The nineteenth century did not invent the family or the thrill of opening its secret doors. The Victorians themselves were conscious of inheriting their obsessions: they looked back to the domestic poetry of Cowper, back to the scandals of the late Georges, back to Wollstonecraft, Bute, Wilkes. Beyond these eighteenth-century sources, they scanned all known history for intimations of their own family love and household trouble. And yet the conditions of mid-nineteenth-century English life—the sheer extent of the home fetish, the maturing apparatus of information (newspapers, journals, telegraph), the campaign for legal reform of the family (infant custody, divorce, married women's property), the self-consciousness of modernity—gave it a special claim on its own attention, and now give it a special claim on ours.

Even to list these diverse interests is to acknowledge the need for scholarly partnership. The present study grew out of the patient collaboration of its two authors, each knowing that they couldn't command the whole field alone, and also knowing well that their research would rely on a much larger collaborative context. During the past two decades, many scholars working within the disciplines of English and history have uncovered important materials, produced adventurous interpretations, and constructed new webs of literary and historical relationships. Among the contributions we acknowledge at the outset are the studies of family and class by Catherine Gallagher and Mary Poovey; the analyses of the household by Leonore Davidoff, Catherine Hall, and Elizabeth Langland; the architectural reconstructions of Mark Girouard; the account of respectability by F.M.L. Thompson; the revisionary narratives of Queen Victoria by Margaret Homans and Adrienne Munich; the demographic researches of Michael Anderson; the legal history of Mary Lyndon Shanley; and the history of transgression offered by William A. Cohen.[19] These precedents serve as a background, a framework, even a lattice for our own acts of historical recovery and cultural understanding.

5

The Spectacle of Intimacy begins with the cataclysm endured by Caroline Norton, as she was made to pass from the most elite alcoves of metropolitan society onto the harshly lit stage of scandal. The object of fascination and revilement during the adultery trial, she was also the active, canny writing subject, who under the stress of personal emergency invented a voice that let her challenge her husband, transform her fiction and poetry, and agitate successfully for the passage of the Infant Custody Bill. The second chapter turns to the young Queen Victoria, not yet twenty, who in 1839 startled both the duke of Welling-ton and all the rest of Britain when she refused a change of government on the grounds that it would disrupt the comfort of the royal household. With Victo-ria's stubborn assertion of her right to be pleased by the ladies of the bedcham-ber, she not only threw politics into turmoil; she also encouraged and confused new thought about the meaning of youth, virginity, womanhood, privacy, and home. These two episodes, the Norton trial and the Bedchamber Crisis, have a central actor in common, Lord Melbourne, prime minister, the accused lover of Caroline Norton and the acknowledged father surrogate to the queen. They are also complementary performances enacted at a moment of felt historical transformation. In the public chaos of these incidents, politics, literature, and the family seemed suspended over an abyss, floating free, open to change. "The Political Theater of Private Life" is the rubric under which we approach these events.

The middle chapters address two strenuous projects of the 1840s: the unre-lenting work of Sarah Ellis to promulgate a new orthodoxy of middle-class family life, and the labor of Charles Dickens, under the rapt gaze of his reading public, to devise a household utopia. Here are two influential attempts to create affirmative scenes of privacy as antidotes to public disgrace. In the case of Ellis, we propose a revisionary understanding of a writer who has too often been reduced to a succession of catchphrases. By looking at forgotten writing, by situating Ellis's vocation close to her husband's (William Ellis's) work as a Christian anthropologist, and by recovering the political critique within the domestic celebration, we mean to restore the improvisation and mobility within the discourse of home and to change the connotations of orthodoxy. Dickens's absorption in the fireside idyll begins by protecting it from threats outside the window and beyond the walls, but as he elaborates his project and consolidates his reputation, the house becomes an uneasy cauldron of bliss. Even within the ostensibly anodyne Christmas books, the self-enclosed family creates the disruptions it fears. How to manage the demands of sexual desire? How to turn literary popularity to the purposes of domestic peace? These are different questions, but we read the Dickensian project of the forties as an attempt to assemble a flourishing home by way of negotiations between sexual-ity and popularity.

The Deceased Wife's Sister Bill of 1848, the bloomer fashion of 1851, and the return of Florence Nightingale from the Crimea are the subjects of the third part of the book. Each has its rewarding specificity, but what they shared was the power to disturb the consensus on home conduct forming among the middle classes. The intense privacy of a widower's decision to pursue marriage with his wife's sister moved from the realm of secret wish into the hands of investigators, into the speeches of parliamentary commissioners, and finally into the boisterous taunting of polemicists. The strange episode makes an exemplary instance of the transformation of an intimacy into a spectacle. The bloomer, on the other hand, was never concerned with secrecy. The decision of English women to wear the American bloomer and to walk without fear through streets and squares was a challenge thrown down in public and repudiated by public men. The bloomer stands as the cultural contrary to Patmore's Angel in the House, and the outrage directed at her strolling form became a rhetorically inflated contest of wills. The trembling panic of men generated a nightmare vision of bloomer revolution that with one sharp shift in valence would become the positive basis of a feminist program. It also prepared the ground for the momentous case of Florence Nightingale, who came back from the Crimea as a heroine too strong for the plots brought out to contain her. The compulsion to fix the meaning of her life became a national vocation. If she had only drifted into benevolent reticence, then the ideologists might have reached a comfortable accord, but like Caroline Norton, Nightingale was the willful subject as well as the much-gazed-upon object of domestic virtue. Through a reading of *Notes on Nursing* within the context of the cultural appropriations of the Lady with the Lamp, including the appropriations of Anna Jameson and F. D. Maurice, we identify Nightingale as one who offered too much for the culture to absorb. Seeming to bear solutions for all women—work for spinsters, responsibility for wives—Nightingale flew across the boundary separating home and hospital, confusing the difference between them.

In Part Four we look to the role of the built environment within the drama of privacy, especially the attempt to design barriers against the exposure described elsewhere in the book. "On the Parapets of Privacy" is a study of the "wall," both as social force and imaginative resource. The wall makes a boundary between street and home; it facilitates the partitioning of the household; it invites anxious reflection on psychic and social borders, edges, and limits. Here we also address the horrified image of the wall-less poor, moving into the streets and then crowding in hordes within their rookeries. Henry Mayhew occupies the focus here. The second chapter of this section engages Robert Kerr's *The Gentleman's House*, a highly successful book of the mid-1860s. Kerr promised to teach a nation how the profession of architecture could at last provide the twinning triumph of "comfort" and "convenience," and how it could deliver principles of design bringing the glory of gentlemanly life to every domicile of the "better sort" from the parsonage to the palace. The firm settlement of domestic orthodoxy is written into Kerr's treatise. It appears both in his architectural history and in the elaborate plans and sketches that fill this long book. No tone could be more authoritative, no doctrine more untroubled, but we look to the recalcitrant materials that are compounded within the gentleman's complacency and that disclose themselves when Kerr, at the height of his professional success, turns to solve "The Problem of Providing Dwellings for the Poor in Towns."

The final section takes up social disruptions ignored by one such as Kerr but strongly felt elsewhere in the culture—the passage of the Divorce Bill in 1857, the provocations of female singleness, the death of Prince Albert, the emergence of the bigamy novel, the insurrection in India—and shows the close web of connection linking these events. "The Empire of Divorce" pays particular attention to two issues. First is the agitated relation between a more entrenched respectability and the sensation of single women; second is the subterranean tie between the imperial shock created by the Indian revolt and the debates over a new law for divorce. The final chapter, "Bigamy and Modernity," offers readings of two sensation novels by Mary Elizabeth Braddon, *Lady Audley's Secret* and *Aurora Floyd*, in the context of the new divorce culture and the relationship between scandal and respectability.

The structure of the book depends on an alternation between public sensations and the attempt to guard home against such sensations, between spectacle and the defense against spectacle.[20] Parts One, Three and Five address visible shocks to the privacy of home; Parts Two and Four take up the sedulous attempt to build a safe domestic space. It will turn out that these activities are not as opposed as they might first seem, but we adopt this structure in order to underscore the double rhythm of Victorian domesticity: its infolding and outflaring, its daily obscurity and sudden notoriety. If we begin and end with moments of visible difficulty, this is because the pursuit of home peace depends so fundamentally on flights from disaster.

In an age recognizing the powers of public opinion and the double-edged resources of journalism, our age as well as that of the Victorians, culture plays out a rhythm of predictability and astonishment, familiarity and monstrosity. In addressing a number of cases when the conventional transforms into the sensational, we remain guided by the belief that these stormy episodes are not mere exceptions or wild anomalies. Hectic and overwrought they may be, but they remain part of the social field, sometimes as revealing symptoms, sometimes as keen diagnoses, but always tied to the daily life they challenge.

Yet, such events do not simply reproduce the agitation and contradictions of the usual, nonsensational routine. Reproduction occurs. But under the conditions of spectacle, everyday affairs change their aspect; other forms of life are glimpsed; consciousness is forced. A shockingly public occurrence can create a widespread perception that some deep truth has been disclosed, but it remains part of the logic of spectacle that the significance of the truth is so often obscure. How fully do the actors in the sensational drama represent us, who gaze and chatter? How much has changed in the chemistry of visibility? We know them, we even know the queen, as participants in a shared history: the most distant social superiors have certain intimate emotions in common with the rest of us. They, too, share air. But under the pressure of the spectacle, the familiar becomes uncanny. Events that clearly emerge from the movements of interconnected social lives take on a monstrosity that excites, but can also defy, interpretation. Even when they subside, lose their fascination, and take their place in popular legend, we are frequently uncomfortable remembering what we have seen. A culture that has been beguiled by a public fetish is never sure what it now knows.

"Spectacle," of course, has had a spectacular career in its own right. As the name for a grandeur in large arenas, a melodrama on every screen, it suggests cultural absorption on a vast scale, an absorption eagerly measured by industrial statisticians.[21] We, too, are interested in the cometary event, the event that cannot not be seen, that forces the notice of public opinion. But we are equally concerned to break the grip of gigantism, and on several occasions we change the angle of vision to show the intimacy of spectacle. A more flexible notion of the public sphere is needed, one that recognizes how "publicity" and collective revelation can also occur in small groups, around a fireside as well as in a courtroom. A society perfecting the forms of private pleasure repeatedly found its secrets exposed to view; it now remains for us to gaze at those gazing Victorians.

PART ONE

The Political Theater of Domesticity

Chapter One

THE TRIALS OF CAROLINE NORTON: POETRY, PUBLICITY, AND THE PRIME MINISTER

1

When in the last years of the 1830s Caroline Norton fought her successful campaign for the Infant Custody Bill, she displayed in the clearest possible terms the politics of domestic life. Arguing that the law of custody had never been understood and that misinformed women persistently believed that they possessed legal recourse against established immorality, Norton turned away from her imaginative writing in order to produce a series of fiercely polemical works—privately printed or published pseudonymously—that exposed the legal nullity of the wife and mother. Vilely abusive husbands who separated from their wives still enjoyed full and incontestable custody of their children; pining mothers petitioned the courts in vain. Accumulating painful recent stories of marital disaster, Norton took her own life as the most compelling of examples. If history has granted her the dignity of heroic begetter of the Infant Custody Act of 1839, she purchased her reputation with humiliating exposure to the wide public eye.

But to speak of the politics of domesticity here is to refer not only to the systematic constraints of family law but also to the less formal, but no less palpable, workings of domestic power. At a time of rapidly changing attitudes, the failure of Norton's marriage became a spectacular figure of domestic pathology. In a letter written in 1837 and published soon after, Norton etches the bloody outline of the struggle.

> I can prove (if indeed Mr. N will ever dare the investigation) that not only was he a *careless* husband, but that he was a most violent and cruel one; that in his rage there is nothing he has not attempted, short of murdering me, and that on the most trivial occasions of dispute. I can prove, that when I was within three months of my confinement of my youngest child, he kicked the drawing-room door off its hinges, and dragged me out by main force, flinging me down the stairs; and I mention this instance not because it is worse than others, but because, by a fortunate chance, *I have the admission and defence of it in his own handwriting to my brother.*[1]

They were married in 1827; he was twenty-six, and she nineteen. George Norton was younger brother to the present Lord Grantley, with whom he was on the most fragile terms, but whose childlessness meant that the lordship was likely to pass into George's family. A staunchly Tory line, the Nortons liked to trace their pedigree back to the Conquest. For her part, Caroline Norton saw her grandfather Richard Brinsley Sheridan as the eminent precursor, referring to herself, at moments of argumentative stress, as the "granddaughter of Sheridan." The playwright had no blood pedigree, but through a long, low ebb in British drama, his achievement kept its luster, and then, too, Norton's relation to this patriarch carried far more than literary implication. Sheridan was still remembered as the celebrated partisan, the legendary parliamentary orator, whose intimacy with the great Whig families would have important bearing on his granddaughter's marriage.

Alongside the sharp contrasts in temperament, these party differences might have counted for less, had it not been that the problems in the Norton marriage coincided with the political crisis of the late 1820s. In the intensity of debate over Catholic Emancipation, in the weakening and then the fall of the long Tory rule, and then, climactically, in the agitation over the Reform Bill, party politics assumed a scarcely precedented intensity. For the young Norton marriage, the public turmoil was no greater than the private shudder. George Norton, who had been MP for Guildford, lost his office in the landmark election of 1830: it certainly cannot have encouraged marital harmony that his political career foundered in the reformist campaign blithely championed by his wife.

And yet, Caroline Norton's staunch reformism, her willingness to challenge entrenched customs through barbed prose polemic or sentimental verse, needs to be placed in the still more immediate context within which she suffered and wrote. Her relation to Whig politics came not only, or first of all, through her commitment to the ideals of social renewal; it came through her family relations to the great Whig aristocrats who led the party and, beyond that, to the royal patronage extended by the prince regent. After the death of her father Thomas Sheridan, son of the playwright, her mother was given apartments in Hampton Court, where the seven Sheridan children came into daily contact with the titled and the parasitic. Lacking both high birth and high fortune, the Sheridans nevertheless cast their social identity with those at the summit of power. The three daughters in the family, each of legendary beauty, entered a difficult marriage market, where their charms had to stand in place of blood and money and where their liberal politics counted less than their deportment. Set on parade in the London season, they endured such rituals of display as the "Fancy Quadrille of the Twelve Months," in which each of the year's debutantes danced with a different basket of flowers and fruits on her head.[2]

Norton's coming to a writing career and her coming to consciousness of her body met violently, met productively, and no reflection on the material conditions of her literary life can ignore that first materiality, the young female body, marked as sensuous and adorable, the body paraded, gazed at, discussed, and engraved, the only sure resource within a close system of sexual and marital exchange. This is the body, glowing as a burnished artifact, that writes itself into the early poetry, as in this characteristic passage from "The Undying One":

> ... beautiful is she, who sighs alone
> Now that her young and playful mates are gone:
> The dim moon, shining on her statue face,
> Gives it a mournful and unearthly grace.[3]

"Statue face" captures well the artifactual self-possession that Norton knew in excruciating precision.

For her eldest sister, Helen, the ceremonies of the London season yielded a marriage to Price Blackwood, later Lord Dufferin; for the youngest, Georgiana, it ultimately brought a still more glittering match with Lord Seymour, eldest son to the duke of Somerset. But for Caroline the events of the season brought no husband. Three years earlier George Norton had been told that she was too young for his love; when he renewed his offer in 1827, the portionless Caroline agreed.

The Sheridan family would bitterly claim that Norton had badly misled them about his personal fortune. Misleading or not, his position was hardly lustrous, and early in the marriage it became clear that George's best hopes lay with his wife's connections. By her account he bullied her into trading on her grandfather's reputation in order to appeal to Whig grandees. Fatefully, Lord Melbourne, the former William Lamb, then home secretary in the government of Lord Grey and soon to be prime minister, gave a favorable response, visiting the Norton household and then arranging a comfortable position for George Norton as magistrate for Lambeth. Thus in an act of conventional patronage began a relationship destined for an awful celebrity.[4]

All the while she wrote, and if in her entrance to Georgian society Caroline Norton found the exquisite refinements and ceremonies of the marriage market, in her accession to poetry she found Byron. In the 1830s Byron's dead face looms up everywhere in the universe of the literary annuals. In the poetic remains of Caroline Lamb, in the romantic melodramas of Mary Shelley, in the lush engravings of dying lovers, all the dangerous transports of love are performed with props from Byron's theater. Here is Norton in a characteristic lyric entitled "The Favourite Flower" (the engraving for the poem appears as Figure 1).

> Thine be the starlike jasmine; pale,
>   And cold as cloister'd maiden's face;
> Thine be the lilach, faint and frail,
>   And thine the clustering rosebud's grace;
> But me the burning poppy bring,
>   Which evermore with fever'd eye,
> Unfreshen'd by the dews of spring,
>   Stands gazing at the glowing sky;

Figure 1. "The Favourite Flower." From *The Keepsake for MDCCCXXXVI* (London: Longman, Rees, 1836).

Whose scarlet petals flung apart
  (Crimson'd with passion, not with shame),
Hang round his sear'd and blacken'd heart,
  Flickering and hot, like tongues of flame!
Scentless, unseemly though it be,
  That passion-lorn and scorch'd up flower.[5]

Norton's poetry was certainly not alone in favoring the overheated stress of passionate abandonment, but she was a privileged figure in the poetic throng. In the best-remembered judgment of her literary gift, Hartley Coleridge would firmly link her to Byron, praising her as the first female poet of the age: "This lady," he wrote, "is the Byron of our modern poetesses."[6] Coleridge's opinion is unsurprising, and yet its sententious certainty has misleadingly frozen the career of a writer whose power lay in her political and literary improvisations.

Certainly, Norton began within the Byronic medium where always, there at the start, she pursued the long, reaching rhythms hurtling toward sensual extremity. Sometimes the scene of erotic transport lies along the rocky shore, often in the dark forest, sometimes in the waste spaces of nowhere; the costume can be medieval or oriental; but always the performance ends in the fatality of passion, the cataclysm of desire. And yet within the frame of such a Byronism, Norton quickly saw and keenly felt that a woman is not a man. Her first challenge was to shift poetic attention within the circuit of power and to take as her great early subject the abjection of female passion.

In the long ambitious narrative of "The Undying One," a close forgotten counterpart to Tennyson's "Tithonus," Norton evokes the Wandering Jew, Isbal, condemned to live out a spectacularly un-Tennysonian immortality. In her version of the tale, the never dying man becomes an emblem of resistless male power, an erotic conqueror, invulnerable to the corrosions of time. Not for this Jewish Tithonus to sink into the withering loss of bodily strength—rather for him to exercise an ever young erotic fascination, attracting lovers through the centuries, who must then age and die, while he lives on, loves on, with the next in a series of captivated women. Edith, Xarifa, Miriam, and Linda, each dies in extravagant submission, while the undying male continues the quenchless Byronic career. In scarifying anticipation of Brontë's Heathcliff, Isbal digs Marion out of her grave, props her body next to him,

And we once more were seated side by side—
The half-immortal, and his victim bride.

(*Undying One*, 101)

Norton's earliest poetry achieves a startlingly deep solidarity with the erotics of victimage. The narratives hover around a sexual agon organized within the recurrent terms of the "haughty" and the "convulsive"—male haughtiness exacting and inciting the convulsions of the yearning, pleading woman. In

"The Reprieve," a prostrate and groveling speaker begs for the life of her husband; here is the inevitable fate of the female statue; she is toppled, broken, degraded.

Yet it is the very extremity of the abjection that will become a resource for transformation. Her earliest success, "The Sorrows of Rosalie" (1829), perfected the apparatus of submission even as it glimpsed the insurrection of the victim. Deserted by Lord Arthur, left with his child, and yet still enthralled by his bright face, the penniless Rosalie sees him with his bride.

> Despair gives strength—with one convulsive bound
> I reached him, clung to him with fervent grasp;
> And when he gazed in wild amazement round,
> And strove to disengage my frantic clasp,
> I burst the bounds of silence with a gasp.
>
> (*Undying One*; *Sorrows of Rosalie*; *and Other Poems*, 158)

The clarity of this insight, that despair can give spasmodic strength, will become a source of Norton's transformation, and it will do so, first of all, within the household economics of a strained domesticity. For it fell to Norton to ease the embarrassed circumstances of her husband through the achievements of her literary career. The great vogue of the literary annual, heavy, gilt-edged, finely illustrated, rich with the names of eminent writers, opened a roomy arena for an ambitious young writer. As she disarmingly put it, "Luckily for me, light serial literature was the express fashion of the day. Nor did the greatest authors we had, disdain to contribute their share to the ephemeral 'Annuals' and Periodicals, which formed the staple commodity of the booksellers at the time."[7] Both as contributor (of poems and stories) and as editor, Norton quickly became a popular annualist much in demand. What she could not have anticipated in her first dreams of literary success is that her genteel achievement in the annuals would become an indispensable part of the family income. George Norton's sinecure as a fifteen-hour a week magistrate did not stretch nearly far enough; it fell to his wife to sustain the marriage on the lower edge of high society.

"Our position in this respect," she later wrote, "was extraordinary and anomalous; inasmuch as instead of Mr. Norton being, either by the exercise of his profession or patrimonial property, what Germans call the '*Breadfinder*,' it was on my literary talents and the interest of my family, that our support almost entirely depended, while I still had a home" (*English Laws*, 23–24). Under the pressures of need, her gentility passed quickly into a professionalism. She produced popular fare at great speed, nurtured her relations with editors, and kept long hours.

I rejoiced then, at finding, —woman though I was, —a career in which *I* could earn that which my husband's profession had never brought him. Out of our stormy quarrels I rose undiscouraged, and worked again to help him and forward the interests of my children. I have sat up all night, —even at times when I have had a young infant to nurse, —to finish tasks for some publisher. I have made in one year a sum of £1,400 by my pen. (26–27)

Part of the scandal of this failed marriage, and no doubt part of the fascination it attracted, came from this tableau of domestic reversal: the male breadwinner grown weak and ineffectual gives way to the energetic female.[8] Within a wider economy that would resolve ever more thoroughly into separate spheres, the affront of the Nortons was precisely to invert the spheres. Given the immediate needs of the household, Norton cast aside an ideal of permanent literary value, settling happily for the rapid manufacture of salable textual commodities—the author as reproducer. "I have written day after day, and night after night, without intermission; I provided for *myself* by means of my literary engagements; I provided for my *children* by means of my literary engagements" (*Letters, etc.*, 12). In her well-earned pride, she displayed satisfactions common to many other newly confident professionals. Although her family history, her childhood milieu, her friendships, and her social pretensions placed her within the most exclusive drawing rooms in the realm, the crisis in her marriage and the conditions of her labor marked her as a vigorous literary entrepreneur.

Her husband, on the other hand, not only embodied aristocratic privilege, his son ultimately succeeding to the title of Lord Grantley; within the context of reform, he also signified a moral decadence. Conspicuously marked as indolent, pampered, arbitrary, and ill-tempered, George Norton became fixed in an image (effectively prepared by his wife) of the unregenerate aristocrat ill-suited to modernity. As one who enjoyed the legal right to his wife's income, he never hesitated to feast on the fruits of her writing labor, as she so bitterly recorded.

The names of my publishers occur as if they were Mr. Norton's bankers. If Murray of Albemarle street will not accept a poem, —if Bull of Holles street does not continue a magazine, —if Heath does not offer the editorship of an Annual, —if Saunders and Otley do not buy the MS. of a novel, —if Colburn's agreement is not satisfactory and sufficient, —if Power delays payment for a set of ballads, — if, in short, the WIFE has no earnings to produce, the HUSBAND professes himself to be "quite at a loss to know" how the next difficulty of payment is to be got over. (*English Laws*, 25–26)

At a time of tense negotiation between the ambitious middle classes and their wary social superiors, the Norton marriage represented the domestic performance of the public struggle. There he lounged, the spoiled child of the aristocracy, desperate to preserve a life of ease and privilege; and there she labored, the professional writer, skillful in manipulating the new resources of publishing in order to earn a substantial income that would preserve the family's precarious gentility.

These are the new conditions, the new material conditions of her marital and her publishing life, that surrounded, and no doubt incited, the first telling transformation in her work: the change from the poetics of the erotic slave to the poetics of the coquette—the coquette who is no longer helplessly infatuated within the scene of romance but who excites infatuation. The image of "The Brighton Beauty" (Figure 2) is one in a series of beauties, not always from Brighton, who no longer swoon but bare their lovely shoulders instead. Against the background of erotic victimage, the self-possession of the coquette represents a rising from the ground, a reconstituting of the statue, an assumption of female haughtiness to match the haughty male.

If it was Norton's first poetic act to reanimate an erotics of power and victimage, in which authoritative males—men in uniform, in eastern dress, in animal skins—curl every lip above the prostrate form of subdued women, this second act was to extend the power of disdain from men to women. In the early 1830s, she publishes a series of sketches, stories and poems, in which the central female figure is no longer passion's slave but the mistress of passion. Now men begin to lower their bodies, and to sigh and sing for love, and in poems like "Fashion's Idol" Norton allows her superb coquettes to relish the fruits of that romantic victory,

> When, victims to thy practised wiles,
> Hundreds bow'd down the willing knee.[9]

But from the first appearance of the figure, her victory is marked as doomed. The coquette enters a body of poetry already imbued with the lesson drawn from female victimage, the lesson of the finitude of woman's sensual delight. Indeed, history appears first in Norton's work as no doubt in her life, as the history of fashion and flirtation, as a quick temporality that ensures the fading of beauty and the loss of social power.

The coquette, then, is an emanation of women's strength immediately condemned to fatal corrosion: the object of satire, who must learn painfully to abandon "the temptations and pleasures of England."[10] But what then is the alternative to such pleasure?—nothing other than the pursuit of that erotic sublimity that had trapped her women within their desperate victimage. Through the early thirties Norton wrote a series of sketches for *The Court*, collected in *The Coquette and Other Tales and Sketches*, that tirelessly rehearses a narrative of passionate transport thwarted by the artifice of empty social norms. Norton typically follows out all the degraded effects of vain fashion, only to conclude by submitting her frivolous protagonists to the violent shock of recognition. The coquette of the title story (Bessie Ashton) stands as the chief defining figure for all Norton's writing during these years. Pos-

Figure 2. "The Brighton Beauty." From *The Keepsake for MDCCCXXXVI* (London: Longman, Rees, 1836).

sessed by "the restless love of conquest,"[11] she enjoys a garland of admirers, and when it comes time to allow one to be her husband, she turns away from the intensely passionate lover (Claude Forester, for whom she genuinely cares), in order to choose wealth and position. Her "spirit of coquetry" (*Coquette*, 1:6) lives on past the wedding day; she encourages many new flirtations, including one with a Lord Linton who neglects his "little fair consumptive sister" (1:25) in slavish pursuit of the coquette. In the strongly trumpeted climax, a distracted Bessie, confused by the return of the passionate Forester, becomes lost in the vortex of her own vanity. Having cajoled the dangerously ill girl into attending a ball, Bessie accepts her brother's devotions, while the sister dances to her death. Stunned by the disaster, Bessie gives up her coquetry and cleaves to her husband.

Norton never shrinks from the melodramatic dictate of "light serial literature"; unembarrassedly, she keeps her moral contrasts severe and her thematic burden simple. The interest of these early pieces lies not in the writer's subtle departure from convention but in her very willingness to unbind the affect concealed within her light forms. Without challenging the terms of her chosen genre, she embraces them in such full rhetorical flourish that she lets them parade all their instabilities.

Norton's first "solution" had been to set the authenticity of passion against the falsities of fashion. Those who yield to the tyranny of social form give up the integrity of passionate love, and in Norton's early poems and stories they always pay a high price for their desertion. Norton follows sentimental orthodoxy—passion is natural, fashion artificial—as she caresses the ideal of an uncorrupted love beyond the reach of mere vanity. And yet in working through this convention, in following where it leads, Norton comes to the unsettling recognition that erotic passion is also vain, and that vanity has passions of its own. The male lover, who had first appeared as a sensuous rebel living in a realm of authentic, unconstrained, extralegal love with all its sexual implications conspicuously displayed, entirely loses his oppositional character. No longer a rebel, he becomes a fashionable rogue, who is still capable of arousing a love "approaching to idolatry"[12] but who remains a "slave to the opinions of others."[13] Desire, after all, is no opening to a life elsewhere; it is instead the dangerous power generated by the very society it threatens to dissolve. Norton's tales become crowded with images of men who retain the aspect of erotic rebels—coarse-featured, harsh-eyed, irresistible—while working their temptations from secure positions within the fashion system.

Despite this harsh recognition, Norton will sometimes allow her coquettes (and her readers) to dream of a redemptive sensuality with the one true gloomy lover, while in other moods she bitterly displays the fatality of the sensual, its entanglement in fashion and privilege. Up through the middle of the decade, Norton's work oscillates fitfully between two forms of failure: vanity or desperation, the woman as hollow statue or as dying animal.

It would be right to call this an impasse, if it didn't, at the same time, represent such a professional success. Norton won great popularity among the readers and editors of literary annuals; in 1836 she won a plum commission to edit that year's *Keepsake*, a clear mark of her prominence and an opportunity to offer a richly engraved presentation of her work. We began by speaking of Norton's body, her beauty, the "statue face," as the only sure resource during an uncertain youth, but now her literary professionalism can be identified as a condition of freedom from the beauty market, even as her heroines remain tightly bound within the scenarios drawn for them.

2

In 1835, the year before her life changed forever, Norton made a sustained effort to think beyond the genres that she had exploited. The novel *Woman's Reward* was a commercial failure that kept Norton away from novel writing for the next fifteen years, but from our standpoint it can be seen as a distinct historical success, a work that condenses many transformative pressures—domestic, literary, political—into a vision of epochal change.

Norton's telling recognition was that her family peril and her political-social milieu held an emblematic force within the literary conventions where she had made her imaginative home. Now she could write fiction with polemical vengeance. In an audacious challenge that would surely have enraged her quick-angering George if he had troubled to read the book, Norton scarcely places any mask over the mannerisms of the vile Lionel Dupré, leaving him as transparent counterpart to her husband. With his "wild and violent temper," his "demoniac beauty," his "cold and sarcastic" manner, his Tory politics (once elected, then defeated), and his intolerable fussiness while traveling, the fictive Lionel becomes the occasion for the author's revenge on his original.[14] Melbourne, too, walks through the fiction with the thinnest of veils. He appears under the name William Clavering, the rising Whig star destined to be leader of the party, graceful in his aristocratic bearing, with a "soberer style of feeling" (*Reward*, 1:168). He shows himself as the man of true pedigree who needn't stage his emotions, but whose self-command allows him to command others. When the Whigs come to power late in the novel, Clavering, like his source, becomes the prime minister. The novel evokes the image of the grand politician, who "in the midst of public applause, and private temptations" walked through "the cold fogs of a London November . . . to forget the toils and tasks of the day, in the pleasure of [Mary's] gentle converse and kind smile" (1:136). It would be only a matter of months before all the world learned of Melbourne's habit in the early 1830s of passing from the "toils and tasks" of Whitehall to the intimate Norton drawing room, where he and Caroline were closeted for hours.

For reasons that will become clear, Norton places herself not as Lionel Dupré's cruelly abused wife, but as his long-suffering sister, Mary. By their father's dying request, she has committed herself to her brother's care, and the inherited obligation clearly captured Norton's sense of her marriage as not merely a mistake but as an original, involuntary, and fateful entanglement. The self-denying, scrupulous Mary accepts her brother's unfair demand that she break with Clavering without even allowing him the right to an explanation.

But the most cunning turn that Norton gives to the edgy roman á clef is to double its work of salacious reference. It is impossible to know when she realized that her growing antipathy to Byron had merged with hatred of her husband. Nothing is clearer than Norton's early debt to early Byron, but any fair measure of her literary and political importance depends on seeing that by the time Hartley Coleridge called her "the Byron of our modern poetesses," Norton's work was built upon a determined anti-Byronism. The effect of reading *Don Juan*, she wrote, was "like hearing some sweet and touching melody familiar to me as having been sung by a lost friend and companion, suddenly struck up in quick time with all the words parodied." The celebrated poem is one "which no woman will ever like" (Perkins, 117). Norton located Byronic irony as part of the culture of vanity, but the problem with the poet was much greater than this. His parody was only a mask over his carnality: in the opening pages of *Woman's Reward* she describes Byron as "one of the most selfish sensualists, who ever pretended to deep feeling" (1:12). George Norton was her very own "selfish sensualist," and with an ingenuity supported by outrage, the novel traces a double narrative in which her unhappy triangle with her husband and Melbourne overlays that spectacle of twenty years earlier played out by Byron, Melbourne, and Caroline Lamb.

If it were no more than a clever code for literary gossip, the novel would illuminate very little. But as she teases out the parallel catastrophes, Melbourne's humiliating loss of Caroline Lamb to Byron in 1812 and her own recent misery, Norton offers a vigorous interpretation of the passage from Georgian decadence to a "post-Georgianism" that we cannot yet call Victorian. Lionel Dupré/Byron/George Norton has imaginative gifts, but they are coarsely reduced to the call of bodily pleasure. He of "the folded arms, the haughty head, the flashing eye" (1:135) writes the following verse as an act of seduction.

> Mine be thy love! the wild, the first,
> Which cold experience hath not nurst.
> > Which knows nor bound nor measure;
> What time thy young and startled heart,
> Shrank from the god's unerring dart,
> > And fear'd the painful pleasure. . . .

Till Passion, Love's degraded son,
Usurps his abdicated throne,
   Mad tyrant of an hour,
Creates a wild and treacherous flame,
And spends in deeds of crime and shame
   His transitory power.

(1:98)

What is most immediately striking about Lionel's poem is that it might so easily be read as a pastiche of Norton's early work, even as the novel securely locates it as a pastiche of Byron. Within the terms of the novel's literary-political revisionism, Byron's actual politics are willfully ignored. A carnal, selfish Byronism is reconstructed as a natural Toryism; indeed, a central aspect of the book's polemical mission is the effort to show that domestic cruelty, poetic extravagance, and Tory traditionalism stand in deep and frightening congruity.

The novel's figure for Caroline Lamb, Lady Clarice Lyle, is a prodigious condensation of Norton's many portraits of female vanity. If she follows her source closely in such "perversities" as dressing like a page, Lady Clarice steadily accumulates so many vices that she becomes the very type of the degraded coquette: "Such women, in romances, break their hearts and die; such women, in real life, destroy the destinies of others" (2:31). The cruel Tory poet and the vain pleasure-seeking *poseuse* thrill and agitate one another until they lose all self-command: "Wayward herself, she loved even the way-wardness of Lionel. The capricious changes from gaiety to gloom, from tender-ness to anger, from devoted passion to the coldness and tyranny of selfish love—these fed her restless spirit, and charmed her fevered imagination" (1:169). In Norton's reconstruction of the notorious infidelity, Melbourne/Cla-vering never suffered, because he had never lost himself in the destructive charms of the restless siren. Let the Tory Byron have her; Melbourne was made for other things.

He was made for Mary. Through the portrait of this ardent but self-denying woman, Caroline Norton paints herself into her narrative as patient and de-voted, gentle and amiable, humble and pure-hearted, willing to wait through the decades, while her lover grows gray and heavy, until she can receive "Woman's reward" for her forbearance. When the blocking agents have all died, Mary Dupré marries her prime minister, and if they are not ardent lovers, they are "exceedingly comfortable" (2:96). Given that in 1835 Norton could not have imagined the miserable outcome of her domestic difficulty, there is poignancy in the fantasy she allows herself, that no matter how long it will take, she will escape the circuit of family violence and find refuge in the prime ministrations of Melbourne. In working through that fantasy, the novel com-pletes its political interpretation of domestic desire. In Norton's polemical construal, Tory love is Byronic passion, which after treating others cruelly, turns to consume itself. The alternative in *Woman's Reward* is the enlightened Whiggery of its hero and heroine, a Whig politics and poetics, which chastens sensuality, defers pleasure, seeks justice, and reads, not Byron, but Tom Moore. We can only guess where Norton would have taken this new figuration of Woman and domestic hope if a next event had not changed all the conditions of her life and writing.

3

When in the spring of 1836 George Norton haplessly decided to accuse Lord Melbourne, the prime minister of Britain, of an adulterous relationship with his wife and to bring a formal suit of criminal conversation, Caroline Norton wrote a chilling note to Melbourne: "I perceive *your* enemies join *mine*."[15] There is an awful profundity in the remark. It captures the sudden convergence of her private torment with the most public of political struggles. Her enemies were her husband's brother Lord Grantley and his guardian Lord Wynford. Both were staunch Tories living unhappily in the midst of Whig rule; Wynford, in particular, played an active and influential role in Tory strategy. In the early months of the year George Norton had investigated a healthy sample of his wife's male acquaintance, searching for evidence that might lead to divorce proceedings. At a certain point he, or more likely his advisers, fixed on Melbourne, and what had been an unhappy private misery became a richly notorious scandal.

The prime minister would receive a decisive verdict of innocence. But not since the trial of Queen Caroline, observers regularly said, had there been as sensational an event as this. For weeks the papers were full of first whispers and murmurs, and then hoots and bellows. Even after the rapid and unequivocal judgment—the jury not even retiring to deliberate—it took many days for the aroused voyeurism to subside. The *Times*, which had breathed heavily on the embers of scandal, entered a shouting match with the *Morning Chronicle*, naming the Whig paper "the most worthless print in England"—to which the *Chronicle* brazenly replied: "We hope it will not be thought that we feel much hurt at being called 'the most worthless print in England,' by the most lying journal in Europe."[16]

More than an occasion for the sordid maneuvering of political factions, the trial also staged an exemplary tableau of aristocracy in the age of reform. Melbourne's vindication represented not merely a moment of personal deliverance in his political career, or only a triumphant stroke for the Whig Party; it stood equally as a drama of upper-class redefinition. Both through George Norton's failure at the trial and through his wife's subsequent pamphleteering, he assumed the aspect of a rogue aristocrat, content to sue his patron in greedy pursuit of ten thousand pounds in damages. For all the pedigree of the Norton line, by the time it reaches the scheming, brutal George it now appears as enfeebled, diminished, decayed. Melbourne, on the other hand, stood at the summit of political power, where he genteely embodied the Whig ideal of a reforming aristocracy, at once refined in manners and responsive to political change. Whatever the ultimate weaknesses of the Melbourne ministry, at the time of that extraordinary trial and its immediate aftermath, it enjoyed the great advantage of a contrast between a treacherous Toryism, relic of an obsolete past, and its own moderate, accommodating Whiggery.

Among the fine social ironies of the long day's spectacle was that the contest between these two aristocracies was performed through the testimony of domestic servants, the question of Melbourne's adulterous guilt turning on the evidence of the lady's maid, the housemaid, the footman, and the coachman. It was easy enough to establish the pattern of Melbourne's visits beginning in 1831, but because no one would have seen the confirming act itself, the plaintiff's argument rested on building a circumstantial case founded on the servants' memories of suspicious incidents, telltale gestures. A housemaid testified that she was instructed not to enter the drawing room when Lord Melbourne was visiting Caroline Norton: "No visitors were ordered to be admitted. [She] had known Mrs. Norton to come up stairs to alter her dress, to put her collar and hair to rights, which were generally tumbled when she came up stairs. She put fresh rouge on her face."[17] A lady's maid reported that she had "seen Lord Melbourne and Mrs. Norton in the room together—they were both sitting on the sofa with Mrs. Norton's hand in Lord Melbourne's" (*Trial*, 11). But the most sensational testimony was that of John Fluke, former Norton coachman, who recalled an incident in which he knocked at the drawing-room door to bring a message and, receiving no answer, passed through the door.

> He there saw Lord Melbourne sitting on the left hand side of the fireplace, with his knees together and his elbows upon them, looking at Mrs. Norton, who [was] lying on the hearth rug on her right side; the moment witness got into the middle of the room, Mrs. Norton's clothes were in disorder; her left leg was uncovered, and witness saw as far up as thick part of the thigh; witness immediately turned round and retired from the room, and went down stairs, but he did not mention any of the circumstances at that time. (14)

Melbourne's lawyer, Sir John Campbell, the attorney-general, brutally discredited all of this testimony. Fluke, the chief witness, was marked as a drunkard, who had been dismissed after a quarrel with his employers, who had been brought to the Grantley estate at Wonersh in the days before the trial, who had been paid large sums of money, and who had boasted of his role in this legal challenge to the prime minister. But for Campbell, Fluke was only the most flagrant instance; the other witnesses were all "discarded servants—a race, the most dangerous in all cases, but particularly in cases of this sort, wholly unworthy of belief" (18). The attorney general invokes Edmund Burke who, in talking of domestic servants, had said that they sowed the seed of discord, and surrounded the bed and table with snares—that no man's life was safe or comfortable—and that they were nothing but instruments of terror and alarm. What family, he would ask, could be safe, if at the distance of years, discarded servants could come forward and make such statements, concealed for so long a period, and which they themselves admit excited no suspicion while the circumstances were recent, and while they were there to make these observations? If they were brought forward at the end of years, excited with the hopes of reward and of making their fortunes, what safety could there be, what protection for innocent persons? (19)

Here is a harshly direct statement of what will become a chronic anxiety within the Victorian domestic daydream: that within the private sanctum of the respectable household loom the unrespectable eyes of prying servants, and that the achievement of domestic gentility carries with it this inescapable flaw.

In the Melbourne trial the weakness of the servants' testimony—all of it weakly circumstantial, possibly tainted, and none of it pertaining to recent events in the Norton marriage—helped to clinch Campbell's argument, but worth emphasizing is that, beyond the particular weaknesses, the mere fact that these were servants' words marked them as suspect. Thus the leader of the reforming party, the historically responsive viscount, won his verdict through an attack on the credibility of the servant class. And within the allegory of class relations written into this glowing public drama, the determining voice was that of a third force: of the twelve members of the jury, eleven were classed as "merchant." Blazoned before the newspaper-reading public, the trial staged a resonant scene of social transition, in which middle-class merchants passed judgment on aristocratic virtue by evaluating and finally repudiating the testimony of servants. Here is an emblem of the great rapprochement between those accommodating elements of the gentry (and aristocracy) and the eagerly advancing middle classes that had brought the reform of 1832—an accommodation that offered precisely nothing to the "race" of servants.

But where was the woman within this allegorical spectacle? She was nowhere. Two years later Caroline Norton would bitterly describe the unhappy legal condition,

> that where an action for damages is brought by the husband against the supposed lover of the wife, *she can make no defence*; that she is not an acknowledged party to the suit, although *hers* is the character at immediate issue; although in fact *she* is the person prosecuted; although the sole object of the suit is to prove her guilty. While the advocate engaged by her husband is employing all the ingenuity of rhetoric against her; assuming her guilt, and working upon the feelings of the jury by a description of the husband's distress . . . *she* is condemned to remain perfectly neuter; perfectly helpless; excluded, by the principles of our jurisprudence, from all possibility of defence.[18]

Caught between men, the wife vanishes into legal impotence. As Lord Brougham bluntly put it, "the wife has no defence, but behind her back, by the principles of our jurisprudence, her character is tried between her husband and the man called her paramour" (quoted, *Plain Letter*, 79). Merged in the legal identity of her husband, she was condemned to be the object, not the subject, of inquiry.[19]

Yet, as Norton came painfully to realize, worse still than her legal vanishing was her spectacular presence in the realm of scandal. It was as if she had disappeared from the legal arena only to reappear more extravagantly in the press. She, who had passed through the most select drawing rooms of London, found her tarnished name blown about the streets on the fluttering daily papers. In its war with the Tory press, and especially with the *Times*, the *Morning Chronicle* clucked an angry tongue at the indecency of its rivals. In their "unmanly eagerness," they have succeeded

> in dragging a beautiful, accomplished, and talented woman (now a helpless woman, made so by their foul slanders,) but most innocent lady, before the public, but they have failed, signally failed, in attaching to her one stain of guilt. We blush for the English Press. Decency and forbearance to that sex before which it is the glory of man to bow with reverence and affection, which it is our duty to protect at every hazard, have been most ruthlessly thrown aside. What shall we have next?"[20]

An answer to that question is, more notoriety for Caroline Norton, carried again into a degrading prominence, this time by those ostensibly devoted to protecting her from the glare of attention.

By the 1820s, as Jonathan Parry has recently shown, the power of "public opinion" had become a commonplace theme.[21] The steep growth in the number of newspapers combined with the intensity of party competition to create the preconditions for a modern media society. The case of *Norton v. Melbourne* represents an early crystallization of the pattern of scandal and publicity, in which secret, scarcely mentionable events become violently assimilated within the circuit of rumor, gossip, and endless idle speculation. And when the energy of sensation fails, then the sensational organs, the hungry newspapers, feed on themselves.

The compound of sex, rank, and party made the Norton affair irresistible, but of these elements, it was unquestionably sex that drove the carriage of public fascination—and this not because the details of the sexual encounter were deliciously lewd, but because the mere act of exposing such an intimacy produced the thrill of humiliation.[22] The tension between the inviolable privacy of respectable womanhood and the avid press created a central exciting taboo, which the press was ready both to acknowledge and to violate. So one finds the sorry comedy of the *Morning Chronicle*, complaining of the filth that it greedily stirs.

In 1835 when she first left her husband after he seized their children, Norton endured the indignity of an advertisement in the daily newspapers, notifying all the world that George Norton was no longer responsible for his wife's debts. When he later accuses her of speaking "disrespectfully," of him, she acidly responds that "It never appears to occur to him that not only has he spoken 'disrespectfully' of *me*, but that he has caused *all England* to speak lightly of me; that wherever newspapers go, he has sent foul and unmanly abuse of me."[23] However great the embarrassment of the advertisement, the trial naturally surpassed it by a long margin. To Melbourne she describes the anguish of a "public ribaldry and exposure" that has made her "appear a painted prostitute in a Public Court before a jury of Englishmen" (*Letters*, 96, 98). To John Murray, editor of the *Quarterly Review*, she wrote that her name "has grown to be only the watchword of insult and cruel abuse": "I have one poor boast, and that is, that my foes are all among strangers; it is reserved for those who never knew me personally, who perhaps never saw me in their lives, to erect themselves into judges of my character and motives, to erect an imaginary Mrs. Norton, something between a barn-actress and a Mary Wollstonecraft, and to hunt her down with unceasing perseverance" (Perkins, 151).

What she saw with bitter clarity was that the legal vindication counted for little when set against the guilt of public attention.[24] For a woman, the "very fact of the publicity" counts as her disgrace (*Plain Letter*, 29). Melbourne, who had been exonerated, returned to the pinnacle of government, and in the following year when Victoria acceded to the throne, he ornamented his political power with a new role as personal advisor to the young queen. One needn't strain to imagine how galling it was to be told by Melbourne that as long as the queen was unmarried, Mrs. Norton's presence before her would be unseemly.

The fall into publicity had been frightful, but Norton soon understood that the wound couldn't be healed by a retreat into safe seclusion. Wherever she might conceal herself, her name would remain a radiant sign, ready to be circulated by all who traffic in disgrace. Without any doubt the central insight was that having fallen into the theater of publicity, she would find her best hope in performing on that open stage. Publicity had been her curse; it would become her cherished instrument.

Norton came to realize that for the men who had left the trial to resume their lives, public revelation was now far more terrifying than it could ever again be to her.[25] She had lost her good reputation; George Norton and Melbourne still had reputations left to lose. Before the trial the prime minister had written revealingly that "You describe me very truly when you say that I am always more annoyed that there is a row than sorry for the persons engaged in it" (Perkins, 82). Then, after the great row of the courtroom, he rushed to draw down the mantle of reticence, quickly accepting an end to their intimacy, aware that any close tie between them could arouse a new catastrophic scandal. In her shock at his abrupt withdrawal to a safe personal distance, Norton dangles the possibility of publishing the letters between them, and it is clear enough from the surviving correspondence that very few items would have been needed to compromise Melbourne's claim to perfect decorum. Melbourne must have responded with some anger, because Norton tauntingly responds, "I never *threatened* to publish your letters—I said I *could*" (*Letters*, 96). There the tense matter stood, Norton loyally keeping silent until after his death when she told the long story of an innocent friendship. But even as she kept his secrets, she couldn't resist prodding at his invulnerability. Under the name of Pearce Stevenson, Norton acidly describes how the vindicated Melbourne

> stands free from the charge brought against him of having seduced a woman young enough to be his daughter, under the guise of friendship and patronage to her husband; enjoys the highest place in the councils of this kingdom; and sways the helm of state, distinguished by a peculiar degree of favour from royalty; insomuch that it would almost seem as if he combined in his own person the offices of guardian to an orphan, and prime minister to a beloved sovereign. This is the position of the *man*, involved in that charge, absolved by that acquittal. (*Plain Letter*, 89)

With her husband, on the other hand, there was no need to disguise her panting fury. To her public humiliation, he had added intense private pain, by refusing to let her see her children, often refusing even to let her know where they were—and this the law gave him every right to do. In the year after the trial the couple entered a cautious correspondence, he eager to secure himself against her debts, and she fiercely intent to recover the children. First by way of their legal representatives, then in direct correspondence, and finally with the help of a mediator, they perform an excruciating dance of proposal and counterproposal, insult and recrimination. Will she promise to raise the three boys with due strictness? Will he bring her the children? Will she take steps to settle her debts with the dressmaker? Will he deliver the children next week as arranged? Will she accept support of three hundred pounds a year? Where has he put her children?

George Norton threatens her with "revolting exposures," which "must ensue if amicable arrangement does not take the place of hostile proceeding"—to which she responds, "I do not fear such a result; the worst *I* can ever suffer has been suffered." From this point the threat of exposure becomes the sharpest edge between them. When she makes clear that she is fully prepared to publish these letters of negotiation, in order to reveal his duplicity, George splutters with rage: "Do you allude to those communications which were entered upon under the most distinct and mutual assurances of secresy? Do you mean to say the thought has entered your nature to divulge to others, and even convert into evidence against me, what was made secret between us?"[26] Indeed it has. She calls the correspondence a "weapon" in her hands, "a weapon, not of *attack*, but of defence."[27] The fact that we can quote the letters here is the clearest sign of her resolve.

The mediator in this impossible negotiation was John Bayley, who had served as one of George's lawyers in the suit against Melbourne and who had taken the new role on the understanding that his proposals would be binding. But in the course of the remarkable correspondence of 1837, Bayley found himself scandalized by the conduct of his former client. Attempting to hold fast to a conventional notion of marital privacy—"I think there are things which should be seen by no one but man and wife"—he came to share Caroline's view that only the threat of publicity could bring George back to moral reason. Bayley began to read the ongoing correspondence to those who might bring strong influence to bear on the stymied negotiation. He wrote to Caroline that "if Mr. N's letters were made public they must ruin his character."[28] Still, despite his threats Bayley was unable to put his late intervention to much use. The correspondence broke down, leading Caroline to make good her threat to use the "weapon" of publication. Stuck in this mud, Bayley himself would write a letter to the *Times* defending his role in the excruciating affair; George, we know, had already chosen the newspapers as a forum of insult. Then in 1838 Caroline prepared for her own textual militancy, composing a work to be privately printed under the title, *A Plain Letter to the Lord Chancellor on the Infant Custody Bill*.

This remarkable volume brings together in a startling way the two enterprises that Norton pursued so intently after the debacle of the trial. On the one hand, she engaged in the long, fruitless correspondence with her husband and his legal advisors, in the desperate hope of recovering her children, or at least gaining permission to see them at some place other than the office of her husband's attorney for a mere half an hour. On the other hand, she took up the cause of a parliamentary bill to reform the law of custody, recruiting to the campaign Thomas Noon Talfourd, a young MP and barrister, who had assisted in Melbourne's defense and who had also served as counsel in two dreadful cases of child custody.[29] Talfourd brought the bill forward in early 1837, just as Norton began to compose a series of pamphlets on the injustice of the current law.[30]

We can now look back on the struggle to pass the Infant Custody Bill as the first Victorian attempt to reform family law. The ultimate passage of the legislation would open the way for the reform of divorce law and the law of married woman's property later in the century. But in 1837 history had not yet revealed its intentions. For Norton the decision to publish her views on custody was an anxious new movement into the civic space.[31] It was one thing to threaten to publish her husband's letters; it was another to turn her own suffering into a political cause. During this time she was in correspondence with Mary Shelley, to whom she confided her difficulty, noting that "There was such a division in my family as to what I might and might not do, and such an outcry about the indelicacy of public appeal" (Perkins, 137). And yet, as she nerved herself for the act, her own view hardened: "I think there is too much fear of publicity about women; it is reckoned such a crime to be accused, and such a disgrace, that they wish nothing better than to hide themselves and say no more about it" (Perkins, 134). Willing this turn into the harsher light of exposure, refusing the conventions of female silence, Norton began a two-year campaign of political advocacy, finally validated by passage of the bill in 1839.

Part of Norton's political shrewdness was to link the proposal to the (modestly) emancipatory aims of a reformist decade.[32] The fact that custody now remained as the exclusive privilege of the father, no matter how grotesque and cruel his conduct—that "the Father's right is absolute and paramount, and can no more be affected by the mother's claim, than if she had no existence"[33]—was, in Norton's portrayal, a last vestige of obsolete tyranny. "It is a strange and crying shame," she writes,

> that the only despotic right an Englishman possesses is to wrong the mother of his children! That compelled as he is by the equal and glorious laws of his nation, to govern even the *words in which his anger is expressed* to his fellow men and subjects, he may act what cruelty he pleases by his own fire-side, and he who dares not in the open street lay a finger on the meanest man there, may stand on his own hearth and tear from the very breast of the nursing mother, the little unconscious infant whose lips were drawing from her bosom the nourishment of life! (*Separation*, 24)

A father may live in open adultery, may engage in every moral profligacy, may never see the children whom he sends off to another caretaker, and still there was no legal recourse for the mother.[34] She could claim no right either to see the children or to share in the plans for their care. A series of cases, which Norton's pamphlet summarizes, had demonstrated that the existing law regarded the father's rights as legally unassailable. Against this archaism, the bill proposed nothing like equal rights for the mother but would merely allow her to apply to the courts for the modest privilege of access. It would offer "a case of simple protection of liberty and rights of the subject, and not of any encroachment on the authority of a father as the master of the house and the head of his family" (7).

The alliance between Norton and Talfourd in 1837 must have offered sweet satisfaction after the embarrassment of the trial. Her legally enforced silence now gave way to a garrulous engagement in her own cause, enlivened by the prospect of a parliamentary victory that would begin to relieve her domestic misery. Unhappily for Norton, the reforming initiative met strong resistance. Her husband's guardian Lord Wynford and her erratic ally Lord Brougham both spoke strongly against the measure, leading to the defeat of the bill in the House of Lords, and during this period when the outcome was uncertain, a stinging critique appeared in the prominent journal *British and Foreign Review*, edited by John Mitchell Kemble.[35] For well over a hundred pages of woodenly apocalyptic rhetoric, it attacked the bill as "the most immoral and unconstitutional law that was ever attempted to be carried through the Parliament of this country."[36] The downfall of the Roman Empire, the French Revolution—these were the historical precedents. "If ever there was a dangerous and revolutionary measure, this Custody of Infants' Bill is one; not the less dangerous, because the danger has been cunningly veiled" ("Custody," 385). The family is at once the mirror of the state and its foundation. To begin to legislate reform is to open cracks that will only widen to corrupt national integrity.

> [O]f all faith, that due by a wife to her husband is the most intimate and most important. It is the first condition and pledge of faith in the life of the family; without it the family could not exist; a man could not know which were his own children. But, as the family is the first element and very foundation of the state, —the state in miniature,—and the state itself nothing more than a system of co-ordinated families, it is plain that if the chief bond of the faith of families be weakened, the faith of society at large is weakened in the same degree. The state thus demoralized in the very elements of its social existence loses all its moral principle, and with that its national power. (276)

Everywhere behind this anxious document stands one uncanny fear: that if women can have access to their children from outside the marriage, then many of them will rush from the marital nest: "a door of temptation will be thrown open to innumerable separations" (291). The picture is of swarms of wanton women, given to "frivolous and heartless dissipation" (284), who are now only restrained by their desire to appear (if not to be) good mothers, but who will lose all such restraint after the passage of such a morality-mocking bill. Its proper name is "A Bill to facilitate Separations, Seductions and Adulteries" (295), because its passage will destroy the one sure bond keeping alive the fragile faith of dissipated wives. Let them be free of a husband's absolute rights of custody, and they will rush to be separated mothers, soon to be adulterers.

The unrelenting intensity of the argument gives one sign of the disruption created by Norton's campaign, but an even stronger sign appeared in the decision to appraise not her bill but her good name. A journal that came to its readers offering high-minded disquisitions on history and politics suddenly turned to searing personal criticism—and that this was a highly charged decision is acknowledged within the essay. The *British and Foreign Review* will never stoop to the tactics of "those base innuendo-making dastards who dare to make insinuations against persons, which they dare not afterwards substantiate"; its abiding principle is to "avoid all personalities." In this case, though, "It is not we, but Mrs. Norton, who has forced her case upon the public": "She has courted publicity" ("Custody," 367–68, 376). Under these special circumstances, the editor must set aside his scruple.

What follows then is a teasing, taunting account of Norton's marital disaster. Coy allusions evoke the trial, the letters in the newspapers, and various unproven charges, such as that she ran her husband into serious debt or that she improperly circulated his private letters. Then, beyond the character-staining aspersions, the essay charges that the bill before Parliament is an astounding political affront based on nothing more than Caroline Norton's anomalous domestic history. Passages from Talfourd's parliamentary speech and Norton's pamphlet are set side by side to suggest that behind the apparently disinterested principles of the legislation stood the partial emotions of one notorious wife. That "the paternal rights of a whole nation should be violated" just to satisfy the suspect claims of a single woman—this is a truly "monstrous injustice" (378). In perhaps the most wounding charge, the essay suggests that the delays in the proceedings requested by Talfourd in the summer of 1837 were due to Norton's temporary change of heart, when it seemed that the negotiations with her husband had taken a promising turn.

It was bitter enough for Norton to be painted as a wanton adulterer by the daily press. But it was still more painful (and enraging) to be subtly sketched as a scheming revolutionary in this high Tory essay, with its influence on MPs and its cachet within polite society. Given her social milieu, the guffaw on the street corner was less hurtful than the titter in the drawing room. When in 1839 she published her longest defense of the Infant Custody Bill, the anonymous author of the essay drew her fiercest anger.

> Where was the *mother* of this man? —in her grave, or on this earth, when he undertook to speak of the whole female sex, as of animals who required caging and chaining? —of English wives and mothers as if they all desired to forsake their homes—as if they all hated and rebelled against their husbands—as if they all only waited for some revolting watch-word of liberty, to give loose to every wild and profligate feeling that stains our commingled nature? Did this author never see that very usual and customary sight, a modest and affectionate wife? Did he never see a woman watching the cradle of her sick child? Did he never see a mother teaching her little one to pray? (*Plain Letter*, 96)

No one can doubt that Norton's defense of motherhood emerges from the raw ache of her deprivation. Her devotion to her children was often remarked; it was even admitted by hostile witnesses in the Melbourne trial. George Norton's removal of the three boys devastated her; her health weakened under the strain of her attempts to win them back. Norton's letters to Mary Shelley rest on a solidarity between mothers, and at one point she speaks of Felicia Hemans, whom she never met, as writing "in a true mother's spirit" (Perkins, 134).

And yet for all the passionate immediacy of her maternal lament, no less marked is Norton's deft rhetoric of motherhood. Condemned to be a suffering mother, she turned her predicament to telling polemical advantage. Indeed it is notable that in her early literary success—itself a product, as she says, of her need to feed her children—mothers were of distinctly meager account. The first poems and stories take the agony of romance as their perpetual theme. The vanity of conquest, the cruelty of passion, the lure and danger of romantic pleasure—these recurrent subjects leave mothers and children aside. But in the catastrophe of open scandal, Norton evidently recognized that the strongest response to charges of wifely indecency was to insist on the supremacy of maternity. Mocking the view that maternal love was merely an instrument to keep wives loyal, Norton reversed the hierarchy, insisting on a stark asymmetry at the root of domestic life: "*a man cannot love his wife better than a mother loves her child*" (*Plain Letter*, 47). From this point forward, both her pamphleteering and her literary work employ the resources of a defiant motherhood.

Her next published book of verse, *The Dream and Other Poems*, did not appear until 1840—the year, that is, after the victory of the infant custody fight—and it bears all the marks of the struggle. In the long title piece, a daughter recounts a Keatsian dream of splendor, a night that is a plenitude of romantic garden delight, with grotto and waterfall, bower and arcade, cypress and pine, music and poetry, and the beckoning male lover, guide to the gorgeous mysteries. Yet, no sooner is that luscious dream told, then the daughter's mother reads its meaning with an interpretive edge that can still shock:

> In what an idle luxury of joy
> Would thy spoil'd heart its useless hours employ!
> In what a selfish loneliness of light
> Wouldst thou exist, read we thy dream aright!
> How hath thy sleeping spirit broke the chain
> Which knits thy human lot to others' pain,
> And made this world of peopled millions seem
> For thee and for the lover of thy dream![37]

Here is the brazen maternal refusal of the lure of the sensuous life and the maternal demand for a life of social engagement. The mother enters Norton's transformed poetic, not as a sweet creature who can soothe the irritations of domesticity and ease the reign of the patriarch, but rather as one who has known Man, who has endured the vicissitudes of eroticism, and who can therefore warn the young to choose concern for the "peopled millions" before "low desire" (*Dream*, 51).

Under the pressure of her extremity Caroline Norton devises this new figure, the figure of maternity, not as a source of nurturing private love but, far more ambitiously, as the one who has lived through its failure. This mother has felt the cheat of male passion; she has understood Tory oppression within the confines of the bedroom. In Norton's fierce construction the mother gives birth to a rival affection—maternal love not as the consummation of erotic life, but its saving alternative; maternal love as

> The *only* love which on this teeming earth
> Asks no return from Passion's wayward birth;
>
> *(Dream*, 20)

These lines, let us remember, are composed by the author of "The Undying One," "The Reprieve," "The Brighton Beauty," "Fashion's Idol," and so many others. Within ten years the Byron of modern poetesses, belatedly so called, has reinvented herself as a Whig poetic mother, a public mother resolved to teach the lessons of reform.

The culmination of this conspicuous political labor of poetic maternity is "The Child of the Islands," a poem of 1845 dedicated to the young Prince Edward. If the happy little prince is made to appear as the universal type and ideal of the child's rightful pleasure, Norton fashions herself as the universal mother, who in recurrent apostrophe to that "Child of the Islands," conducts a sweeping synoptic lesson in the urgency of reform—the need to ease the bite of hunger, the plague of ignorance, the pride of class superiority.

The poem is one long scene of maternal instruction, Norton gently but firmly displacing that other mother, that queen, who might have given her little prince his lessons in life. Instead, it is Norton who assumes the high rights of poetic maternity, in order to show the prince, and the prince's subjects, what should and should not be.

> Here lies a man who died of Hunger-pain,
>   In a by-street of England's Capital.
> Honest, (in vain!), industrious, (in vain!)
>   Willing to spend in useful labour all
>   His years from youth to age. A dangerous fall
> Shattered his limbs, and brought him to distress.
>   His health returned: his strength was past recall:
>   He asked assistance (earnings growing less,)
> Received none, struggled on, and died of Want's excess.[38]

A body, a professionalism, a notoriety, and a maternity—there is no deep logic in this succession, no narrative of liberation. Norton's invention of the poet-mother was not a solution to an impasse, or a merry escape from a difficult trap—it was something finer: on a difficult public stage, it was the quick improvisation of a threatened poet, who had to knit her costume while she walked the boards, and who knit the dream veil out and knit the millions in.

Her torment and her strategy thus coincide. What she felt she also performed. The *British and Foreign Review* derided the sentimentality of Talfourd's speeches and Norton's pamphlet; if the author had read the poems, he would no doubt have scorned them too. But what was named sentimentality might just as well have been called social force, because it was Norton's great stroke to release the emotional charge of maternity within a culture that was now beginning to construct its domestic vocation in earnest.

THE YOUNG QUEEN AND THE PARLIAMENTARY BEDCHAMBER: "I NEVER SAW A MAN SO FRIGHTENED"

1

> It is really a most painful thing to be thus speaking of ladies at all
> in a public debate, or to discuss a question in which they are
> mixed up. But their position and their fortunes have become a
> matter of state. Ladies of the bedchamber are now made public
> functionaries; they are henceforth converted into political
> engines; they are made the very pivot upon which the fate
> of ministry turns.
>
> —Lord Brougham[1]

This note of mock sorrow and sincere outrage dates from the end of a fiercely turbulent May in 1839, when the irrepressible and vengeful Lord Brougham rose in the House of Lords to throw scorn upon his former allies in the Whig government. Windily recounting the events that we know as the Bedchamber Crisis, Brougham recalled the sequence of misadventures in the early days of the month: the resignation of Lord Melbourne's Whig government after the loss of a sustainable majority; the young queen's turn to the Tories, first to the duke of Wellington and then to Robert Peel; the painful clash over Peel's right to replace the members of her royal household; the Whig defense of Victoria's royal prerogative; the highly theatrical breakdown of the negotiations between the queen and Peel; and the abrupt return of the Whigs to the power they had abandoned just a few days before. In a mood of bitter satire Brougham observes that the government has come slinking back into office without a program or a principle.

> The friends of the Government have nothing to say for themselves or their employ-
> ers—no merits of their own to plead—no measures to promise for the future—no
> defence to make for the past; —all the cry they utter is the name of "Queen!
> Queen! Queen!"—all the topic they dwell on is the supposed feelings of their
> Royal Mistress, the court difference, the Bedchamber quarrel about promotion;
> and, to sum up all, in one sentence . . . the event is announced as matter of ministe-
> rial gratulation that Sir R. Peel has in the attempt to form a government, been
> defeated by two ladies of the bedchamber! (404)[2]

It was no part of Brougham's account to consider why the episode so violently disturbed the course of political life, why it created so much visible discomfort in elite social circles, or why it generated a sense of failure everywhere, of personal humiliation, of chaos in public opinion. Like so many contemporary observers, Brougham assumed a rigorously public standpoint from which the mere mention of Ladies of the Bedchamber could only seem grotesque interference in the decorum of political office. But his very tone of disgust points back to the disruption caused by the young queen's refusal to allow any tampering with her ladies.[3] The general nervousness stirred by Victoria's action, the private agitation and the public hysteria, gives a clue to the radically unsettling character of the episode. For Brougham, as for the angry Tories, the debacle was only one more sign of Whig dereliction, but if one escapes the party political wrangle, then it becomes evident that the general moral tipsiness was not only a product of Lord Melbourne's weak ministry but the effect of a confusion whose roots ran deep into the affective life of an unstable culture.

Who can doubt that the Bedchamber Crisis was a spectacle that had been waiting impatiently to display itself? The accession of a young queen, the first reigning queen in more than a hundred years, came at a time when the rites of household privacy were achieving unprecedented prominence; the conditions were thus well prepared for a violent conflict between those private ceremonies epitomized by Victoria's sheltered upbringing and the demands of public political theater. The history of kingship has always been a record of tense dealings between the private and public bodies of the sovereign, but in the case of Victoria the tension inevitably sharpened.[4] The problems of her sex and her age, or, more exactly, the problem of her sex aggravated by the problem of her age, meant that Victoria came to symbolize a mythology of private experience—its vulnerability, its innocence—even as she was held, and held herself, to the exacting standards of impersonality.[5]

The emergency reveals itself immediately in one of Lord Melbourne's letters to the queen in the early hours of the episode.[6] He tells her of the government's weak majority on the Jamaican Bill, its failure to persuade enough Radicals to join the measure imposing direct rule on the colony, as a way of insisting on the abolition of slavery. Announcing that the vote will force the Whigs from power, and still anticipating that the Tories will indeed form the next government, Melbourne writes to prepare the queen for the convulsion.

> Lord Melbourne is certain that your Majesty will not deem him too presuming if he expresses his fear that this decision will be both painful and embarrassing to your Majesty, but your Majesty will meet this crisis with that firmness which belongs to your character, and with that rectitude and sincerity which will carry your Majesty through all difficulties.[7]

Within three years Melbourne had moved from one spectacle to another. The elegant, experienced aristocrat was the point of contact between these two tempests of the later 1830s, the Norton trial and the Bedchamber Crisis. He had told Caroline Norton that what he hated most was a "row," and now his first response to the young queen is to plead for calm, self-possession, and consciousness of position. Yet, the note struck in his message, the careful allusion to Victoria's emotional life and the plea for her resolve, shows Melbourne's awareness that the political change will bring a personal revolution. Through the tense correspondence that unfolds hour by hour, it becomes plain that the queen and her first minister had enjoyed a familiarity so comfortable that affairs of state had been absorbed into the pleasures of friendship. This is what Caroline Norton found so irksome, that Melbourne was able to float easily into the lap of royal favor. During the spring of 1836 he shared with her the taunts and insinuations of the press, but slightly more than a year later, while she was still a prisoner of public humiliation, he was the queen's most cherished intimate. Norton must have taken some satisfaction in the turn of events in 1839: even as she was winning a victory with the Infant Custody Act, Melbourne had fallen again under the public glare. No one, of course, accused the prime minister of sexual impropriety this time, but the sheer fact of their affection was enough to excite this second round of civic frenzy.

In a second letter of May 7 Melbourne warns the queen that in her dealings with the Tories she must be "very vigilant" in approving "all measures and all appointments": "It is the more necessary to be watchful and active in this respect, as the extreme confidence which your Majesty has reposed in me may have led to some omission at times of these most necessary preliminaries" (*Letters*, 196). Those "omissions" were acceptable within the spirit of intimacy. But now the queen must finally assume her formal comportment. Yet, for all Melbourne's ceremonial prose and his delicate advice, he cannot prevent the scene of emotional violence. The following morning brought him a distraught note.

> The Queen thinks Lord Melbourne may possibly wish to know how she is this morning; the Queen is somewhat calmer; she was in a wretched state till nine o'clock last night, when she tried to occupy herself and try to think less gloomily of this dreadful change, and she succeeded in calming herself till she went to bed at twelve, and she slept well; but on waking this morning, all—all that had happened in one short eventful day came most forcibly to her mind, and brought back her grief; the Queen, however, feels better now; but she couldn't touch a morsel of food last night, nor can she this morning. (197)

—to which Melbourne sagely responds, "The situation is very painful, but it is necessary for your Majesty to be prudent and firm" (197). The initial structure of the crisis reveals itself here: the queen, a center of turbulent affect, must chasten the riot of feeling, while the prime minister must tutor her in the athleticism of self-restraint. In this urgent exercise Melbourne will self-consciously play steady father to wayward daughter. Thus the queen, in thanking him "for his excellent advice, which is at once the greatest comfort and of the greatest use to her," notes that "she trusts Lord Melbourne will help her and be to her what she told him he was, and begged him still ever to be—a father to one who never wanted support more than she does now" (203).

Yet, even as Victoria asks for a fulfillment of the promises implicit in their relation, Melbourne recedes with a dainty firmness, insisting that the rituals of office be maintained. The negotiations for a new government are now under way, and therefore, intones Melbourne, "it will never do, whilst they are going on, either for appearance or in reality, that Lord Melbourne should dine with your Majesty, as he did before this disturbance" (198). Melbourne's careful use of the third person signifies the will to impersonality, but for the queen, who had not yet been trained out of the motions of subjectivity, the confusion reaches into the deepest strata of self-representation. Is she an "I" or is she the queen? Can one possibly be both? In an overwrought letter of May 8, when it still appears that the queen will turn to the Tories, she reports to Melbourne on her encounter with the duke of Wellington, the shifts in self-reference exposing her uncertainty.

> The Queen then said that she felt certain he would understand the great friendship she had for Lord Melbourne, who had been to her quite a parent, and the Duke said *no one felt and knew that better than he did, and that no one could still be of greater use to the Queen than Lord Melbourne.* The Duke spoke of his personal friendship for Lord Melbourne, and that he hoped I knew that he had often done all he could to help your (Lord Melbourne's) Government. The Queen then mentioned her intention to prove her great *fairness* to her new Government in telling them, that they might know that there was no unfair dealing, that I meant to see you often as a friend, as I owed *so* much to you. (199)

It was a scene of forced maturation, then, staged there at Buckingham Palace during a few days in May. But though in the first hours, Victoria fought the very idea of a change, she quickly saw the inevitability of the fall into political impersonality—a fall as it were, into the British constitution—and so actively took on the role that was in any case forced upon her. On the morning of May 8 she is distraught, but by the evening of the 9th she has fashioned a political face. After a tense meeting with Peel she informs Melbourne that "I was calm but very decided, and I think you would have been pleased to see my composure and great firmness; the Queen of England will not submit to such trickery" (205).

2

Although the immediate effect of the shock was to force the queen to assume the public airs of her royal role, the equally important result—still more important for being disavowed—was the entanglement of public men within the web of private life.[8] The crisis *reactivated* the engine of private experience in those who habitually conducted government under the cloak of impersonality. Nowhere is this clearer than in the fortunes of the word "confidence" during these anxious days.

The Melbourne ministry had resigned on May 7 because its margin of only five on the Jamaican question demonstrated a failure to sustain parliamentary confidence. As Melbourne put it to the Lords, the vote showed "such a want of confidence on the part of a great proportion of that House of Parliament, as to render it impossible that we should continue to administer the affairs of her Majesty's Government in a manner that can be useful or beneficial to the country" (*Hansard* May 7, 1839, col. 974). To construe the issue of parliamentary "confidence" in terms of a voting margin is clearly (and uncontroversially) to follow well-established political conventions that ignore the emotional state of the members. "Confidence" here is a matter of public votes on public questions.

Against the background of a technical, political "confidence," the reaction of the queen appeared all the more disruptive. In the first hours after Melbourne's resignation, Lady de Grey had sent to Peel her astute anticipation of what would now happen. "The Queen," she writes bluntly, "has always expressed herself much impressed with Lord Melbourne's open manner, and his truth. The latter quality you possess, the former not." Then having praised Peel's character, she indicates her fear "that even with such qualities you may not succeed in gaining the Queen's confidence, as I think your bearing too reserved and too cautious."[9] Indeed when the queen meets the Tory leader, she responds as Lady de Gray had imagined, informing Melbourne that she finds Peel "such a cold, odd man she can't make out what he means. He said he couldn't expect me to have the confidence in him I had in you (and which he never can have) as he has not deserved it. My impression is he is not *happy* and sanguine. . . . The Queen don't like his manner after—oh! how different, how dreadfully different, to that frank, open, natural and most kind, warm manner of Lord Melbourne" (*Letters*, 200). The queen, in effect, restores confidence to its full semantic density and its older political meanings, according to which the confidence of the sovereign is not merely a matter of political congruity but implies deep affirmations of a personal will. Confidence, then, takes on extralegal meanings, both older ones that we know as ancient regal prerogatives and newer ones that belong to an age of private life; in both senses, it belongs to a family of emotions and attitudes including trust, fondness, devotion, care.

The powerful collision of these meanings occurs when Robert Peel decides that his own political weakness requires a special show of queenly favor. Indeed later, after the game has been lost (or perhaps won through the losing), he will defend his dogged insistence on the Bedchamber Question, asking Parliament whether he could "overlook this important fact, that in the House of Commons I should not commence my career commanding a majority? . . . Being invited to take upon myself the responsibility of conducting public affairs, and taking it without the confidence of the House of Commons, could I ask for less, than that I should have, at least, the unqualified confidence of the Crown" (*Hansard*, May 13, 1839, col. 988). Exactly because he was weak in Parliament, he felt the need to be strong with the queen. Bulwer Lytton, speaking in high Whig dudgeon, disdained this principle, pointedly asking whether a ministry *"not having a majority in the House of Commons should make that very reason the pretext for demanding a peculiar show of countenance from the Crown?"*[10] Could Peel's political weakness possibly justify the personal, the intimate, demand? The further question, of course, is why the "peculiar show" of favor should have become so tightly bound to the fate of the royal household. Why should the Ladies of the Bedchamber have come to matter like this?

It cannot have been because the queen's domestic arrangements were remotely representative. She was surrounded by all those attendants with their long-sanctioned titles, their annual incomes, and their political connections to the parties who appointed them. To see these functionaries, paid to be prompt, as close intimates of the queen made no sense to such as Brougham. But in the case of Victoria, who had such a depleted personal world, should it have been surprising that she would invest affection even in people who understood themselves to be performing public functions? It may well have been precisely the exceptional character of these private investments and the exceptional demands placed upon them that made the queen's bedchamber a privileged scene in an unfolding narrative of domesticity. Just to the extent that common private needs existed here, too, in the most public of private lives, they took on an amplification that gave dramatic urgency to the crisis. When Peel demanded that the queen exhibit her confidence by yielding him the power to appoint the membership of the royal household, and when she blankly refused to accept him on those terms, the two laid the ground not only for a new constitutional struggle over the relations between Crown and Parliament, but also for a struggle over the definition of the privacy.

3

How did it happen? How did they all arrive here in the swamp of public confusion? It had started so well two years earlier, the meeting of the queen and her minister in the first hours of her accession: he with his solicitous ceremony, she with her eager desire to learn the posture of her power. On June 20, 1837, after her first long day as queen of England, she recorded the charged encounter in her journal.

> At 9 came Lord Melbourne, whom I saw in my room, and of *course quite alone* as I shall *always* do all my Ministers. He kissed my hand, and I then acquainted him that it had long been my intention to retain him and the rest of the present Ministry at the head of affairs, and that it could not be in better hands than his. He again then kissed my hand. He then read to me the Declaration which I was to read to the Council, which he wrote himself and which is a very fine one. I then talked with him some little time longer, after which he left me. He was in full dress. I like him very much and feel confidence in him. He is a very straightforward, honest, clever, and good man. (*Letters*, 98)

Here at the start can be seen the exciting confusion of personal and public connections, neatly captured in the slippage between a figure of speech and the formal touch of two bodies: the ministry "could not be in better hands than his. He then again kissed my hand." Within her wariness of the fawning officials around her, she decisively chose Melbourne as the one to trust: "the more I see him, the more confidence I have in him" (103), and he quickly transformed his life to nurture this new tie.

Together constantly, even in violation of rules of precedent, they felt more than easy affection; they clearly met needs for one another. On Melbourne's part, the friendship with the queen utterly changed his official standing; after the sharp awkwardness of his relation with King William, Melbourne now bathed richly in the warmth of his tie to Victoria. And then, beyond the happy political reversal, he clearly enjoyed the emotional luxury of their tie—as Greville put it, "I have no doubt he is passionately fond of her as he might be of his daughter if he had one, and the more because he is a man with a capacity for loving without having anything in the world to love."[11] Months later, Greville expands on the remarkable change that has allowed Melbourne

> to overcome the force of habit so completely as to endure the life he leads. Month after month he remains at the Castle, submitting to this daily routine: of all men he appeared to be the last to be broken in to the trammels of a Court, and never was such a revolution seen in anybody's occupations and habits. Instead of indolently sprawling in all the attitudes of luxurious ease, he is always sitting bolt upright; his free and easy language interlarded with "damns" is carefully guarded and regulated with the strictest propriety, and he has exchanged the good talk of Holland House for the trivial, labored, and wearisome inanities of the Royal circle. (*Memoirs*, 129–30)

The queen, needless to say, saw her court and her minister with other eyes, but then on her side of the relation, there were still more subtle adjustments to make. Melbourne had only to change his manner; she had to determine the conditions of her sovereignty. In that project, she chose him not only as the trusted minister who would give clarity through the political haze, but she also frankly understood the paternal relation that bemused those around her. Transcribing the intensities of the coronation ceremony, she recalled that "My excellent Lord Melbourne, who stood very close to me throughout the whole ceremony, was *completely* overcome at this moment, and very much affected; he gave *such* a kind, and I may say *fatherly* look" (*Letters*, 155). The queen and Melbourne together built a delicate structure of affect, within which he was both deferential minister and doting father, while she was his sovereign and his daughter.

To say that the daughterly role was only a reassuring metaphor while the sovereignty was real is to miss the necessarily fictive aspect of those first years of queenship. So little was given to Victoria, so much had to be invented. With no precedent of a queen regnant in over a hundred years and with a succession of recent kings who had offered so many incompatible styles of sovereignty, Victoria's political role was no more firmly scripted than the role of friendship. Throughout the early relation with Melbourne, it was never quite clear whether she was a queen impersonating a daughter, or a daughter impersonating a queen.

What is at once uncanny and also impressive is Victoria's resourcefulness in using each side of this ambiguity to control the instability of the other. Obligingly, and with desires of his own to satisfy, Melbourne offered himself as a prop in the queen's delicate drama. As queen, she could allow herself to indulge gestures of intimacy, secure in the thought that sovereignty set crisp limits to the claims of filial emotion. And as daughterly young woman to aging fatherly man, she could keep her distance from the royal harness, experimenting with tones and styles of queenship. In effect, she played at being a daughter as she played at being a queen, with Melbourne shifting easily between the father above and the minister below. Early on, she saw that Melbourne would be "of the greatest use to me both politically and privately" (*Letters*, 103), and, as it happened, the best use of all was to move so quickly between those realms that the distinction lost its clarity.

And then, of course, though it was Melbourne supremely, it wasn't Melbourne alone who disturbed the division of realms; it was the set of his political friends and allies who joined the court; and most fatefully, it was the Ladies of the Bedchamber. Was it Whig cunning or only Whig exuberance? Whatever the motive or the cause, the result was that the royal household was populated with the relations of Melbourne's cabinet ministers, their wives, their sisters, and their daughters.[12]

For the Tories this was a political construction of the bedchamber that only reinforced the conditions of Victoria's early upbringing. Lord Ashley captures party frustration when he writes to Peel that "from her earliest years she has been taught to regard us as her personal enemies. I am told the language at Kensington was such as to inspire her with fear and hatred. And certainly

Melbourne's hedge of male and female Whigs was not adapted to remove this prejudice by letting in Tory light" (Peel, *Papers*, 405).[13] In a prescient piece of invective published in the *Quarterly Review* in 1837, J. W. Croker—still a leading Tory tactician, and polemicist—had brightly italicized the objections to the Whig arrangement.

> It is neither constitutional in principle, nor convenient or becoming in practice, that the Sovereign should be *enclosed* within the *circumvallation* of any particular *set*, however respectable—that in the hours of business or amusement, in public or in private, she should see only the repetition of the same family faces, and hear no sound but the different modulations of the same family voices; and *that the private comfort of the Queen's interior life should be, as it inevitably must, additionally exposed to the fluctuations of political change, or what is still worse— that political changes should be either produced or* PREVENTED *by private favour or personal attachments.*[14]

Croker evokes the specter of political indoctrination, what would come to be called "brainwashing," achieved through the relentless manipulations of private life—the looming nightmarish control exercised by those "same family faces."[15] The essay devises a theory of influence that circulates wildly through the Bedchamber Affair and according to which the domestic sphere is a closed realm that can create tastes, dispositions, and ultimately political beliefs.

And yet, nothing is clearer than that this theory does not apply universally; not everyone, not every monarch, is vulnerable to the pressures of intimacy. The theory, which comes bearing general principles, in fact exists to explain the glaringly special case of Victoria, whose sex and youth expose her to the power of those family faces. It was not simply that for more than a hundred years the country had known only male monarchs; it was also that the female monarch was twenty years old. As Croker laid out the case, "A princess of the age of eighteen years and one month, who had been educated in a perhaps proper, but certainly very remarkable seclusion from general society, and whose experience of what is called the world was even less—if less be possible—than might have been expected from her tender years, is suddenly called to the government of a great empire" ("Household," 235). And then beyond these provoking conditions of sex and age, lay the changing character of domestic life, at once more sharply defined and more passionately valued than in the time of the most recent and most ambiguous precedent, Queen Anne. Lord Ashley recalls Peel saying, "I remember that I am to provide the attendants and companions of this young woman, on whose moral and religious character depends the welfare of millions of human beings. What shall I do? I wish to have around her those who will be, to the country and to myself, a guarantee that the tone and temper of their character and conversation will tend to her moral improvement" (Peel, *Papers*, 393). An image of the drawing room as the privileged site of *Bildung*, perhaps the only site, creates the much-expressed Tory worry that the queen will have not only partisan opinions but that her character will harden permanently into Whiggish shape.

For their part, the Whigs, no less than the Tories, invested the domestic circle with extravagant significance. Only in their case, the high value of the private household lay not in its power to create public character but precisely in its distance from the workings of power, its status as refuge from the field of politics. From this standpoint, the application of Peel's principle would bring a domestic catastrophe. It would mean, in Bulwer Lytton's words, that "the Sovereign was to be debarred from the privileges enjoyed by her meanest subject—condemned to feel that every association, every intimacy, every friendship, was held upon the tenure of ministerial jealousy and fear—chopped and changed with each fluctuation of party—living not in a home but an inn" (135). This, indeed, is how the queen understands the challenge. In a journal entry of May 9, she records the difficult conversation with Peel earlier that day, in which she had defended her right to keep the Mistress of the Robes and the Ladies of the Bedchamber: "I said . . . that I never talked politics with them" (*Letters*, 208). She recalls taunting the duke of Wellington with the question, "Was Sir Robert so weak that *even* the Ladies must be of his opinion?" (209) To Melbourne she writes: "The Queen would not have *stood so firmly* on the Grooms and Equerries, but her *Ladies* are *entirely* her own affair, and *not* the Ministers" (206), and when on the following day, May 10, the danger seems averted, she writes to say that "she must rejoice at having got out of the hands of people who would have sacrificed every personal feeling and instinct of the Queen's to their bad party purposes" (211).

It is right, but only partly right, to see the two parties as holding incompatible views on the relation of domestic and political life. But behind the round rhetoric of high principle stands a dirty tactical conflict. The Whigs, having seized the ground of the queen's private comfort, trap Peel into the role of political bully, insensitive to the ideals of home life. Once control of the household has become the sign and token of power, Peel has little choice but to persist in his demand for that special show of confidence, what he calls the "public proof of your majesty's entire support and confidence" (*Papers*, 397). To the degree that the queen placed the bedchamber outside the reach of politics, as a *refuge* from politics, to that very degree it became an arena of political desire. Only by winning his point in that sacred space—by winning "permission to make some changes in that part of your Majesty's household which your Majesty resolved on maintaining entirely without change" (397)—would Peel feel that he had achieved the "confidence" to govern.

The Whig polemic moved on ground just as treacherous. The lofty claims in behalf of sacred domesticity and personal affection grew murky, even paradoxical, when the private emotions were those of the monarch. Quickly and inevitably, the Whig argument shifts from a defense of domestic privacy to an improbable defense of the rights and privileges of the sovereign—("Strange doctrine in Whig mouths," wrote Greville in his diary (183). On May 9 an aroused and perhaps renewedly ambitious Melbourne writes to the queen that "if Sir Robert Peel presses for the dismissal of those of your Household who are not in Parliament, you may observe that in so doing he is pressing your Majesty more hardly than any Minister ever pressed a Sovereign before." And further: "They press upon your Majesty, whose personal feelings ought from your circumstances to be more consulted, a measure which no Minister before ever pressed upon a Sovereign" (*Letters*, 204). At this point it becomes clearer why the episode aroused such immediate popular passion: the sovereign, and indeed sovereignty, had become cast as the emblem of personality oppressed by party politics; the queen had suddenly become the spectacular limiting case of the rights of private freedom within a coarsely public world. In these un-canny circumstances of the crisis, to defend those rights was to defend the high privileges of monarchical will. In his speech before the House of Lords, justifying his return to office, Melbourne concludes with a grand rhetorical gesture that sustains the flourishing confusions of sovereignty and domesticity.

> I now, my Lords, frankly declare, that I resume office unequivocally and solely for this reason—that I will not abandon my Sovereign in a situation of difficulty and distress, and especially when a demand is made upon her Majesty, with which I think she ought not to comply—a demand, in my opinion, inconsistent with her personal honour, and which, if acquiesced in, would make her reign liable to all the changes and variations of political parties, and render her domestic life one constant scene of unhappiness and discomfort. (*Hansard*, May 14, 1839, col. 1015)

That the royal household should be the household of a reigning queen, that she should be a young queen, that she should begin her reign at a time of both great political instability and increased devotion to domestic security—all this created a richly welcoming context for the mutual transgressions of politics and domesticity. No one knew what to say; awkwardness was everywhere. Continually, the principals in the close drama improvise verbal routines that have the look of ceremonial formality; but in fact the guiding conventions by which these figures would understand themselves—the dependence of a girl or the strength of a monarch, the quiet of home or the deep voice of political authority, the merely technical meaning of "confidence" or its urgent psychic claim—all collide and disarm one another. The absurdity of the episode was well appreciated by those caught within it. "It seems the fate of these household discussions," wrote Lord Brougham, "to be attended with constant misappre-hension, and to involve all concerned with them in ridicule and discredit" (*Speeches*, 418). But the sense of farce should not mislead us. Much can be discharged and displayed within the convulsions of embarrassment.

4

Brougham's consternation, though rhetorically exaggerated, had ample justification: "Never before did I know, never did I hear, of a Whig Government
establishing itself upon a bedchamber question, —resting its whole claim to the
support of the country upon its care for the personal feelings of the monarch"
(*Speeches*, 416). He did not add, though he might well have, that the sight of
Tories as jealous defenders of parliamentary right against the claims of the
monarch carried its own strong peculiar savor.[16] Croker, who saw the tangle,
complained to Lord Hertford that the queen, in turning against the Tories, has
rejected "her natural allies."[17]

Certainly, the comedy of such party cross-dressing should tickle anyone
with a taste for political ironies. But what throws a new knot into the confusion
is the recognition that the monarchy was itself undergoing a profound historical
evolution, which could not have been fully grasped by the participants in the
comic drama. One way to describe the change is to see it as the *feminizing* of
the monarchy, a development begun well before Victoria's reign but given
heightened force by the conspicuous fact of her sex.[18] The loss of monarchical
prestige under the fourth of the Georges; the flailing, largely futile, attempts
of William IV to impose his political will upon Parliament; and the popular
mythology of those heartier days "when George III was king" all contributed
to a notable weakening of a still potent image of the sovereign as the concentrated sight of masculine authority. Then, too, stands the fact that more even
than in the case of royal sovereignty, Parliament had always been the quintes-
sential male preserve, a condition giving added point to the queen's satiric
comment that she would retain her Mistress of the Robes because Peel had
"said *only* those who are *in Parliament* shall be removed. I should like to know
if they mean to give the *Ladies* seats in Parliament?" (*Letters*, 206) The court,
on the other hand, whether or not led by a reigning queen, had retained a space
for its ladies. Always less uniformly male, by the end of the age of Victoria,
it began to seem essentially female.[19]

No one could have known that when William IV dismissed the Melbourne
ministry, this was a last, and indeed a desperate, attempt to employ the sovereign right of dismissal in order to assert royal influence on government policy.[20]
In the event, William was unable to keep the Tory ministers he desired, and
so his defiant gesture only dramatized the limits of monarchical authority
(Newbould, 160). Within the long historical logic of parliamentary rise and
monarchical decline, the tempest in the bedchamber appears less random and
foolish; it suggests the painful locking into place of the "womanly" character
of all modern sovereignty. Melbourne's very choice of metaphor in describing
Peel's assertion—Peel "is pressing your Majesty more hardly than any Minister ever pressed a Sovereign before"—teases out the sexual figure in the relationship between a Parliament, conscious of the potency of its broadened legiti-

macy, and a monarch placed in a condition of female vulnerability. No doubt part of the challenge of a queen sitting on the throne at this historical moment is that it *confirms* this feminizing of sovereignty—as if the truth about changing power relations between Parliament and the monarch were finally revealed in the accession of Victoria: relative to Parliament, the monarch is placed in just that defensive and vulnerable position that women held in relation to men.

5

In the immediate aftermath of the Tory defeat, J. W. Croker wrote another essay in the *Quarterly Review.* Long, tense, clotted, and partisan, "The Household and the Ministry" is an inviting document, rich in productive contradiction, writhing with all the contortions of the Bedchamber Affair. What makes it particularly notable is that the essay can be recognized as a polemic commissioned by Robert Peel. A memorandum from Peel to his friend Croker reads as marching instructions to a sharp-tongued controversialist; it lays out the argument to be developed, the historical references to be cited, and the central question to be relentlessly posed: "What in a constitutional point of view, had the country to do with the youth of the sovereign, or the sex of the sovereign? No more than with the nature, or the beauty. A great public principle is under consideration" (*Croker Papers*, 341).[21] In the published essay Croker dutifully burnishes the edge.

> To raise any distinction on this great question from the age or the sex of the sovereign is a constitutional error and a personal indignity: the constitutional law which admits females to the throne, and fixes their majority at eighteen, takes no other cognizance of age or sex; the sovereign is KING OF ENGLAND. ("Household," 262)

Under the banner of this principle, Croker like his chief argues for the constitutional purity of the claim on the bedchamber. Can the sovereign disregard the advice of the duly chosen minister and seize the prerogative to appoint those whose right to office exists only through an act of Parliament? Can age or sex possibly bear on that great constitutional question?

These are the questions that Peel's Croker tauntingly poses, and yet when he takes up the questions that have bedeviled historians—Why did the Tory leader fix on the question of the bedchamber? Why did his constitutionally sanctioned prerogative choose to meet the queen on this sore subject?—then sex and age suddenly recover their pertinence. Trying to explain why Peel did not simply refuse the queen's demands, Croker weakly notes that "though the *age* and *sex* of the Sovereign can and ought to have no influence on questions of constitutional rights and prerogatives—(which are abstractedly the same, whatever be the head on which the crown may be placed)—yet they very naturally affect the forms and manner in which the Sovereign is to be treated"

("Household," 242). In fact, as Croker develops the argument proposed by Peel, the sex, if not the age, of Queen Victoria will turn out to be exactly the historical matter.

In his parliamentary explanation after the return to office, Lord Melbourne recalled that in that first visit to the queen he hadn't even mentioned the Ladies of the Household, because he never imagined they would be at issue. Instead he undertook only to inform Victoria of her historical responsibilities. A howling, sneering Croker wonders how this *"historical lecturer"* could have construed his responsibilities if he ignored the nightmarish precedent of Queen Anne's reign—"a period in every way remarkable, but in none more so than in the important, the overwhelming influence which *female ministers* under the title of *court ladies*, had obtained over the destinies of England and of Europe" ("Household," 245). The "momentous struggle between Godolphin and Marlborough on one side, and Oxford and Bolingbroke on the other, was conducted in the recesses of the Queen's apartments between the Mistress of the Robes and the Woman of the Bedchamber" (255)—this is what Melbourne had failed to recollect for the queen. He had ignored Mrs. Masham ("she was only a bedchamber-woman, but she soon became the pivot of the political world") and had kept a ludicrous silence on the subject of the duchess of Marlborough: "Not a word of her! though she is the strongest example, perhaps in the history of the world, certainly in the history of this empire, of the abuse of female favoritism, and the most flagrant instance of the incalculable influence of household familiarity on the destinies of mankind" (253). And so on, crescendo beyond crescendo.

Between the view that age and sex are constitutionally nonexistent (a queen is the king of England) and the view that the court drama around Queen Anne shows the dangers of female favoritism, female influence, and female ministers, Croker moves with utter insouciance. Peel, he holds, was right to make his demand because no sovereign, male or female, could enjoy a limitless prerogative, but he was also right because a female reign risks catastrophes peculiar to the sex.

A much nearer precedent, which Croker had special reason to remember but also political reasons to forget,[22] loomed behind the present frenzy. For all of its complex determinations, the Queen Caroline Affair of 1820–21—her return to England after long estrangement from the prince regent, her demand for queenly prerogatives at his coronation, and his attempt to divorce his wife in Parliament—left lingering images. Laqueur has persuasively identified Caroline's cause as "perhaps the first of those nineteenth-century political causes—opposition to the bastardy clauses of the New Poor law was another—in which women acted as defenders of familial values and communal morality."[23] Davidoff and Hall have extended this insight in order to argue that the episode marked a first precipitate of an emerging discourse of marriage and domesticity: "Public opinion had decreed that the royal family must indeed be a family; kings and queens must be fathers and mothers in their own home if they were to be fathers and mothers to the people."[24] Set against the figure of a sexually degraded male sovereign, Queen Caroline came to stand as the improbable site of domestic virtue.

But it is one thing to identify a queen consort as the image of injured respectability, whose reputation has been mutilated by a king's rude morals, and it is quite another to make the young queen regnant into a compound of wounded domesticity and unchallenged sovereignty. If the compound became more stable later in the reign, this was due both to the reassuring mythology of Victoria's marriage to Albert and to her recession into the safer space of symbolism. But in 1839 the queen still figured as a concretely embodied woman, who hadn't yet disappeared behind the harness of ceremony.

A pro-Tory pamphlet called *The Household, or What Shall We Do with the Ladies?* criticized the queen's letter of refusal, which described Peel's request as not only "contrary to usage," but also "repugnant to her feelings." *Feelings*, insists the anonymously aggrieved pamphleteer, must always be sacrificed "upon the altar of duty" (Croker, "Household," 260). And yet everywhere in the affair there appeared the disruptive presence of feeling, of rebellious emotion beneath the rites of politics. Undoubtedly, much of what made the affair so absorbing to the public mind was that the political stresses became a frame around a crisis of feeling that took on the aspect of family catastrophe. Exceptional though her position remained, the queen gave a heavily stylized performance of several distinct domestic gestures that were recognizable, in many ways representative. Victoria, who asks Melbourne to give her a father's support, will mock the Tory "attempt to see whether she could be led and managed like a child" (*Letters*, 206).

But it's worth emphasizing that the role of the vulnerable child was only one disruptive implication. A scandalized Greville tells his diary that "the Queen was in communication with Sir Robert Peel on one side, and Lord Melbourne on the other, at the same time" (*Memoirs*, 182). Although Greville is only referring to the political indelicacy, his words evoke a picture of the queen in the role of unattached young woman choosing between two suitors. When she has broken with the "cold, odd" Peel—failed father, failed suitor— she gaily invites the graceful Melbourne to dine. Especially against the background of the sordid Norton episode, the resolution of the Bedchamber Crisis represents a chaste version of public romance. Melbourne steals the queen back from Peel, much as he was accused of stealing Caroline Norton from George, but in this case the triumph is to preserve, not to stain, the woman's virtue. As the generous, not wolfish, suitor, Melbourne wins the queen in order to preserve her inviolate sovereignty.

The constant chanting together of those words "age" and "sex" can reasonably be taken as a substitution for the unutterable word "virgin." At a deep level of the collective psyche the disturbance of the Bedchamber Affair must have gained great energy from the unspoken conflation of "sovereignty" and "virginity." The awful hush before the queen, the excessive scruple, the zealous preservation of distance, all so conspicuous in the behavior of the male principals, might be seen as an overdetermined product of both her constitutional authority and the authority of her intact innocence. Although the parliamentary speech and the various written texts naturally avoid the taboo of the queen's sexual status, the preoccupation with her "unworldliness" suggests an appreciation, at whatever level of consciousness, that the queen was not yet initiate in the ways of normative adult sexuality.

Indeed what is perhaps most challenging of all in the event, and what gives special edge to the sexual implication, is the queen's aggressive assertion of a world beyond the realm and reach of men. Those "ladies," with whom she never discusses politics, mark out a female household space, which according to usual understandings existed as refuge and support for the responsible male domestic authority. But in the young queen's inner household she herself embodied that authority. When she recounts the tale of her refusal, she speaks as the proud head of household, fiercely reluctant to imperil a single member of the circle: "the Queen maintains *all* her ladies. . . . her *Ladies* are *entirely* her own affair, and *not* the Ministers." To the images of queen as daughter to paternal ministers and as blushing adolescent caught between two eligible admirers, we have to add the still more startling figure of the queen as chief among a tribe of women.

The conversations among those women disappeared in the surrounding air. Among the many documents in this heavily textualized affair we have no register of what the Mistress of the Robes said to the First Lady of the Bedchamber; their laughter is unrecorded. But we have every reason to suppose that during this perplexing week when their intimacy was the subject of raucous public debate, these women used their tongues in self-defense. Whatever was said and whatever its tone, it would have helped give Victoria the temerity to speak back to the looming men. "Sir Robert Peel has behaved very ill," she reports to Melbourne in the second of three letters on the May 9, "and has insisted on my giving up my Ladies, to which I replied that I never would consent, and I never saw a man so frightened" (*Letters*, 204).

Few at the time could have known of the queen's flashing anger and her pleasure in Peel's fear. But though the details have had to wait for history, the form of the conflict was perfectly conspicuous. This strong-willed hedged-in adolescent of a queen had defeated the usurping Tory male. Among all the circulating images of crisis, the one most sharply etched was that of the "roused woman" refusing to surrender the rights of her bedchamber. Just six months later the engagement of the queen to Albert would begin her assimilation into the role of wifely exemplar. But for the space of that period of crisis and its aftermath, Victoria lived out an assertion of royal privilege that was at the same time a glaring disclosure of stresses within an emerging domestic ideal. From the summit of her high anomaly, she exposed the emerging crux of private life: the more prized, the more pillaged.

PART TWO

Beneath the Banner of Home

Chapter Three

SARAH STICKNEY ELLIS: THE ARDENT WOMAN AND THE ABJECT WIFE

1

> With regard to asking for advice, I believe I did not state the case
> properly, for I often ask, but seldom take advice, and this you will
> find one of the lamentable consequences of marrying a middle-
> aged independent woman; for what should I have done had I not
> been able to act without advice? The kind of life I have led has
> tended very much to confirm a strength of will which, in my
> childhood, was, I believe, almost without equal. What will you do
> with such a companion?
>
> —Sarah Stickney[1]

> There is an honest pride which every true heart has a right to feel,
> and England's pride should be in the inviolable sanctity of her
> household hearths. When these are deserted, the sentence of her
> degradation will be sealed.
>
> —Sarah Stickney Ellis[2]

Our first epigraph comes from a letter written by Sarah Stickney to her husband-to-be, the anthropologist and missionary, William Ellis. Its sentiments should come as something of a shock to those who know "Mrs. Ellis" only through her influential series of domestic celebrations heavily clustered in the 1840s, which have earned her the contemporary reputation as "probably the best-known idealogue of domesticity."[3] Ellis herself would no doubt have rejoiced in the description. But our epigraph is a first effort to make Ellis strange again: she has been familiar for too long.

But we also want to make strange a question that has preoccupied cultural historians for some time: what brought domestic mythology to prominence in the later 1830s and 1840s? Some compelling answers have been given, including the influence of Evangelical morality,[4] the growing separation of home and work,[5] the example of the married queen,[6] the new centrality of household management,[7] a lingering romantic cult of the child,[8] a refusal of the new economy,[9] a retreat in the face of an urbanism seen as insanitary, overcrowded, anarchic.[10] For as long as the question is put, all of these dimensions of explanation need to be respected, and in these next two chapters we follow still other emphases: in particular, the influence of missionary-ethnography and the resource of aesthetic experience. We also emphasize that home was not merely understood in negative terms, as a retreat or a refuge, but that much writing of the 1840s aimed to create a profusion of positive values. In *Barnaby Rudge* Dickens writes of "every little household favourite which old associations made a dear and precious thing."[11] Part of the task of the 1840s was to produce the conditions of inward-turning nostalgia as a defense against the public storm. Home will be the place where personalities, objects, and traditions entwine, manufacturing "precious" value out of "old associations."

Still, what makes the question strange is that domesticity is no single object. The Victorians often talked as if it were, and contemporary historians are necessarily bound by a limited vocabulary that can imply a unitary referent: home, family, hearth. And yet part of what the publicizing of family life revealed was that the house was no consistent zone of privacy, but a miscellany. Wives were unlike husbands, children unlike lodgers, sexuality distinct from friendship; the middle-class home differed from Irish rookeries, as aristocratic domestic service contrasted with middle-class housekeeping; the kitchen was not the parlor, nor the garret a dining room; the lines of status and gender, work and wealth, conviviality and solitude, food and cleanliness intersected at countless points. Home contained a thousand regions and a thousand pleasures, but it can go wrong in a thousand ways.

Our discussion of Caroline Norton and Queen Victoria suggests how the eye of spectacle uncovers the disorderly character of private life. In the conditions of the 1830s, the public thrill revealed the confusion gathering around such terms as youth, beauty, and innocence, and also mother, wife, and friend. It's right to see a movement from the unsettled agitation of the thirties toward certain recurrent conventions, ritualized phrases, and formulaic images. But one claim of the present study is that no orthodoxy ever reached a settlement. The conventions of home were in perpetual motion. Even as codes of normality came into prominence, they were revised, abandoned, and then replaced by new statements of the code. A privileged class found itself constantly adjusting the terms of its home sanctity. One reason lay in the challenge of those beyond the walls of respectability, who were living examples of life outside ostensibly universal norms of comfort. But, as the next three chapters emphasize, much of the difficulty was internal to the family mythology. The heterogeneity of both the household and its affirmations meant that contradiction was inescapable, and that, as the domestic discourse conducted itself in the public sphere, it continually changed the terms of conversation.

2

Sarah Stickney Ellis must stand alongside Dickens as one of the deep designers of the midcentury family imagination. Her titles alone indicate the relentless powers of concentration: *The Women of England*, *The Wives of England*, *The*

Daughters of England, The Mothers of Great Men, and on and on. But before she became the great domestic apologist of the 1840s, Sarah Stickney was an ambitious writer of the previous decade, the prolific author of fiction in a popular soft-moralistic mode, including the successful *Pictures of Private Life*, as well as the energetically speculative book of criticism, *The Poetry of Life*. Living at a home with her aging father, a farmer who suffered increasing financial hardship, looking on happily as her siblings married, watching horrified as all three of her sisters died young, and then tending their children when and as she could, Sarah Stickney saw writing as the one road out of a tightening domestic entanglement.

In her resolve to write speedily and to publish widely, to win many readers and to earn significant sums, Stickney was, and knew herself to be, a member of a remarkable generation of women writers, who understood that turns in the publishing market and in popular taste meant that they could achieve the material success of literary production. Caroline Norton has been our first example here, but other important figures surround her, including Laetitia Landon and Mary Shelley. The young Sarah Stickney belongs in this company, as one who trades on the conventions of sentiment, but who does so from the standpoint of an unsentimental professionalism.

To return to the Stickney Ellis of the 1830s is not only to recover the prehistory of a domestic polemicist; it is, as we go on to suggest, to change the terms by which we understand that polemic. In Ellis's early works the virtues of hearth and home sound as only one chord among many others, and indeed the characteristic subject of the first successful stories is not family virtue but family cataclysm. Blighted hopes, chronic unhappiness, moral degeneracy are recurrent figures in the portrait of "private life," a pattern that should alert us to a signal feature of early Victorian domestic reverie: namely, the extent to which the celebration of home life emerges from the spectacle of failure. The tumult of the Queen Caroline affair and the trials of Caroline Norton represented conspicuous examples within the visible public arena, while the stories of Sarah Stickney display the persistence of disasters performed within the small theater of home.

By the end of the decade, with the publication of *The Women of England*, Ellis began to establish herself as the semiofficial portraitist of an aspiring middle-class domesticity. But we do well to remember that neither her orthodoxy nor her reputation dropped from the sky. To reread Ellis must be to recover the forgotten sources of her domestic faith, and when that is done, the faith will show itself as no serene condition of moral repose but as a willful social critique that sets one cultural affirmation against another, and as a summons to action far more challenging than a few catchphrases can convey. We easily recall that she called women "relative creatures"—but what did she call men?

3

A great turn occurred in Sarah Stickney's career when she met William Ellis, who first appeared in her life in the guise of editor, initially willing to publish her poetry and one of her early stories, and then eager to recruit her as an active participant in his new ventures. Ellis, who had spent long years in the South Sea Islands, published his magisterial book *Polynesian Researches* (1829) on his return. Accepted as definitive, it stands as one of the early landmarks of a Victorian anthropology coming to a difficult birth in the writings of missionaries. Certainly, the only thing greater than Ellis's faith in exact scientific description was his faith in an unseen God. Even as he presents an exhaustive multivolume compendium of the "moral, intellectual and physical character" of the Polynesians, he attempts, by means of the same evidence, to offer a "satisfactory history of the origin, progress, and results of the Missionary enterprise, which, during the last thirty years, has, under the Divine blessing, transformed the barbarous, cruel, indolent, and idolatrous inhabitants of Tahiti, and the neighbouring Islands, into a comparatively civilized, humane, industrious, and Christian people."[12] It would be right to speak of the difficult double aim of the labor—to document and to convert—were it not that documentation was already so pervaded by the motives of conversion that the distinction loses its grip.[13] Nowhere is this clearer than when the far-traveling Ellis looks at the native village and asks, Where is home?

A decade after his *Polynesian Researches* Ellis published a second large work, the *History of Madagascar*. Taken together, these two books not only dramatize the union of the ethnographer and the missionary; they also offer specific renderings of what Ellis understood as the barbarous pathology of native family life, the most sensational example being the practice of infanticide. His account of the South Sea Islanders' claims that "two-thirds of the children were murdered by their parents" (*Polynesian*, 251), and in the work on Madagascar, one finds this shocking passage.

> The tendency of all the systems of absurd and degrading superstition which enslave and afflict mankind, is to triumph in fiendlike despotism over the first, the strongest and tenderest dictates of humanity; yet, perhaps, amidst the various exhibitions of its malignant domination, it does not unfold a scene of more affecting wretchedness than is presented on these occasions. An infant, a new-born, perfectly helpless, unconscious infant, smiling, perhaps in innocence, is laid on the ground in the narrow entrance to a village, or a fold, through which there is scarcely room for cattle to pass; several cattle are then driven violently in, and are made to pass over the spot in which the child is placed, while the parents with agonizing feelings stand by waiting the result.[14]

Infanticide is the ghastly horror designed to transfix the reader, but within the rhetoric of Ellis's ethnography it cannot stand alone. It appears rather as the horrific symptom of a broader disease: the islanders' complete and systematic failure to constitute domestic order. Within the ethnographic sketches, native families always stagger on the point of collapse; even to call them families is made to seem an act of charity. The same failure of affection that allows the murder of children loosens the bond between men and women and encourages the second horror, the practice of polygamy. Of the South Seas Islanders, Ellis writes that "the marriage tie was probably one of the weakest and most brittle that existed among them; neither party felt themselves bound to abide by it any longer than it suited their inclinations and their convenience," so that marriage "was dissolved whenever either of the parties desired it . . . ; the husband took other wives, and the wife other husbands" (*Polynesian*, 273). Polygamy, he writes in the Madagascar study, "is a curse to the land"—and one only pauses before this judgment because infanticide had already seemed to hold the title of reigning abomination (*Madagascar*, 172). If the abominable emanates from every direction, this is because for Ellis the native family is less an example of alternative, even immoral, cultural norms, than the essential antitype of domesticity.

Indeed the antitype shows itself most clearly in those cases where the sensational polygamy and infanticide recede into the background, leaving the intact family, such as it is, to display its routine domestic anarchy. The children of Madagascar "are not subjected to the least restraint, but are, as soon as able to act for themselves, allowed to follow their own inclination" (*Madagascar*, 161), while in the South Sea Islands, "No regular parental discipline was maintained. As soon as the child was able to will or act for itself, it was generally exempt from all control, and given up to the influence of its own inclinations. Their years of childhood and youth were passed in indolence, irregularity, and the unrestrained indulgence in whatever afforded gratification" (*Polynesian*, 261). From such scenes of disorder, Ellis draws the homiletic conclusion that "filial affection is rarely seen where enlightened and judicious parental discipline is not uniformly manifested" (*Madagascar*, 161).

This last formulation is perfectly representative, enacting a reflex movement from "accursed" native customs to contrasting norms of English family health. Ellis's ethnography continually stimulates a regulative domestic imagination, with the result that the "enlightened and judicious" standards—whether these concern the appropriate age of marriage, the naturalness of monogamy, or the necessity of parental discipline—stand not merely as tacit background assumptions but as richly embroidered presentations of all that native life denies. The local custom is always awaiting the comparative gesture, as in the following summative judgment.

> The father and the mother, with their children, never, as one social happy band, surrounded the domestic hearth, or, assembling under the grateful shade of the verdant grove, partook together, as a family, of the bounties of Providence. The

nameless but delightful emotions, experienced on such occasions, were unknown
to them, as well as all that we are accustomed to distinguish by the endearing
appellation of domestic happiness. (*Polynesian*,128)

The historical significance of such judgments extends beyond the imposition
of foreign social norms by the missionary ethnographer. Writing about Polynesia, Ellis writes about England. The sensationalism of the narrative becomes
an argument for the purification of the reader's family life. By studying its
negative image, the English home might become the exemplary theater of
human flourishing, where the "social happy band" will perform those acts
of judicious discipline leading to warm affection.[15] The recoiling from idolatrous "depravity" in the lower hemisphere toward regulative norms of family
life in the north—Ellis performed this gesture that his work asks his readers
to imitate. At a moment of self-conscious historic transition, the inhabitants
of Madagascar and the South Sea Islands are recruited to play a role in the
development of early Victorian family discourse. They did so in company of
another, even more sensationalized figure, one who was also helped to an awful
celebrity through the labors of William Ellis: the Hindu wife, victim of suttee,
the Indian ritual that allowed so many English citizens to become engrossed
in their outrage.

In 1833 Ellis edited an annual called *The Missionary; or Christian's New
Year's Gift*, a new and sober entrant in the field of expensive, once-yearly
publishing. In deliberate contrast to the light fare of other annuals, Ellis's volume collected memoirs, ethnographic sketches, poems, stories, and engravings, all pursuing the themes of the missionary enterprise. The opening essay
was a scarifying exposition of Hindu widow sacrifice, its author, Reverend
James Hough, insisting that of all the customs that had been recently recorded
by missionaries to the East and that had aroused "deep and extensive" reaction
in England, "none excited a more painful sensation in the Christian world than
the practice of burning the Hindoo widow on her husband's funeral pyre."[16]
Hough's claim to originality lies in claiming that alongside widow burning
was found the even more frightful ceremony of burying the live woman within
the husband's grave. As if this catalog of horrors were not enough, Ellis's
annual included a second essay on "The Suttee," an anguished eyewitness
account by the Reverend Henry Townley.

What such writings confirm is that the growing power of the domestic ideal
in the 1830s emerged not only within a national frame but within the context
of a global ethnography that fed scandalous images into the machinery of
respectability. There can be no doubt that Reverend Hough was right to speak
of the "deep and extensive" reaction to such images, and if this were the only
link to the discourse of domesticity, the importance of the ethnographic context
would be secure. As it happens, the link could not be more direct.

It was in William Ellis's 1833 volume of *The Missionary; or Christian's New Year's Gift* that Sarah Stickney published her first story for him. Called "The Young Hindoo," it fits easily within the religious ethnography that gives the volume its identity. Yet, even as it participates in the strongly defined editorial project, the story turns in a direction that will prove astonishingly fruitful. Stickney avoids the tones of indignation that pervade the collection and that identify Indian life, in the words of one contributor, as a "repulsive deformity and sanguinary despotism."[17] Her "young Hindoo" has indeed known "the horrors of idolatry, for he had seen the abominations of Juggernaut, and the cruelties of superstition."[18] But having experienced the transformative power of conversion, his past has been exorcized. By the time he arrives in Stickney's story, he has become a paragon of Christian virtue, whose fictive role is not to enforce the depravity of Hinduism but to expose a spiritual weakness lurking in England.

Within the Beverly family that welcomes the convert to its comfortable home there lives one Isabella, a fastidious daughter who trembles at the thought of a "frightful black man," an "odious Indian" ("Hindoo," 146), living in the house. The work of the story is to reverse the task of conversion. Isabella, who has been taught by a governess to "value the accomplishments of fashionable life before the graces of the humble Christian" (147), must learn to give up the vanities of fashion. The climax occurs when she finally recognizes the spiritual authority of the Christianized Hindu, who in forgiving her coarse prejudice welcomes her to a reborn faith.

The reversal of the ethnographic gaze, which Stickney alone performs in the 1833 volume, will become the guiding tactic of her fiction of the later thirties. Self-consciously, she takes up the role of the "keen observer of the varieties of human character" (150), whose task is to study England as if it were a Polynesian island. Christopher Herbert has shown with compelling force how the researches of the missionary ethnographers came to be applied to the working classes at home, with the result that categories of "Polynesianism" become the basis for diagnosing social behavior within a national and urban frame.[19] What one finds in Sarah Stickney's fiction of the 1830s is the application of such categories to the genteel classes perched high atop the social pyramid. All through her *Pictures of Private Life*, Stickney reviles the decadence of an aristocracy and gentry, which provide flagrant examples of the "depravity" that had been located in antipodal southern islands. What William Ellis describes as the wild pursuit of "inclination" in Madagascar and Polynesia reappears in the country estates of England. The infidelity of husbands and wives, the catastrophic neglect of children, the absorption in the artifice of fashion, these obsessively reiterated scenarios represent the northerly correspondences to the polygamy, the infanticide, and the pagan ritualism of the south.

In a letter of 1838, written soon after their marriage, Stickney Ellis records that she and her husband "have just completed a volume of Missionary Records which ought to have been done three months ago, and on the instant it was finished he agreed with a publisher to have out his "History of Madagascar" by next May; so that I shall have no hope of anything but write, write, writing for the next four months to come" (*Home Life*, 89). The letters show her intimate relation to her husband's work: indeed, whatever her creative role in his publications, she evidently spent a good deal of time "write, write, writing" the sentences that appeared under his name. It should then be no surprise to find that her own writing exhibits full consciousness of the arguments and intentions of ethnography.

Stickney Ellis comfortably assumes the rhetorical standpoint of the emerging discipline—its science of "temperament" and its acts of distancing from the customs it records. However, her relation to the other part of the tense coupling, the Christian missionary project, is far less certain. As an aspiring writer eager to publish widely, Stickney adjusted the content of her fiction to its container. Within Reverend Ellis's *The Missionary; or Christian's New Year's Gift*, she conformed to the topos given by the missionary enterprise, though not without leaving the impress of her own concerns. But in other stories in other annuals, or in her own collections of fiction, she allowed the tone of orthodoxy to drop entirely. Notoriously, in a story called "Marriage As It Might Be," she represented a hard-riding Anglican clergyman as a moral monster, whose wife must dread each day

> the noisy entrance of a blustering man, calling with impatience for his dinner, to which he would sit down without either grace or gratitude; and when his keen appetite was a little abated, came the luxury of recounting his "glorious leaps," and magnificent exploits, added to that of drinking my health, with the health of any other, man, woman, or child, who might "prove an excuse for the glass," and then followed the deadly stupor of exhausted animal nature, with the heavy eyelids closed, and the whole face stiffened into the stupidity of sleep.[20]

Elsewhere, she merely leaves religious life in the shadows—a display of indifference that quickly exposed her to criticism. In a preface to the later editions of *Pictures of Private Life*, she defends herself against the charge that "the religious sentiments it contains are not sufficiently DECIDED," asking her readers to remember that "my object is rather moral than religious" (viii).

Whatever effect other critics may have had on her work, the opinions of William Ellis became inescapable, as the two grew closer in the middle thirties. *The Missionary; or Christian's New Year's Gift* survived only long enough to be the gift of a single year, but two years later William Ellis began to edit *The Christian Keepsake and Missionary Annual*, which would have a hardier publishing life. Ellis's preface acknowledges the swarm of annuals competing for readers, but, as if in answer to Stickney's own apology, he announces that his will be a "volume more decidedly religious."[21] Indeed the title itself throws down a direct religious challenge to its gorgeously secular rival, *The Keepsake*, within whose pages Caroline Norton was just then displaying her self-acknowledged facility for "light serial literature."

In this new annual, Sarah Stickney again assumes an important writerly role, but surviving letters suggest that she and Ellis performed some difficult editorial negotiations. She proposes an essay on "Temper"—"Now, don't be so rude as to say that I, of all people, ought to understand the subject" (*Home Life*, 67)—while he counters with a request for an essay on Maria Jane Jewsbury. Expressing disappointment and doubting that she can muster enthusiasm for "Miss Jewsbury," she asks him to think again. Perhaps he did. But the Jewsbury essay duly appeared under the title "Mrs. Fletcher, late Miss Jewsbury" whereas the work on "Temper" had to wait until the next decade.

Though taken on with reluctance, the essay on Jewsbury/Fletcher discovers a way to keep faith with the challenge of "temper," refusing to produce the moral paragon that William Ellis evidently had in mind. In this, it stands as a pendant to Stickney's revealing study of Felicia Hemans published in the *Christian Keepsake* the year before. Her Mrs. Fletcher, like her Hemans, is a complexly divided woman, riven between the "ambition of superior intellect" and the demands of family attention.[22] "The wonder," writes Stickney, is that "knowing and feeling herself to be thus endowed, she should have devoted her time, her care, and her affectionate attention, to the household duties of her father's family" ("Mrs. Fletcher," 33). In Stickney's sketch, "Mrs. Fletcher" arrives at spiritual purity and home virtue only after a long passage through self-mortification. And the case of Hemans is even more urgent. Her domestic example sits uneasily alongside the poetic achievement, the fame, the scandal of her broken marriage, the untimely death. A "diffusion of holy calm over feelings too easily excited"—this is the enviable but strenuous attainment.[23] Stickney evokes the scenario of genius, imagination, and ardent affection, all "combining against the domestic peace of woman by their power to excite, to bewilder, and to lead astray" ("Mrs. Hemans," 67). The key thought in both essays is the overcoming of intensely turbulent, "bewildering" emotion in an extraordinary act of domestic self-subdual; this thought will follow a twisting course through the writing of "Sarah Ellis."

4

Only just barely, letters survive that allow us to place the negotiation between evangelizing editor and young professional writer in the closer context of their courtship, and within the small arena of personal life can be found the subtle disturbances that will live on within the multivolume domestic opus inaugurated in 1839.

The epigraph at the head of our chapter, where the self-described "middle-aged independent woman" comically asserts her indifference to her fiancé's advice and (perhaps only half-comically) warns him of her "strength of will . . . almost without equal," links Sarah Stickney to the writing women whose lives she was recording in the *Christian Keepsake*. She plainly understands herself as yet another woman of talent, for whom writerly "ambition" and "domestic happiness" stare warily at one another.

To see her as an unwilling participant in her husband's life of Christian activism would be badly mistaken. From her early wish not "to exclude a certain degree of moral or religious sentiment" (*Home Life*, 52) to her eagerness to contribute to the *Christian Keepsake*, she continually acknowledges, even when she resists, the growing claims of "serious Christianity." She converts to Congregationalism in marrying Ellis; she also accepts the workaday responsibilities of an evangelizing life.

Still, though she resolutely faces the change in her life, she disarms neither her will nor her irony. Anticipating a party that she and her husband will give for "upwards of forty missionaries," she writes, "Only think the figure I shall cut as a minister's wife."

> In my capacity of Mrs. Ellis I sit amongst these London people, who neither know nor care where I come from, what are or have been my pursuits, or thoughts, or feelings; and what is worse, who never would care for me if I were to live with them for fifty years. I often wonder how they would look if I were to startle them with an outburst of North Country enthusiasm. (*Home Life*, 84)

In addition to visiting the poor and serving on a "Penitentiary committee," she becomes the superintendent of a large Sunday school, a position "which requires a great deal of attending to" and which she describes as "much against my inclination" (95). Even after several years of marriage and of extraordinary success as celebrant of home, she can still assume the tones of domestic subversion, mocking her husband for his failure of imagination.[24] At the very moment of submission—"What a blessing it is to feel that, whether weary or at rest, we are in the hands of one who knows what is best for us!"—insurrection quickens: "Still there are natural yearnings of the heart that will not be subdued" (118). Can it be a surprise then that even the celebrated author of *The Wives of England* imagines the doom of marriage? Having heard that "Mrs. Jameson," "an irreproachable woman," has separated from her husband, she meditates that "There seems to be no luck with authoress-wives. Mary Howitt and I have stood it out yet—but there is no saying what may come" (128).

The connecting strand in this web of ironic reflections on marriage is an ideal of "enthusiasm" or "yearning" or "imagination" at odds with a religiously or morally regulated home life. A sign of the conflict came in an exchange during the late stages of the courtship, when William Ellis asks whether she is fond of devotional poetry, to which Stickney sharply replies,

I fear you will be disappointed when I tell you I *am not*. In early life, when my love of poetry was intense, my taste was formed first by Burns, then Milton, then Shakespeare, and afterwards by Byron and Moore. I regret that the *beauties* of such writers are so seldom found in devotional poetry. (*Home Life*, 70)

Whatever such a forthright opinion meant for her marriage, it certainly meant a good deal for Sarah Ellis's domestic mission. Just here we come on a second, distinct strain of thought that will wend its way into the public statements of her household triumphalism. What her edgy response to her husband-to-be reveals is that Sarah Stickney was a committed late romantic author, whose writing career, like her marriage, would play out the struggle between romanticism and Evangelicalism.

In her early, successful publication, *The Poetry of Life* (1835), Stickney began by identifying her subject not as a genre of literature but as a condition of character—"poetry" as a receptiveness to impressions, a susceptibility to passion combined with a faculty of arrangement. What gives force to the otherwise banal idea is Ellis's view of a new social crisis of poetry. Her generation of writers must now acknowledge that in recent decades England has so advanced as "a commercial country" that economic pressures threaten the survival of poetry.[25] She understands the task of her book as a counteroffensive to a post-Napoleonic business ethic, an act of refusal that insists that "poetry has a world of its own—a world in which, if sordid calculations have no place, the noble, the immortal part of our nature is cherished, invigorated and refined" (13). Invoking the many disabilities of modern economic life, she pointedly asks "who would choose to explore the wild and magnificent beauties of mountain scenery, with one whose ideas were bounded by the limits of the Bank of England?" (19) The leading characteristic of poetry, then, is that in the age of "sordid calculation" and political economy it preserves and burnishes a world apart.

In exactly such terms Ellis will soon define the successful home. Before she has identified her publishing program as the invention of a modernized domestic ideal, Ellis locates poetry in the place where the hearth will soon appear: the site of a heightened affectivity under threat from coarse commercialism. A career that begins in the tones of wistful cultural nostalgia—how might we preserve the fading voice of poetic genius that once sounded in Shakespeare, in the Bible, and in Milton?—turns to a purposive and confident social mission: how can we build a properly modern home life that will avoid the degradations of commerce?

And yet wasn't the social force of Ellis's writing a sustained critique of the lure of aristocracy? Wasn't her moral target the indolence and the amoralism of the genteel classes? So we have said, and this is indeed a vigorous emphasis throughout her work. But much of the force of Ellis's domestic project depends on a double object of critique. On the one hand, she offers a stiff rejection of the failure and obsolescence of aristocracy and gentry. *The Women of England* (1839), the book that begins the long succession of tracts, holds that the lustrous title "the women of England" belongs not to those of great rank who possess "a *hired* hand for every kindly office," nor those "amongst the indigent and most laborious of the community," but to those standing in the broad ground between, "who are restricted to the services of from one to four domestics, —who, on the one hand, enjoy the advantages of a liberal education, and on the other, have no pretension to family rank."[26] The women of the middle-class, in their balance of privilege and constraint, are the bearers of the great domestic opportunity that history has bestowed.

The Women of England, that is, affirms the special dignity of the middle classes, even as it offers withering appraisal of the economic life of commercial England. And if any sense is to be made of midcentury domesticity, this tense subtlety must be respected. It turns up in Dickens as regularly as in Ellis: the distinction between middle-class capitalism and bourgeois domesticity. Instead of identifying these forces as the same historical process, we need to recognize the extent to which early Victorian home life appeared not only as distinct from the new economy but as its saving alternative.

Against this background of Ellis's divided inheritance, we return to the blunt action, repeated anew in each publication: the assertion of woman's inferiority and her consignment to the space of home. Early in *The Daughters of England* she offers a formulation that can stand for countless others: "As women, then, the first thing of importance is to be content to be inferior to men—inferior in mental power, in the same proportion that you are inferior in bodily strength."[27] This is the absolute condition of the abjection: an asymmetry at once prior and final. Ellis offers no argument for conditions that she regards as naturally and spiritually ordained. Here is the notorious essence traditionally extracted from her oeuvre, and there can be no doubt that such brazen aphorisms influenced the popular philosophy of home life. The many editions of her works should be enough to convince us of the reach of her views; later in life she would write proudly of the "sympathy with public feeling which sold 'The Women of England' " (*Home Life*, 190). We have good reason to believe that in the family legal struggles of the next few decades, the diffusion of Ellis's opinions, as "sympathetic" precipitates of the public consciousness, helped to forestall changes in the laws of married women's property and divorce.

What, then, are we now to make of Ellis's publishing struggles with her editor, her assertions of independence with that editor turned husband, and her ironic appraisal of their married state? Shall we see her public assertion of female inferiority as a suppression of attitudes and tones indulged outside the pages of her tract? We should and must. But this is precisely the wrong place to curtail reflection. If the *Women*, *Wives*, and *Daughters* of England represent a victory for her husband's missionary Evangelicalism, it is a victory whose spoils begin to burn in the hand.

Take, for instance, this characteristic (but still uncanny) address to her women readers: "It is quite possible you may have more talent [than your husband], with higher attainments, and you may also have been generally more admired; but this has nothing whatever to do with your position as a woman, which is, and must be, inferior to his as a man."[28] The distribution of talents among actual men and women has nothing to do with the doctrine of "inferiority," because it is an a priorism, a moral formalism that depends on nothing so coarse as an empirical encounter. The asymmetry of men and women is a structure independent of the content of particular lives.

Ellis periodically invokes her a priorism as if to remind herself and her readers of a foundational belief. And yet, as soon as her writing leaves the abstract formalism, as it so quickly does, the picture of fireside comfort changes its colors. Nowhere is the change more dramatic than in her representation of men.

The inveterate profligacy of men—this is the glaring sign of Ellis's challenge. Those men, whose superiority is ensured by axiom, nevertheless show a dazzling gift for moral degradation. Through her fiction passes a collection of repellent male failures, including the alcoholic doctor, the misanthropic landowner, the faithless dandy, the anxiously ineffectual ironmonger, the brutal and hypocritical clergyman. When Ellis begins the writing of her domestic tracts at the end of the 1830s, this gallery of male shame shows itself to be part of a systematic understanding of domestic character.

It is hard to reason with a man, she notes in *The Wives of England*, because of "the incapability under which he labours, of placing himself in idea in the situation of another person, so as to identify his feeling with theirs, and thus to enter into what they suffer and enjoy, as if the feeling were his own" (177). Accordingly, men are "comparatively destitute" of the power of sympathy. But allowances must be made, given an upbringing that encourages "precocious selfishness": "we may grant [men] to be selfish, and pity, rather than blame them that they are so" (68–69). The debility appears so fundamental that it can be described as an "inborn selfishness" (*Women*, 61).

If the male child begins life as a primal egotist, he soon enters a world that aggravates rather than heals the wound. The boy, watching the fate toward which he is tending, "sees before him every day and every hour, a strife, which is nothing less than deadly to the highest impulses of the soul" (*Women*, 60)— and this because the new economic circumstances, in England and beyond, "are rousing men of every description to tenfold exertion in the field of competition in which they are engaged; so that their whole being is becoming swallowed up in efforts and calculations relating to their pecuniary success" (64). Considerations of "worldly aggrandisement" are "constantly misleading their steps, closing their ears against the voice of conscience, and beguiling them with the promise of peace, where peace was never found" (60). In her sustained and trenchant criticism Ellis sees that "the fault is in the system" (65), which allows no one to escape the logic of competition:

> [T]here is no union in the great field of action in which he is engaged; but envy, and hatred, and opposition, to the close of the day—every man's hand against his brother, and each struggling to exalt himself, not merely by trampling upon his fallen foe, but by usurping the place of his weaker brother, who faints by his side, from not having brought an equal portion of strength into the conflict, and who is consequently borne down by numbers, hurried over, and forgotten. (60–61)

Here in *The Women of England* Ellis formulates the theory of domesticity that she will articulate over the next two decades, at whose center stands the repudiation of an economy that has created unprecedented material wealth only by corroding human dignity. A just reading of Sarah Ellis must restore this critique to a central place in her work, much as a just reading of Victorian domesticity must acknowledge that the fetish of home life created both a spatial logic and a discursive tonality that allowed "fireside comfort" to serve as the basis for repudiating the emergent competitive economy. Needless to say, the fireside was always a flickering and unstable basis, and with the rise of more conspicuous consumption after midcentury, middle-class home life became an ever weaker alternative to "worldly aggrandisement." Nevertheless, as Ellis's collection of books went through numerous reprintings, they continued to assert the radical incompatibility between the virtues of home and the "eager pecuniary speculations," the "fierce conflict of worldly interests" (*Daughters*, 20).[29] Crucially for Ellis, the terrible problem is not only that the public world, "the mart, the exchange, [and] the public assembly" (*Women*, 61), has become a morally fallen domain; it is also that public life has begun to erode the integrity of men's private character.

> We cannot believe of the fathers who watched over our childhood, of the husbands who shared our intellectual pursuits, of the brothers who went hand in hand with us in our love of poetry and nature, that they are all gone over to the side of mammon, that there does not lurk in some corner of their hearts a secret longing to return; yet every morning brings the same hurried and indifferent parting, every evening the same jaded, speechless, welcomeless return—until we almost fail to recognize the man, in the machine. (*Women*, 56)

The harshness of the critique, its social reach and its psychological depth, cannot be dismissed in the pursuit of a settled category for the infamous "Mrs. Ellis," matron of the separate spheres. What she understands as the "deterioration of the husband's character" is not a tragic anomaly, but the sadly inevitable effect of structural degradation in the public sphere. Not merely depicted within such easy epithets as "refuge" or "balm," home appears as an urgently required therapeutic ward, the only possible site of recovery from the debilitating forces of worldly commerce.

Nor is it only a matter of recovery from the economic disease; men suffer too from a sexual immorality that had shown itself among the rampant predators in Ellis's fiction. Outside the circle of the hearth, men cannot be trusted with women—or, as she sharply puts it, "whatever may be the excellences of man in every other walk of life, it is a subject of something more than regret, that these excellences are so little called forth in his intercourse with women in mixed society. As a father, a husband, a brother, and a friend, his character assumes a totally distinct aspect" (*Daughters*, 306). The great labor of domesticity is to bind men within these family roles, because when he leaves them, he risks becoming a machine or a fox.

In light of these accumulating instances, the temptation is great to see Ellis as engaged in a canny subversion of her official views. Yet the question is more difficult than this. Given the proudly categorical assertions of male superiority blazoned through her writings, there is scant warrant for seeing Ellis as a clever ironist, sapping the foundations of her absolutism.

The special difficulty of her oeuvre is that the slogans, mottoes, and catchphrases of female abjection, so easy to extract, occur within the dense portrait of the household in its distressingly concrete particularity. In the preface to *The Women of England*, Ellis insists that she has no desire to add to the many "dissertations upon female character," that she will instead offer a study of the "particular minutiae" of a wifely life (v–vi). What allows for the challenge of this frank domestic ethnography is that the moral formalism is so securely embedded. Having assumed her foundational principles, Ellis is then free to describe the world in its shocking impurity. At no point does the unblinking scrutiny of male moral failure so much as nudge the absolute principle of women's inferiority. Indeed, it seems just to the extent that she assumed the utter inviolability of her doctrine that she allowed herself such keenly critical remarks on individual members of the species Man.

5

What has been lost in a thin reading of Ellis is an acknowledgment of what she asks women to perform within the domestic theater. An inferiority it forever remains, but an inferiority that presides over the superior realm of home. Eternally vigilant in discouraging the ambition of the middle-class woman to leave their "little sphere" (*Wives*, 121), Ellis goes so far as to reject the work of the governess as a desertion of her natural family. Women cannot hope to accomplish what is given to the other sex to perform in the great world; even to make the attempt is to sacrifice themselves in an alien field of toil. And yet once Ellis has made this root gesture of confinement, she begins an extraordinary act of imaginative investment.

Beginning in 1839 with *The Women of England* and continuing with unrelenting stamina, Ellis turned the home into a profuse garden of meanings. Her
professional ambitions suggest that when she grasped the publishing possibilities in a series of books on "female character," she cannily devised a lengthen-
ing list of domestic virtues. But the motives scarcely matter. The responsiveness of her readers and her own sensitivity to those responses mean that
whatever impelled her to this monumentalism of "minor morals," it circulated
widely as part of the self-understanding of the age.

What distinguished that monumentalism, first of all, was an aestheticizing
of household responsibility that owes everything to her early apology for *The
Poetry of Life*. Ellis is a proponent of "usefulness," no one more so, but a key
step in the elaboration of her domestic mythology is the fusion of the useful and
the poetic, where household poetry chiefly signifies an elevation of common
experience until what had seemed merely instrumental becomes a gorgeous
value in itself. Just here Ellis's most notorious phrase—"suffer, and be still"—
needs to be restored to its immediate context within *The Daughters of England*.
"If for man," she writes,

> it be absolutely necessary that he should sacrifice the poetry of his nature for the
> realities of material and animal existence, for woman there is no excuse—
> for woman, whose whole life, from the cradle to the grave, is one of feeling, rather
> than of action; whose highest duty is so often to suffer, and be still; whose deepest
> enjoyments are all relative; who has nothing, and is nothing, of herself; whose
> experience, if unparticipated, is a total blank; yet, whose world of interest is
> wide as the realm of humanity, boundless as the ocean of life, and enduring as
> eternity. (133)

Here, the abjection of women is brutally exposed, and exposed in terms that
will prove so intractable in the legal battles of the next twenty-five years. But
here too is a stirring within the absolutism. It was, after all, a first presupposi-
tion in Ellis and her epigones that women should go willingly into marriage;
should not be coerced into obedience. Although she will speak in revealing
moments of wives and daughters as a "community of slaves" (282), the clearest aim in the writing project is to persuade women that they ought freely to
embrace what they cannot in any case escape: an inferiority, a dependence,
a suffering.

Toward that rhetorical end, the series of books constructs an intricate articulation of the symbolic system of home. The realm of man remains impalpable
and mysterious. They go away, the brothers and the husbands, into the degraded public space, simplified by its worldly coarseness, leaving the household not only as the site of value but as the bristling locus of an intricate social
world: diverse, multifarious, dramatic.

Indeed, the theatricality of domesticity becomes one of the recurrent motifs in Ellis's project. The mechanism of the household requires constant vigilance, because the dimensions are so various, their balance so fragile. The wife who commands this intricacy will glow with a moral radiance. She who has arranged the stage and who at last can say "I am ready," enjoys one of the "most precious" moments of life: "To be ready a little before the time, is like pausing for a moment to see the great machine of human events at work, to mark the action and the play of every part, and to observe the vast amount of feeling which depends upon every turn of the mighty wheel" (*Daughters*, 52). Family life is a perpetual drama, in which "Every passing event, however insignificant to the eye of the world, has its crisis, every occurrence its emergency, every cause its effect; and upon these she has to calculate with precision, or the machinery of household comfort is arrested in its movements, and thrown into disorder" (*Women*, 28–29). Unmarried women may think of wifeliness as disagreeable or commonplace, but

> could they really know what deep and thrilling interests are to be involved in this her duty, what high and burning zeal—what quenchless ardour—what enthusiasm, what feeling, are expended upon the avocations of each day, marked as they must be, by the ebb and flow of affection's ceaseless tide. Could they see all this, how would they start astonished at their own mistake. (*Wives* 339)

The trembling sense of constant crisis, the thrill of permanent emergency, the demand for an ever vigilant readiness—this is the pervasive image.

No doubt such views suited the book of those men, and also those women, who sought to discourage any wifely impulse to leave the circumscription of the fireside. Home was no prison; it was a theater: this is a conveniently alluring vision, fit to dissolve restless daydreams. Why be curious to test the world beyond four walls, when those walls contained such prodigious opportunities?

But to accept such a message was not after all to bring the negotiations of family life to an end. In the campaign to invest home not merely with value but with such an elaborate articulation of roles and responsibilities, thrills and emergencies, the effect is that whatever the immediate interests served by the ideology of confinement, the wife grows into a figure of looming consequence. She is the one who must manage the servants, anticipate the husband's needs, bring up the children, and maintain the good spirits of home.[30]

In significant part this accrual of power is due to woman's gentle theft of the lamp of spirituality. With her lively sense of the worldly debasements of public life, Ellis identifies the home, rather than church or chapel, as the vital spiritual center. Indeed, the proposal is more startling than first appears. For though the religious sense may be the redemptive end of life, in Ellis it cannot be the origin. On this point she is provocatively explicit. In *The Women of England*, she argues that there is no other sure foundation for good morals, than correct religious principle; but I do believe, that, with the Divine blessing, a foundation may be laid in very early life, before the heart has been illuminated by Divine truth, or has experienced its renovating power, for those domestic habits, and relative duties, which in after life will materially assist the development of the Christian character. And I am the more convinced of this, because we sometimes see, in sincere and devoted Christians, such peculiarities of conduct as materially hinder their usefulness—such early-formed habits, as they themselves would be glad to escape from, but which continue to cling around them in their earthly course, like the clustering of weeds in the traveller's path. (viii–ix)

In her ethnographic narrative, family life is more than a spiritual enclosure safe from the encroachments of the world; it is the only sure source of enlightenment; it is what keeps religious character from growing "peculiar." The awkward habits, the "weeds" that she noticed even in such earnest Christians as her husband, can only be softened by the warmth of the hearth. Faith is a last, best grace that owes as much to the English wife as she owes to it.

The English wife should, therefore, regard her position as a central one, and remember that from her, as the head of the family and the mistress of a household, branch off in every direction trains of thought, and tones of feeling, operating upon those more immediately around her, but by no means ceasing there; for each of her domestics, each of her relatives, and each of her familiar friends, will in their turn become the centre of another circle, from which will radiate good or evil influence extending outwards, in the same manner, to the end of all things—to the disruption of all earthly ties, and the union of the great family of heaven. (*Wives*, 344–45)

The Wives of England imagines nothing less than a womanly counterworld, an alternative network of social relations, that offers the radical prospect of the "disruption of all earthly ties"—specifically, the earthly bonds of commerce and public life—achieved through a marriage of spirituality and domesticity.

Men sustain their formal preeminence; and no one should diminish the strength of the formalism. But beneath the uncompromising surface, much occurs. Ellis's men show the real weakness lurking everywhere beneath the ideal form, even as her books endow women with more responsibilities, more meaning, expanded in each successive text. By the mid-1840s the result is that the wife presides over a complex social domain, which in effect becomes the truly flourishing political unit, no longer to be found in the public realm. As Catherine Gallagher puts it, " 'family,' the term often contrasted with 'society,' at length becomes its surrogate."[31] The "little world" of home has been so minutely subdivided that it serves as no mere alternative to social life but a rival social world, which must face the problems that parliamentarians, professionals, financiers, and industrialists have failed to solve. It falls to the wife

Chapter Four

̄OM'S PINCH: THE SEXUAL SERPENT BESIDE THE DICKENSIAN FIRESIDE

1

̄the end of *Martin Chuzzlewit* the fortune-seeking parasite Chevy Slyme ̄ears in the improbable guise of a police officer, no longer hopeful of ̄cting wealth from his distant relationship to old Martin, but no less round ̄resentment or less brazen in his pomposity. Slyme, having been called to ̄ Jonas Chuzzlewit for murder, turns to Martin and flaunts his degradation ̄t were a deadly weapon: "Can you see the man of your family who has ̄ talent in his little finger than all the rest in their united brains, dressed as ̄ce officer without being ashamed? I took up with this trade on purpose ̄ame you. I didn't think I should have to make a capture in the family, ̄h."[1]

̄ pair Dickens with Sarah Ellis, first because the two figures created the ̄highly visible representations of family life during the decade of its se-̄entrenchment. With the confidence of their publishing success, both un-̄k to amplify and ramify the affirmations of home. More than any other ̄gures of their moment, they stirred the circulation of domestic imagery. ̄all, the romance of the hearth didn't come ready-made; it required strenu-̄bor to saturate the home with intimations of pleasure. But the second ̄n for the pairing is that Dickens and Ellis show how affirmation is shad-̄ by insecurity, even how affirmation generates its enemies. The wreck of ̄huzzlewit family, only heightened by the folly of Slyme, alerts us to the ̄hat if Dickens's work of the 1840s becomes the very type and ideal of ̄stic pleasure, it remained sharply attentive to family catastrophe. Dickens ̄ doubt a visionary architect of home comfort, but he was also a theatrical ̄cer of household Slyme.[2]

̄ late stages of *Martin Chuzzlewit* unfold under the bright success of *A ̄mas Carol*, a story that not only opened new literary possibilities but ̄romised a cure for the commercial disappointments of the novel. Dickens ̄ed a hand-rubbing relish in the first weeks of 1844 when the scale of his ̄ph became clear. "Its success is most prodigious," he wrote to a corre-̄ent on January 2, "And by every post, all manner of strangers write all ̄er of letters to him about their homes and hearths, and how this same ̄ is read aloud there, and kept on a very little shelf by itself."[3] Here is the ̄tful fantasy. A tale of the hearth stands on a shelf near the hearth; an

"to establish throughout the household the principles of order, justice, and benevolence" (*Wives*, 263), guided by the principle that "every member of her household has some rights which others ought not to be allowed to infringe." Like any other honorable official, she must apply "her love of justice in the settlement of all difficulties which may arise out of the clashing of individual interests" (272–73).

The construction of separate spheres carried with it two possibilities for female abasement. The first, securely achieved through both legal prohibition and moral discouragement, was the establishment of home as the proper sphere for middle-class women. The second, perpetually contested, was the relegation of women to subordinate relations within that little world. After all, it was never simply assumed that having been deprived of power in the public sphere, women would retrieve it in private life. The iconography of mid-Victorianism abounds with figures of the patriarch, having returned from the exercise of authority at work to wield it a second time at home.[32] A tacit but tense struggle played out though the 1840s was over the question of domestic supremacy. Would this, too, belong to Man?

In the 1837 novel *Pretension*, Ellis describes how the heroine's mother becomes the family potentate, noting that "we generally find it is the most active, not the most powerful spirit that gains the mastery" (*Pictures*, 62). One might take this as a motto for her own struggle in her books, to assign so much activity to women that they will attain the command of home, a command that is by no means unchallenged. In what she calls an "aside" to her woman readers, a "whisper upon paper" (*Wives*, 118), she satirizes the inefficient bustle of men about the house, asserting the rights of women to the "sphere of domestic arrangements," where they should be permitted to "rule with undisputed authority" and in which men should participate only at her request.[33] "In all respects," the wife should be "the mistress of her own house," and "the interior of her establishment must be kept sacred to her alone" (*Wives*, 41).

The ongoing insinuations of male failure belong to a pattern of polemical advocacy, discrediting the claims of men to the station of household patriarch. Not only do they bumble when they are home; home is where they so seldom are. In one scathing passage, she imagines a visitor to England who expects to find a resplendent hearth within the rising middle-class suburbs but finds something quite different.

> What would a foreigner think of those neat, and sometimes elegant residences, which form a circle of comparative gentility around our cities and our trading towns? What would he think, when told that the fathers of those families have not time to see their children, except on the Sabbath-day? and that the mothers, impatient and anxious to consult them about some of their domestic plans, have to wait, perhaps for days, before they can find them for five minutes disengaged, either

from actual exertion, or from that sleep which necessarily steals upon them imme-diately after the over-excitement of the day has permitted them a moment of re-pose. (*Women*, 57)

The persistent motif of the man as elsewhere-than-home makes a revealing appearance in a publication of 1845, *The Young Ladies' Reader*, where Ellis offers a selection of extracts for a regular program of family reading. (One of her recommendations, we note, is "The Sacrifice of the Hindoo Widow," while her old favorite Byron is nowhere in sight.) Where solitary reading breaks family unity and invites "habits of exclusive, selfish and unprofitable musing," reading aloud lets the mother ensure that her children will "do nothing in secret, and have no enjoyment in which she, as their truest friend, might not partake." Good for the entire family, the routine has a still more pointed benefit: it "would do more towards keeping families united than the establishment of a new police for forcing fathers, husbands, and brothers to remain within their own doors" (*Young Ladies' Reader*, 11, 16, 18).

The theme of woman's self-subdual, first broached in those early essays on Hemans and Jewsbury for the *Christian Keepsake*, thus takes on a keener meaning. From a late-twentieth-century standpoint, self-repression stands nat-urally opposed to emancipation; for Ellis, however, this was not the historically urgent contest. The relevant distinction was that between a husband's disciplin-ing of his wife and the wife's self-discipline. Very soon, this choice would be recognized as a barren one not worth making, but in the late thirties and forties, it played a significant part in the defensive parrying of patriarchal encroach-ment. The self-chastening of the wife offered Ellis a way to represent the inconsequence of the wayward husband. Indeed the terrible image of the wife affixing her own chains gives a figure for the intricate play of abjection and independence.

But as she wrote her way into the 1840s with increasing confidence, the language of abjection begins to yield to the language of independence. As men languished in public places, suffering from the fury of competition, drawn to immoral temptations, Ellis's women require, and tolerate, less "interference" from their exhausted and domestically inept husbands. In her third year of her own marriage she wrote to her stepdaughter, expressing a wish that her friend Anna Sewell would join her coming travels: "I do think it would restore her, and I should have the only thing I really want—the happiness of female society. Perhaps you will think I undervalue your father, but I assure you he has been so kind, so social, and sometimes as entertaining as a man could be. But still I have a pining sometimes for the society of my own sex" (*Home Life*, 113).

The mixture of motives in Sarah Ellis is stirred too fully to separate. Partly, she joins in her husband's missionary project, now understood as a national mission to regulate household life by convincing women to accept their abjec-tion and dependence. And partly she writes out of a "pining" for a female

society that rises out of abjection and is increasingl[y] enough to sustain a flourishing counterworld to the so[ ] men. Antithetical as they are, the two strains develop [ ] quite logical, relation. The very energy of the attempt [ ] the home sphere is a worthy moral arena prepares for [ ] own life exemplifies: that the middle-class wife super[ ] manifold and profuse—a micropublic world within t[ ] shift of conception will open into the great world be[ ] resolute traditionalism invests femininity with a pow[ ] soon ask for more than Sarah Ellis is prepared to giv[ ] surely right to argue that the New Woman of the late[r] the managerial arena that Ellis and others design.[35]

The paradox of Sarah Ellis—for indeed she speaks [ ] helps with a broader Victorian conundrum: why is it [ ] of the century, as the ideology of separate spheres bec[ ] feminism will rise to a prominence and a visibility [ ] again dislodged? One beginning to an answer lies [ ] traditionalism such as Ellis's began to generate its [ ] cisely in the extreme character of its separation betw[ ] women for an independence. But on this question m[ ] image of household bliss materializes as itself a piece of such bliss. This stirs one of Dickens's most cherished thoughts—namely, that through the good offices of his books, he himself will take a place inside the intimate circle of the family. Within the tale he evokes the magical transformation whereby an affectionate storyteller enters the room as a benevolent household ghost: "The curtains of his bed were drawn aside; and Scrooge, starting up into a half-recumbent attitude, found himself face to face with the unearthly visitor who drew them: as close to it as I am now to you, and I am standing in the spirit at your elbow."[4]

Dickens had few doubts about the accomplishment of *Chuzzlewit*, but many worries about its fraying relations to his readers.[5] The appreciation of a discriminating few (the immediate Dickens circle, especially Forster, and Dickens himself) was not enough to satisfy him; the decision to take a respite from novel writing was a response to the breach in solidarity with his readers. But what he could not have known was that *A Christmas Carol* would heal that breach so suddenly. At a moment of crisis—not only in his relations to his readers but in the state of his finances—a sweetly sung fable revived him. It not only repaired his ties with his audience, spectacularly so, but in the same stroke it confirmed a tonality and a subject matter. A fond author assumes the voice of intimacy, and while evoking dangerous images, both social and personal, he sustains the easy touch on the reader's elbow, in reassurance that a curving narrative will find its way back to the hearth.

Domesticity and popularity—the tight link between them was a signal event in the Dickensian forties. The celebration of the happy private household converged with the public event of the author's renewed success, making an important conjunction not only for Dickens but also for his readers, whose pleasure in the work evidently increased with the awareness that other readers in other homes were turning the same pages, emitting the same joyous laugh, drying similar tears. The ambitious project of the Christmas books in the middle forties depends on the insight that private pleasure is what many thousands might have in common. Recall Scrooge's passage through London in the company of the second spirit.

> By this time it was getting dark, and snowing pretty heavily; and as Scrooge and the Spirit went along the streets, the brightness of the roaring fires in kitchens, parlours, and all sorts of rooms, was wonderful. Here, the flickering of the blaze showed preparations for a cosy dinner, with hot plates baking through and through before the fire, and deep red curtains, ready to be drawn, to shut out cold and darkness. There all the children of the house were running out into the snow to meet their married sisters, brothers, cousins, uncles, aunts, and be the first to greet them. Here, again, were shadows on the window-blind of guests assembling; and there a group of handsome girls, all hooded and fur-booted, and all chattering at once, tripped lightly off to some near neighbour's house. (*Carol*, 49)

Once the tale achieves its startling success, this picture incorporates a new element, now including Dickens's story of Christmas as part of the annual ceremony, indeed a privileged part, which reminds each fireside that it exists within a universe of privacies. Popularity is not external to the domestic vocation of the forties: success is not an incidental bonus. The paradisal image of private affection includes a consciousness of the seeing eye. The publishing triumph ensures that private enjoyment will be publicly consumed. Dickens exults in the acclaim that greets his reading of the story, the thousands that "have been driving me mad at Liverpool and Birmingham, with their loving cheers." Here is the central rhythm of the Dickensian forties: the movement from the closed room to the sea of faces, from isolation to overwhelming visibility.[6]

The crisis of *Martin Chuzzlewit* may have yielded the "solution" of *A Christmas Carol*, but a telling feature of the novel is that it continues past the crisis point. A work that had seen its author's fortunes ebbing can now conclude in the glow of his popular recovery. The domestic apotheosis of Ruth and Tom Pinch in the last quarter of *Martin Chuzzlewit* is a precipitate of the success of the Christmas story. As the extent of the success widened, *Martin Chuzzlewit* built its own hearth for the Pinches.

> Pleasant little Ruth! Cheerful, tidy, bustling, quiet little Ruth! No doll's house ever yielded greater delight to its young mistress, than little Ruth derived from her glorious dominion over the triangular parlour and the two small bedrooms.

> To be Tom's housekeeper. What dignity! Housekeeping, upon the commonest terms, associated itself with elevated responsibilities of all sorts and kinds; but housekeeping for Tom implied the utmost complication of grave trusts and mighty charges. (ch. 39)

And so on, and on, for Tom's "busy little sister" (ch. 39). The treacle in these passages, sickly sweet to contemporary taste, cannot obscure the disturbances lying beneath the surface.[7] All through the last movements of *Martin Chuzzlewit*, worries tremble beneath the hearthstone. The cooing affection of the siblings represents not only the warmth of the fireside but also the response to a chill.[8] What we call the Tom Pinch problem can easily be lost to view in the glare of Dickens's success and his toasting of family cheer. Concentrating on a cluster of works written in a brief period, we mean to show that in the early 1840s as the fiction consolidates its public affirmations, it also designs a pattern of loss and lack. The good Dickensian home is built with mournful mortar.

2

At the start, Dickensian family life was typically an undisturbed interior, a safe cave. In the earliest writings home was an anchor, a value, an emanation, a tone, a taste, an aroma, a pudding. Dingley Dell and Pickwick's Dulwich villa in *The Pickwick Papers*, the Maylie house in *Oliver Twist*, the homes of the Garlands and the Nubbles in *The Old Curiosity Shop*—these are familiar refuges, sites of food and foolishness, laughter and tears, personal safety and emotional release. Yet, for all their positive charge, they remain values without structure, households without articulation, buildings without architecture. Warmly undifferentiated nodes of love, they avoid the stresses of contrast. And much as the rooms of the house repeat one another's comfort, so do members of the family replicate each another's virtues. Between Harry and Rose Maylie or the three Garlands there is so little to choose that affection often seems nothing more than benevolence's tender love of itself.

No less than the family, the house is reassuring in its sameness. Even as it serves as a figure of moral, psychological, and social health, it does so as a single consistent volume unbroken by separate forces and values. The late enraptured vision of Pickwick's house in Dulwich is characteristic.

> Everything was so beautiful! The lawn in front, the garden behind, the miniature conservatory, the dining-room, the drawing-room, the bed-rooms, the smoking-room, and above all the study with its pictures and easy chairs, and odd cabinets, and queer tables, and books out of number, with a large cheerful window opening upon a pleasant lawn and commanding a pretty landscape, just dotted here and there with little houses almost hidden by the trees; and then the curtains, and the carpets, and the chairs, and the sofas! Everything was so beautiful, so compact, so neat and in such exquisite taste, said every body, that there really was no deciding what to admire most.[9]

Impossible to decide "what to admire most," because impossible to distinguish one "beautiful," "compact," "neat" space from another.

In the thirty-fourth chapter of *Oliver Twist* Fagin and Monks loom up outside the window of the Maylie house, where a happy "completely domesticated" Oliver is dozing over his books.[10] This tableau, illustrated by Cruikshank, gives an emblem of Dickens's early construal of the relations between home and its enemies. The threat stands on the outside, on the far side of the window. The interior is where reassuring emotions can circulate warmly, and the mission is to secure this realm of safety, marked by the outer walls.

The desire to secure closed walls and then to accumulate an immensity of artifacts, a plenitude of emotions—this is a deep and widely shared impulse. Dickens uses other words and different rhythms, but he joins Sarah Ellis in a dream of inwardness that depends on an ever increasing profusion of domestic signs. It's not enough to imagine a household fortified against the devils on the street; it's equally important to populate the closed rooms with bottles, lemons, loaves, uncles, and nieces.

Why and even when this changes for Dickens is difficult to say. But as early as *Barnaby Rudge* (1841), the pleasure of inwardness is already mixed with dread. This unsteady novel breaks down the simplicity of the private realm and reveals family life as no idyll of the same but as a vulnerable community containing hidden disruption. In *Barnaby Rudge*, when the apprentice Sim Tappertit lurks in the workshop beneath the Varden home, nursing his desire for his master's daughter Dolly, he embodies the connection between a changing architecture and the social life it contains. The Gothic plan of the Varden home, attractive to Dickens in its eccentricity and irregularity, satisfying in its arrangement into many little pockets, nevertheless brings new threats. In the rooms tucked away below, Tappertit the dandified apprentice fusses over his appearance, while plotting to waylay Dolly. The novel takes pains to make Sim ludicrous, painting him as a "thin-faced, sleek-haired, sharp-nosed, small-eyed little fellow, very little more than five feet high," who nevertheless secretes shocking impulses.[11] His body appears as another Gothic design, one whose architecture conceals its glaring flaw.

> [I]n the small body of Mr. Tappertit there was locked up an ambitious and aspiring soul. As certain liquors, confined in casks too cramped in their dimensions, will ferment, and fret, and chafe in their imprisonment, so the spiritual essence or soul of Mr Tappertit would sometimes fume within that precious cask, his body, until with great foam and forth and splutter, it would force a vent, and carry all before it. (ch. 4)

Where Dickens says soul here, we might easily read sex. Indeed in the novel's political climax, the Gordon riots, Sim's sex comes spluttering out of its cask. When he first approaches Dolly Varden after she has been abducted, she assumes that he has come to rescue her and that her father must be close at hand. Instead Tappertit declares his love and explains the surprise in this way:

> "You meet in me, Miss V," said Simon, laying his hand upon his breast, "not a 'prentice, not a workman, not a slave, not the victim of your father's tyrannical behaviour, but the leader of a great people, the captain of a noble band, in which these gentlemen are, as I may say, corporals and serjeants. You behold in me, not a private individual, but a public character; not a mender of locks, but a healer of the wounds of his unhappy country. Dolly V., sweet Dolly V., for how many years have I looked forward to this present meeting!" (ch. 59)

Political violence merges with erotic revolt. And in the case of Tappertit, politics is rendered as a symptom, not a cause, the pathology of an unrelieved resentment, whose source is the ache of sexuality.

Within *Barnaby Rudge*, Tappertit's assault on Dolly Varden is specifically linked to the fragile equilibrium of the Gothic house. The irregular space gives delight but also permits secrets to fester, and when the secrets are told, sinister defects are revealed. The posturing of the amorous apprentice is the absurd epitome of the problem that pervades the family dramas of *Barnaby Rudge*:

"to establish throughout the household the principles of order, justice, and benevolence" (*Wives*, 263), guided by the principle that "every member of her household has some rights which others ought not to be allowed to infringe." Like any other honorable official, she must apply "her love of justice in the settlement of all difficulties which may arise out of the clashing of individual interests" (272–73).

The construction of separate spheres carried with it two possibilities for female abasement. The first, securely achieved through both legal prohibition and moral discouragement, was the establishment of home as the proper sphere for middle-class women. The second, perpetually contested, was the relegation of women to subordinate relations within that little world. After all, it was never simply assumed that having been deprived of power in the public sphere, women would retrieve it in private life. The iconography of mid-Victorianism abounds with figures of the patriarch, having returned from the exercise of authority at work to wield it a second time at home.[32] A tacit but tense struggle played out though the 1840s was over the question of domestic supremacy. Would this, too, belong to Man?

In the 1837 novel *Pretension*, Ellis describes how the heroine's mother becomes the family potentate, noting that "we generally find it is the most active, not the most powerful spirit that gains the mastery" (*Pictures*, 62). One might take this as a motto for her own struggle in her books, to assign so much activity to women that they will attain the command of home, a command that is by no means unchallenged. In what she calls an "aside" to her woman readers, a "whisper upon paper" (*Wives*, 118), she satirizes the inefficient bustle of men about the house, asserting the rights of women to the "sphere of domestic arrangements," where they should be permitted to "rule with undisputed authority" and in which men should participate only at her request.[33] "In all respects," the wife should be "the mistress of her own house," and "the interior of her establishment must be kept sacred to her alone" (*Wives*, 41).

The ongoing insinuations of male failure belong to a pattern of polemical advocacy, discrediting the claims of men to the station of household patriarch. Not only do they bumble when they are home; home is where they so seldom are. In one scathing passage, she imagines a visitor to England who expects to find a resplendent hearth within the rising middle-class suburbs but finds something quite different.

> What would a foreigner think of those neat, and sometimes elegant residences, which form a circle of comparative gentility around our cities and our trading towns? What would he think, when told that the fathers of those families have not time to see their children, except on the Sabbath-day? and that the mothers, impatient and anxious to consult them about some of their domestic plans, have to wait, perhaps for days, before they can find them for five minutes disengaged, either

from actual exertion, or from that sleep which necessarily steals upon them immediately after the over-excitement of the day has permitted them a moment of re-
pose. (*Women*, 57)

The persistent motif of the man as elsewhere-than-home makes a revealing
appearance in a publication of 1845, *The Young Ladies' Reader*, where Ellis
offers a selection of extracts for a regular program of family reading. (One of
her recommendations, we note, is "The Sacrifice of the Hindoo Widow," while
her old favorite Byron is nowhere in sight.) Where solitary reading breaks
family unity and invites "habits of exclusive, selfish and unprofitable musing,"
reading aloud lets the mother ensure that her children will "do nothing in
secret, and have no enjoyment in which she, as their truest friend, might not
partake." Good for the entire family, the routine has a still more pointed benefit:
it "would do more towards keeping families united than the establishment of
a new police for forcing fathers, husbands, and brothers to remain within their
own doors" (*Young Ladies' Reader*, 11, 16, 18).

The theme of woman's self-subdual, first broached in those early essays
on Hemans and Jewsbury for the *Christian Keepsake*, thus takes on a keener
meaning. From a late-twentieth-century standpoint, self-repression stands naturally opposed to emancipation; for Ellis, however, this was not the historically
urgent contest. The relevant distinction was that between a husband's disciplin-
ing of his wife and the wife's self-discipline. Very soon, this choice would be
recognized as a barren one not worth making, but in the late thirties and forties,
it played a significant part in the defensive parrying of patriarchal encroach-
ment. The self-chastening of the wife offered Ellis a way to represent the
inconsequence of the wayward husband. Indeed the terrible image of the wife
affixing her own chains gives a figure for the intricate play of abjection and
independence.

But as she wrote her way into the 1840s with increasing confidence, the
language of abjection begins to yield to the language of independence. As men
languished in public places, suffering from the fury of competition, drawn to
immoral temptations, Ellis's women require, and tolerate, less "interference"
from their exhausted and domestically inept husbands. In her third year of her
own marriage she wrote to her stepdaughter, expressing a wish that her friend
Anna Sewell would join her coming travels: "I do think it would restore her,
and I should have the only thing I really want—the happiness of female society.
Perhaps you will think I undervalue your father, but I assure you he has been
so kind, so social, and sometimes as entertaining as a man could be. But still
I have a pining sometimes for the society of my own sex" (*Home Life*, 113).

The mixture of motives in Sarah Ellis is stirred too fully to separate. Partly,
she joins in her husband's missionary project, now understood as a national
mission to regulate household life by convincing women to accept their abjection and dependence. And partly she writes out of a "pining" for a female

society that rises out of abjection and is increasingly understood as strong enough to sustain a flourishing counterworld to the sordid sphere of the absent men. Antithetical as they are, the two strains develop in close historical, if not quite logical, relation. The very energy of the attempt to persuade women that the home sphere is a worthy moral arena prepares for the recognition that her own life exemplifies: that the middle-class wife superintends a domestic polis, manifold and profuse—a micropublic world within the home that by a short shift of conception will open into the great world beyond.[34] The initial act of resolute traditionalism invests femininity with a power and an ardor that will soon ask for more than Sarah Ellis is prepared to give. Elizabeth Langland is surely right to argue that the New Woman of the later century develops out of the managerial arena that Ellis and others design.[35]

The paradox of Sarah Ellis—for indeed she speaks against her own doxa—helps with a broader Victorian conundrum: why is it that by the middle years of the century, as the ideology of separate spheres becomes finally entrenched, feminism will rise to a prominence and a visibility from which it is never again dislodged? One beginning to an answer lies in the recognition that a traditionalism such as Ellis's began to generate its own undoing—that precisely in the extreme character of its separation between the sexes, it trained women for an independence. But on this question more remains to be said.

TOM'S PINCH: THE SEXUAL SERPENT BESIDE THE DICKENSIAN FIRESIDE

1

Near the end of *Martin Chuzzlewit* the fortune-seeking parasite Chevy Slyme reappears in the improbable guise of a police officer, no longer hopeful of extracting wealth from his distant relationship to old Martin, but no less round with resentment or less brazen in his pomposity. Slyme, having been called to arrest Jonas Chuzzlewit for murder, turns to Martin and flaunts his degradation as if it were a deadly weapon: "Can you see the man of your family who has more talent in his little finger than all the rest in their united brains, dressed as a police officer without being ashamed? I took up with this trade on purpose to shame you. I didn't think I should have to make a capture in the family, though."[1]

We pair Dickens with Sarah Ellis, first because the two figures created the most highly visible representations of family life during the decade of its secure entrenchment. With the confidence of their publishing success, both undertook to amplify and ramify the affirmations of home. More than any other two figures of their moment, they stirred the circulation of domestic imagery. After all, the romance of the hearth didn't come ready-made; it required strenuous labor to saturate the home with intimations of pleasure. But the second reason for the pairing is that Dickens and Ellis show how affirmation is shadowed by insecurity, even how affirmation generates its enemies. The wreck of the Chuzzlewit family, only heightened by the folly of Slyme, alerts us to the fact that if Dickens's work of the 1840s becomes the very type and ideal of domestic pleasure, it remained sharply attentive to family catastrophe. Dickens was no doubt a visionary architect of home comfort, but he was also a theatrical producer of household Slyme.[2]

The late stages of *Martin Chuzzlewit* unfold under the bright success of *A Christmas Carol*, a story that not only opened new literary possibilities but also promised a cure for the commercial disappointments of the novel. Dickens enjoyed a hand-rubbing relish in the first weeks of 1844 when the scale of his triumph became clear. "Its success is most prodigious," he wrote to a correspondent on January 2, "And by every post, all manner of strangers write all manner of letters to him about their homes and hearths, and how this same Carol is read aloud there, and kept on a very little shelf by itself."[3] Here is the delightful fantasy. A tale of the hearth stands on a shelf near the hearth; an image of household bliss materializes as itself a piece of such bliss. This stirs one of Dickens's most cherished thoughts—namely, that through the good offices of his books, he himself will take a place inside the intimate circle of the family. Within the tale he evokes the magical transformation whereby an affectionate storyteller enters the room as a benevolent household ghost: "The curtains of his bed were drawn aside; and Scrooge, starting up into a half-recumbent attitude, found himself face to face with the unearthly visitor who drew them: as close to it as I am now to you, and I am standing in the spirit at your elbow."[4]

Dickens had few doubts about the accomplishment of *Chuzzlewit*, but many worries about its fraying relations to his readers.[5] The appreciation of a discriminating few (the immediate Dickens circle, especially Forster, and Dickens himself) was not enough to satisfy him; the decision to take a respite from novel writing was a response to the breach in solidarity with his readers. But what he could not have known was that *A Christmas Carol* would heal that breach so suddenly. At a moment of crisis—not only in his relations to his readers but in the state of his finances—a sweetly sung fable revived him. It not only repaired his ties with his audience, spectacularly so, but in the same stroke it confirmed a tonality and a subject matter. A fond author assumes the voice of intimacy, and while evoking dangerous images, both social and personal, he sustains the easy touch on the reader's elbow, in reassurance that a curving narrative will find its way back to the hearth.

Domesticity and popularity—the tight link between them was a signal event in the Dickensian forties. The celebration of the happy private household converged with the public event of the author's renewed success, making an important conjunction not only for Dickens but also for his readers, whose pleasure in the work evidently increased with the awareness that other readers in other homes were turning the same pages, emitting the same joyous laugh, drying similar tears. The ambitious project of the Christmas books in the middle forties depends on the insight that private pleasure is what many thousands might have in common. Recall Scrooge's passage through London in the company of the second spirit.

> By this time it was getting dark, and snowing pretty heavily; and as Scrooge and the Spirit went along the streets, the brightness of the roaring fires in kitchens, parlours, and all sorts of rooms, was wonderful. Here, the flickering of the blaze showed preparations for a cosy dinner, with hot plates baking through and through before the fire, and deep red curtains, ready to be drawn, to shut out cold and darkness. There all the children of the house were running out into the snow to meet their married sisters, brothers, cousins, uncles, aunts, and be the first to greet them. Here, again, were shadows on the window-blind of guests assembling; and there a group of handsome girls, all hooded and fur-booted, and all chattering at once, tripped lightly off to some near neighbour's house. (*Carol*, 49)

Once the tale achieves its startling success, this picture incorporates a new element, now including Dickens's story of Christmas as part of the annual ceremony, indeed a privileged part, which reminds each fireside that it exists within a universe of privacies. Popularity is not external to the domestic vocation of the forties: success is not an incidental bonus. The paradisal image of private affection includes a consciousness of the seeing eye. The publishing triumph ensures that private enjoyment will be publicly consumed. Dickens exults in the acclaim that greets his reading of the story, the thousands that "have been driving me mad at Liverpool and Birmingham, with their loving cheers." Here is the central rhythm of the Dickensian forties: the movement from the closed room to the sea of faces, from isolation to overwhelming visibility.[6]

The crisis of *Martin Chuzzlewit* may have yielded the "solution" of *A Christmas Carol*, but a telling feature of the novel is that it continues past the crisis point. A work that had seen its author's fortunes ebbing can now conclude in the glow of his popular recovery. The domestic apotheosis of Ruth and Tom Pinch in the last quarter of *Martin Chuzzlewit* is a precipitate of the success of the Christmas story. As the extent of the success widened, *Martin Chuzzlewit* built its own hearth for the Pinches.

> Pleasant little Ruth! Cheerful, tidy, bustling, quiet little Ruth! No doll's house ever yielded greater delight to its young mistress, than little Ruth derived from her glorious dominion over the triangular parlour and the two small bedrooms.

> To be Tom's housekeeper. What dignity! Housekeeping, upon the commonest terms, associated itself with elevated responsibilities of all sorts and kinds; but housekeeping for Tom implied the utmost complication of grave trusts and mighty charges. (ch. 39)

And so on, and on, for Tom's "busy little sister" (ch. 39). The treacle in these passages, sickly sweet to contemporary taste, cannot obscure the disturbances lying beneath the surface.[7] All through the last movements of *Martin Chuzzlewit*, worries tremble beneath the hearthstone. The cooing affection of the siblings represents not only the warmth of the fireside but also the response to a chill.[8] What we call the Tom Pinch problem can easily be lost to view in the glare of Dickens's success and his toasting of family cheer. Concentrating on a cluster of works written in a brief period, we mean to show that in the early 1840s as the fiction consolidates its public affirmations, it also designs a pattern of loss and lack. The good Dickensian home is built with mournful mortar.

2

At the start, Dickensian family life was typically an undisturbed interior, a safe cave. In the earliest writings home was an anchor, a value, an emanation, a tone, a taste, an aroma, a pudding. Dingley Dell and Pickwick's Dulwich villa in *The Pickwick Papers*, the Maylie house in *Oliver Twist*, the homes of the Garlands and the Nubbles in *The Old Curiosity Shop*—these are familiar refuges, sites of food and foolishness, laughter and tears, personal safety and emotional release. Yet, for all their positive charge, they remain values without structure, households without articulation, buildings without architecture. Warmly undifferentiated nodes of love, they avoid the stresses of contrast. And much as the rooms of the house repeat one another's comfort, so do members of the family replicate each another's virtues. Between Harry and Rose Maylie or the three Garlands there is so little to choose that affection often seems nothing more than benevolence's tender love of itself.

No less than the family, the house is reassuring in its sameness. Even as it serves as a figure of moral, psychological, and social health, it does so as a single consistent volume unbroken by separate forces and values. The late enraptured vision of Pickwick's house in Dulwich is characteristic.

> Everything was so beautiful! The lawn in front, the garden behind, the miniature conservatory, the dining-room, the drawing-room, the bed-rooms, the smoking-room, and above all the study with its pictures and easy chairs, and odd cabinets, and queer tables, and books out of number, with a large cheerful window opening upon a pleasant lawn and commanding a pretty landscape, just dotted here and there with little houses almost hidden by the trees; and then the curtains, and the carpets, and the chairs, and the sofas! Everything was so beautiful, so compact, so neat and in such exquisite taste, said every body, that there really was no deciding what to admire most.[9]

Impossible to decide "what to admire most," because impossible to distinguish one "beautiful," "compact," "neat" space from another.

In the thirty-fourth chapter of *Oliver Twist* Fagin and Monks loom up outside the window of the Maylie house, where a happy "completely domesticated" Oliver is dozing over his books.[10] This tableau, illustrated by Cruikshank, gives an emblem of Dickens's early construal of the relations between home and its enemies. The threat stands on the outside, on the far side of the window. The interior is where reassuring emotions can circulate warmly, and the mission is to secure this realm of safety, marked by the outer walls.

The desire to secure closed walls and then to accumulate an immensity of artifacts, a plenitude of emotions—this is a deep and widely shared impulse. Dickens uses other words and different rhythms, but he joins Sarah Ellis in a dream of inwardness that depends on an ever increasing profusion of domestic signs. It's not enough to imagine a household fortified against the devils on the street; it's equally important to populate the closed rooms with bottles, lemons, loaves, uncles, and nieces.

Why and even when this changes for Dickens is difficult to say. But as early as *Barnaby Rudge* (1841), the pleasure of inwardness is already mixed with dread. This unsteady novel breaks down the simplicity of the private realm and reveals family life as no idyll of the same but as a vulnerable community containing hidden disruption. In *Barnaby Rudge*, when the apprentice Sim Tappertit lurks in the workshop beneath the Varden home, nursing his desire for his master's daughter Dolly, he embodies the connection between a changing architecture and the social life it contains. The Gothic plan of the Varden home, attractive to Dickens in its eccentricity and irregularity, satisfying in its arrangement into many little pockets, nevertheless brings new threats. In the rooms tucked away below, Tappertit the dandified apprentice fusses over his appearance, while plotting to waylay Dolly. The novel takes pains to make Sim ludicrous, painting him as a "thin-faced, sleek-haired, sharp-nosed, small-eyed little fellow, very little more than five feet high," who nevertheless secretes shocking impulses.[11] His body appears as another Gothic design, one whose architecture conceals its glaring flaw.

> [I]n the small body of Mr. Tappertit there was locked up an ambitious and aspiring soul. As certain liquors, confined in casks too cramped in their dimensions, will ferment, and fret, and chafe in their imprisonment, so the spiritual essence or soul of Mr Tappertit would sometimes fume within that precious cask, his body, until with great foam and forth and splutter, it would force a vent, and carry all before it. (ch. 4)

Where Dickens says soul here, we might easily read sex. Indeed in the novel's political climax, the Gordon riots, Sim's sex comes spluttering out of its cask. When he first approaches Dolly Varden after she has been abducted, she assumes that he has come to rescue her and that her father must be close at hand. Instead Tappertit declares his love and explains the surprise in this way:

> "You meet in me, Miss V," said Simon, laying his hand upon his breast, "not a 'prentice, not a workman, not a slave, not the victim of your father's tyrannical behaviour, but the leader of a great people, the captain of a noble band, in which these gentlemen are, as I may say, corporals and serjeants. You behold in me, not a private individual, but a public character; not a mender of locks, but a healer of the wounds of his unhappy country. Dolly V., sweet Dolly V., for how many years have I looked forward to this present meeting!" (ch. 59)

Political violence merges with erotic revolt. And in the case of Tappertit, politics is rendered as a symptom, not a cause, the pathology of an unrelieved resentment, whose source is the ache of sexuality.

Within *Barnaby Rudge*, Tappertit's assault on Dolly Varden is specifically linked to the fragile equilibrium of the Gothic house. The irregular space gives delight but also permits secrets to fester, and when the secrets are told, sinister defects are revealed. The posturing of the amorous apprentice is the absurd epitome of the problem that pervades the family dramas of *Barnaby Rudge*:

the domestication of conflict, the involution of desire, envy, repression, and revolt, transforming the household from refuge into cauldron.

"Not a private individual, but a public character"—Tappertit's boast puts the issue clearly. The confines of the household can arouse appetites that will drive the family into the street, transforming private into public life, forcing it into visibility, open to view and therefore open to humiliation.[12] The division of the built edifice, the house, into many compartments with diverse partitions cut by various concealed passages, a Gothicizing of domestic architecture, signals the loss of unity within a benevolent family. Certainly Dickens will not give up his devotion to peace and feast within a quaintly irregular physical frame. But the achievement of the home idyll, which appears so reliably at the narrative's end, now requires strenuous acts of invention. Once the difficulty is not beyond the window but down the stairs, not outside the body but within its quickening, then the road to home must follow an eccentric course.

3

Dickens's own infatuation with the young pianist Christina Weller eerily repeats the emergency of Sim Tappertit's passion for Dolly Varden. In Liverpool early in 1844 Weller appeared on the platform with Dickens at a benefit for the Mechanics Institution. He spoke; she played; they chatted; and he sent her a copy of Tennyson. Writing to T. J. Thompson, Dickens rhapsodized: "I cannot joke about Miss Weller; for she is too good; and interest in her (spiritual young creature that she is, and destined to an early death, I fear) has become a sentiment with me. Good God what a madman I should seem, if the incredible feeling I have conceived for that girl could be made plain to anyone" (*Letters*, 4:55). Ackroyd has remarked astutely on the disturbing link between the upsurge of Dickens's feeling and his immediate thought of her early death, as if "as a result of his love for her, she must die young; thus in a way pre-empting her sexual maturity or sexual identity, while at the same time implicitly disavowing any sexual interest in her."[13] But the second part of Dickens's confession is at least as striking: the observation that he would seem mad if his feeling were seen and known. Here then, powerfully condensed, are the two great sexual dreads, the fear that desire will devastate all who feel it, and that at the same time it will expose the helpless desiring soul as a lunatic, crazed with unspeakable yearnings. Two weeks later, when Dickens learns that his confidant Thompson means to propose to Christina Weller, he has a moment of paralyzing shock—"I felt the blood go from my face to I don't know where, and my very lips turn white. I never in my life was so surprised, or had the whole current of my life so stopped, for the instant, as when I felt, at a glance, what your letter said" (*Letters*, 4:69)—but he quickly recovers, and, even as he generously encourages Thompson's cause, he returns to the work of chastening and mortifying his own desire.

Tom Pinch has felt it too. It is his heavy burden to carry through *Martin Chuzzlewit* a passion as consuming as that of Dickens's for Christina Weller, or Sim Tappertit's for Dolly Varden. Tom is no Tappertit, no bombastic, insistent, sexual clown; he too yearns invisibly like his creator, and the demands he places on his novel are great. Stroked and caressed as the truly benevolent man, he still has appetites as pressing as the malevolent men around him. Generous and desirous, Tom compels Dickens to ask a question that he will ask to the end of his career. What does generosity have to do with sexuality?

How to tell the story of Tom's impossible yearning is perhaps the novel's greatest problem—far easier to tell the moral tale of Chuzzlewit egotism. But Tom can neither relinquish nor fulfill the abiding passion for Mary Graham. To pursue it is unthinkable: he knows that her romantic fate is to marry young Martin Chuzzlewit. But to surrender the love would be grotesque, because loyalty to his ruling passion gives Tom his dignity. When it becomes plain that not only will Tom lose Mary to Martin, but he will also lose his sister to John Westlock, then the Pinch problem becomes keen.

Tom Pinch will be given neither the bliss of romance with Mary nor the infinite coziness of life with Ruth. No exclusive tie will be his to enjoy.[14] If this loss gives his claim to pathos, it also gives his claim to centrality in *Martin Chuzzlewit*. Dickens always acknowledged the social and literary pressures toward a marital resolution. Like others who inhabit these narrative conventions, he accepts the celebration of marriage as a response to the demands of plot as well as the fantasies of readers. But much like Freud, Dickens recoiled before the prospect of the exclusive marriage tie, the withdrawal of the married pair from a broader web of affection. His vision of home, not as a mere refuge from the social world but as a rival social order, is incompatible with the isolation of the loving couple, and in this sense the logic of romance is at once an animating force and a perilously false lure.

In the terror of Mercy (Merry) Pecksniff's marriage to Jonas, *Martin Chuzzlewit* gives not merely an image of a personal catastrophe but, more disturbingly, a figure for the danger that inheres in romantic isolation. To old Martin's warning about the marriage, she carelessly replies, "Of course, I shall quarrel with him. I should quarrel with any husband. Married people always quarrel, I believe" (ch. 24). They don't always, but Dickens always worries that they will, if they become caught within the tight airless dyad. In the case of Merry and Jonas, the apparently harmless "kissing and slapping" (ch. 20) of their flirtation turns into brutality behind the closed door of marriage. "I'll know who's master, and who's slave," promises Jonas (ch. 28), and once sexuality breaks down the simplicity of domestic life, the constant threat is that it will replace the simple with the violent.

The last comic flourishes in *Martin Chuzzlewit* are not the inspiration of Mrs. Gamp or Chevy Slyme; they are the achievement of the late-blooming comedian Augustus Moddle, who gloomily suffers the courtship of Charity (Cherry) Pecksniff. Her romantic bullying opens her to unstinting Dickensian aggression. While she waits humiliated for her fiancé to appear, his letter comes instead, asking "Oh, Miss Pecksniff, why didn't you leave me alone!" and confessing that "Frequently—when you have sought to soothe my brow with kisses—has self-destruction flashed across me" (ch. 54). The guffaw can't obscure the sexual terror; it's typically within the broadest comedy that Dickens shows the specter of sex as death. As surely as Jonas's violence, Cherry's hunger shows how, when desire goes undeflected to its object, it can throttle and smother and terrorize. Just as bad, it can manufacture large public embarrassment.

Against this background, the Tom Pinch problem is also a solution. His deprivation is a raw sore, but this is what lets him heal others. The blocked lover with no channel for fulfillment can become the binding agent for the community at whose center he stands. The damming of his desire creates an overflow of benevolence. Dangerous sexuality, either of the sort that leads to Jonas's physical brutality or to Augustus Moddle's fear and panic, recedes in favor of this other state, the elevated responsiveness, the quick, fond sensibility that becomes the basis for flourishing private life.

Tom plays the organ, and Dickens plays (shamelessly) on the sexual pun. When Mary Graham's beauty sends him into sad, delicious reverie, we read that, "She touched his organ, and from that bright epoch, even it, the old companion of his happiest hours, incapable as he had thought of elevation, began a new and deified existence" (ch. 24). The comic sexual slumming can be indulged in the confidence that the plot will finally trammel sexuality. The last scene of *Martin Chuzzlewit* presents an aging Tom alone at his organ, a "mild figure," whose life is "tranquil, calm, and happy," and who heeds the instructions of the narrator: "Touch the notes lightly." The organ brings thoughts of his "old love," Mary Graham, in "a pleasant, softened, whispering memory," and it brings thoughts of her child, who loves Tom "above the rest, if that can be" (ch. 54).

By the novel's end the organ is no longer a stirring bodily part but a musical agent of sublimation, the conversion of desire into domestic gaiety. Tom, as the hero of sublimation, teaches how the family can be built by refusing and then dispersing desires, changing the urge to possession into the energy of generosity, creating a complex of household pleasures as rich as any feast.[15] In the final dinner of celebration, Tom is himself the delicious morsel.

> They all took their tone from Tom. Everybody drank to him, everybody looked to him, everybody thought of him, everybody loved him. If he so much as laid down his knife and fork, somebody put out a hand to shake with him. Martin and Mary

had taken him aside before dinner, and spoken to him so heartily of the time to
come: laying such fervent stress upon the trust they had in his completion of
their felicity, by his society and closest friendship: that Tom was positively moved
to tears. (ch. 53)

Through it all, Tom is beheld by the others. He will not have to perform his
sacrifice and enjoy his rich substitute pleasures alone. He is looked at and
thought about: in the language of this study, a spectacle is made of him. This
is the reverse of the willful publicity of Tappertit. Tom's glory is the conspicu-
ousness granted to the self-denying, sexually chastened man, as if they all
realize that their happiness depends on his denials.

Being acknowledged, being seen and smiled at, being the object of attention
for many pairs of eyes, this is better than sex. In his literary success Dickens
had experienced the full glow of recognition. On March 2, 1844, he wrote to
Thomas Powell that, "It is a brave thing, by Heaven it is, to walk out of the
room where one is shut up for so many hours of such a short life, into a sea
of agitated faces, and think that they are always looking on" (*Letters*, 4:61).
What the author experiences on the large scale, he allows his characters to feel
in cozier corners.

Popularity is a saving alternative to sexuality. From Pickwick onward (and
including such figures as Dr. Strong and Mr. Dick), Dickens invents characters
who will be removed from the heat of desire, and who will bathe their world
with the affection and esteem lavished upon them. The solution to Scrooge's
soulless life is not to find a wife but to devise his own way to be popular.
Tom Pinch's popularity excites a kind of elevated affection in his friends, a
heightened attentiveness, the sensuous solidarity of the group as an alternative
to the troubling energies of the pair.

When Ruth Pinch and John Westlock put an end to false suspense and decide
on marriage, she worries that she will have to leave her brother Tom. "Leave
Tom!" answers the reassuring Westlock. "That would be a strange beginning.
Leave Tom, dear! If Tom and we be not inseparable, and Tom (God bless him)
have not all honour and all love in our home, my little wife, may that home
never be!" He will soon insist again that "The loss of one person, and such a
person as Tom, too, out of our small household of three, is not to be endured"
(ch. 53). The phrase recurs at the end of Dickens's career in *Our Mutual
Friend*, where the romance of Bella Wilfer and John Harmon is sealed through
the involvement of Bella's father, R. (Rumty) Wilfer, late descendant of Pinch,
who joins the lovers in a "partnership of three" (bk. 4, ch. 4).

Tom is the indispensable third in this household of three, indispensable
partly because of the limits and dangers of the romantic dyad, and partly because of the joys of a widening circle.[16] More than a marriage, it is a *household*
that Dickens's novels come to seek, and the conditions of the flourishing house-

hold require at least three, at least that additional one, to break the close circuit of romantic love. This is what popularity can offer. It can enact the sublimation of sexuality into the softly diffuse responsiveness that flickers through the household as a sustaining glow, settling on no one room, no one body, but always hovering in a tremulous web.

4

In a letter to John Forster in the summer of 1845 Dickens proposes a new idea for a periodical. He wants it to be weekly and cheap, including notices of books, theaters, "all good things" and "all bad ones," in the spirit of "*Carol* philosophy, cheerful views, sharp anatomization of humbug, jolly good temper," with "a vein of glowing, hearty, generous, mirthful, beaming reference in everything to Home, and Fireside." He would call it "The Cricket" after the "cheerful creature that chirrups on the Hearth."

> I could approach them [his audience] in a different mode under this name, and in a more winning and immediate way, than under any other. I would at once sit down upon their very hobs; and take a personal and confidential position with them which should separate me, instantly, from all other periodicals periodically published, and supply a distinct and sufficient reason for my coming into existence. And I would chirp, chirp, chirp away in every number until I chirped it up to— well, you shall say how many hundred thousand! (*Letters*, 4:328)

Here again is the convergence between the twin *teloi* of domesticity and popularity. A new, more zealous dash into personal intimacy will bring not merely deeper ties to his readers; it will also bring more readers. Dickens dropped the plan for the new journal, only to revive it five years later in the founding of *Household Words*. Slater has usefully traced the movement from this unborn periodical *The Cricket* to the third of the Christmas books, *The Cricket on the Hearth*, begun soon after the letter to Forster and so clearly a result of the ever more ambitious design for the domestic conquest of his readership.[17]

The plan to come at his readers in a "different mode" is striking in light of the story that emerges from Dickens's turn. Both *A Christmas Carol* and *The Chimes* had their chirping moments, but only in *The Cricket on the Hearth* does the lovable pest sing out fully. So hard on modern ears, so hard because so very soft, the story was the most popular of the Christmas books.[18] In light of Dickens's uncertain readership in the middle forties, its success cannot be seen as mere audience loyalty; it is better taken as a sign of this odd work's congruity with some of the persistent daydreams of early Victorianism.

The story's subtitle is "A Fairy Tale of Home," a phrase that captures this "modal" resolve: to come at his readers in a "more winning and immediate way." Yet it would be a mistake to see the "fairy" course as a flight from conflict.[19] In its gaudily sentimental manner, *The Cricket on the Hearth* not only revives the good and bad dreams of the Dickensian forties; it raises a formidable new problem that it then works to disarm. In so doing, the story consolidates an influential phase of reverie and disposes the author and his audience to a lasting habit of dreamwork.

"What's home?" brays the ogre Tackleton, and then gives exactly the wrong answer: "Four walls and a ceiling!"[20] Dickens's fairy tale means to conquer such abstract space with the usual density of objects and emotions, but it also shows how the question of family space must be a question of family time. Dot Peerybingle is young. Her husband John Peerybingle is not: how old he is remains vague, because what matters is not his age but what Tackelton bluntly calls "the disparity" (*Cricket*, 175). The difference in age between young wife and old(er) husband creates a "Gothic" effect like that of the earlier spatial divisions in household architecture: it stirs mystery, distributes emotions, heightens tension, increases worry and pleasure. But the question of time secures effects not available to the resources of space. Where Dickensian architecture evokes issues of balance, distribution, concealment, and re-arrangement, the problem of age introduces the issue of generation: the discordant rhythms of life rising and falling.

When the stage villain Tackleton announces his engagement to May Fielding, he insinuates a similarity between his situation and John's. There they will be, two aging men with two blooming wives—who can possibly choose between them? It will be the work of the story to show just how clear the choice remains, but not before Dickens forces the reader to test a danger. The writings of Sarah Ellis have shown the ambiguity in the figure of the female helpmeet. Is she, in essence, a mature wife or a fond daughter? Which icon most fully satisfies the dream of female devotion? Ellis moves between the two as she conducts her negotiations with household patriarchy. But Dickens compounds the images, longing for the wifely maturity of daughterly fondness.[21] Notoriously, he gives young motherly brides to mature men and exults in the pattern that develops in *The Cricket on the Hearth*: the doting, tirelessly bustling, young wife (Dot) tending to a benevolently patient, calmly reticent older husband (John).[22] What keeps this seductive arrangement unsettled is the fear that the wife/daughter cannot, and perhaps should not, give herself up. In *Bleak House*, John Jarndyce will draw back from his "mistake"—his hope that Esther will marry him and gloriously complete the pattern of cheerful young matron and kind old husband—in recognition of her right to less chastened, less subdued, desires of her own. But this famous turn in *Bleak House* should not be given more weight than it deserves. It exists within the context of different outcomes and might be taken as the price paid for indulgence elsewhere.

During the awkward festivities that occupy the center of *The Cricket on the Hearth*, when it still seems that Dot is drifting from her honest John, she teases him: "He adds twenty years to my age at least. Don't you, John?" (197). This is the dread that lives within the fantasy, the fear that the pattern of busy young wife and placid older husband will come to grief on the shoals of the wife's desire. The yearning desirous man—Pinch, Jarndyce, Clennam—attracts sorrow and pity and can still be welcome at the table, but a yearning woman threatens to devastate the quiet of the hearth.

In a scene that represents the "spectacle of intimacy" in its harshest, most startling form, Tackleton brings John to see his wife laughing secretly with their mysterious guest: he had been disguised as a confused old man but is now revealed as an "erect and gallant" young man (206). She teases and hugs the handsome stranger, while John looks on with a rapt voyeuristic gaze. He sees what the reader is taught to fear: that youth will turn back to youth and the stable settlement of home will be devastated by the return of suppressed desires.

John's scene of voyeurism passes into his misery by the fireside, where he gives up his anger and comes to accept the wreck of his marriage. He alone has been responsible for the failure. In marrying Dot, he asks himself, did he consider that he was taking her, "at her age, and with her beauty," away

> from her young companions, and the many scenes of which she was the ornament; in which she was the brightest little star that ever shone, to shut her up from day to day in my dull house, and keep my tedious company? Did I consider how little suited I was to her sprightly humour, and how wearisome a plodding man like me must be, to one of her quick spirit? Did I consider that it was no merit in me, or claim in me, that I loved her, when everybody must who knew her? Never. I took advantage of her hopeful nature and her cheerful disposition; and I married her. I wish I never had! for her sake; not for mine! (217)

When the story reveals its great "innocent deception"—the mysterious stranger has returned to love, not Dot, but May; it will not be John who suffers the terrible loss but that "domestic ogre" Tackleton—then *A Cricket on the Hearth* benignly revokes its threat. Dot is no mooning, yearning, restless female: she is a wife. Her appetites have all been gently pinched and channeled; her loyalty is beyond question. In the midst of his agony, when John believes in her infidelity and struggles against his murderous impulse, he recovers through the chirping offices of the household god, the cricket, who conjures images of faithful Dot, secure in her renunciation—as in the picture of a "crowd of young merrymakers" who come in pursuit of her gaiety.

> Dot was the fairest of them all; as young as any of them too. They came to summon her to join their party. It was a dance. If ever little foot were made for dancing, hers was, surely. But she laughed, and shook her head, and pointed to her cookery on the fire, and her table ready spread: with an exulting defiance that rendered her more charming than she was before. And so she merrily dismissed them: nodding to her would-be partners, one by one, as they passed. (212)

Here is the true Dot; all else was error. She never loved the stranger; she only and always loved John; now the once panting reader can smile with the broadly grinning narrator. The tale solicits a sobbing relief: she is true! she was always true! And what is more, only this visible agony could have shown how true.

In *David Copperfield*, the crack in the marriage between old Doctor Strong and young Annie is the suspicion that she has always loved Jack Maldon, a scamp of her own age. What makes it worse is that long ago she did love Jack, so that all the world can think what her mother always implies: that the aging Doctor Strong should be grateful Annie married him, a man she respected but never loved. Annie knows that the doctor believes what her mother insinuates.

The grip of unuttered emotion is only broken when Mr. Dick orchestrates a scene of exposure. In a tense gathering, her husband, mother, and friends hear Annie confess that she and Jack Maldon "had been little lovers" and that she "might have married him." But she long ago learned, and now must say openly, that the match would have been "most wretched," because "there can be no disparity in marriage like unsuitability of mind and purpose." Set next to this fatal disparity of temperament, the contrast in age disappears at a stroke. At last Annie can look openly on Doctor Strong's face, "revered as a father's, loved as a husband's."[23]

The revelation of these secrets leaves the listeners gasping. But this is how good spectacle works. Life's highest values are most intimate; their unveiling must cause pain; but this is the only way to preserve them. Left concealed, the secret world feeds on its entrails. The drama-stirring paradox is that the only way to save privacy is to publish its secrets.[24] This is not so much because muddles can then be clarified, but because the throbbing act of disclosure purifies the private world. It's as if privacy has to make the supreme sacrifice of letting itself be known. Afterward, it can again retreat behind the wall, doubly secure, now that there is transparency between the intimates and also confirmation in the outer world. Annie and Doctor Strong are securely entwined, but just as decisive is the fact that David Copperfield has witnessed their lesson. Annie had spoken not only of the disparity of "mind" and "purpose" but also, famously, of the "first mistaken impulse of my undisciplined heart." David will take these insights back to his own marriage: because Annie has made a spectacle of herself, he will grow wiser in love. Among other things, the sequence amounts to a justification of the early Dickensian project. It dares to register confidential details of home life because, in the alembic of publicity, personal emotions will be refined, and the cleansed emotions will circulate.

The healthy uncovering of secrets is a counterpart to the work of popularity. In those moments when a group of characters gathers for the painful divulgence of a truth, they earn the benefits of the small public sphere, far smaller than the public world outside, but significantly larger than the circle of two. As against the spectacle of social failure, Dickens is seeking, not intimacy, but spectacle on the family scale.[25] The Dickensian idealization of home is no more a flight from politics than from the exclusive couple. To celebrate a household favorite and to ventilate a shadowy secret—these often coincide, each promoting the escape from narrow intimacy into the joys of looking, of chattering, of shared memory, and mobile fondness.

But even the moments of triumphant visibility cannot put all worries to rest. In *A Cricket on the Hearth* what unsteadies the sentimental conclusion is that the story has prepared so well for the other possibility: the undoing of the father-daughter relation and the catastrophe of a marriage built upon "disparity." It's all very well, and cozily reassuring, to learn that Dot will never desert her John; it was all an innocent mistake. But the pleasing outcome cannot cancel the uneasiness.[26] *A Cricket on the Hearth* has gone much too far in putting the claims of rebellious passion. Dot herself has made the case for youth's right to romance. Urging May to resist the pressures of a "respectable" marriage to wealthy Tackleton, she summons memories that excite and disquiet the Dickensian Christmas. "'Remember," Dot instructs May, "how we used to talk, at school, about the husbands we would choose, I don't know how young, and how handsome, and how gay, and how lively." And as May wavers, Dot presses further, recalling the "real live young men—we fixed on sometimes," confessing that she "never fixed on John I'm sure; I never so much as thought of him." When Tackleton cackles triumphantly that those days are over now and asks "Where are your gay young bridegrooms now," Dot retorts with "earnestness and fire" that "Some of them, if they could stand among us at this moment, would not believe we were the same creatures; would not believe that what they saw and heard was real, and we *could* forget them so" (197–98). The reader will soon learn that Dot is not speaking for her own romantic frustration but for the still living hopes of her friend. But what can it mean that the plot doubles in this way, reminding one young woman of the insurgent claims of young desire, while training another in the sublimity of mature abstention?

It can only mean that Dickensian domesticity can fully accept neither condition, neither the discharge of desire nor its sublimation, but must be restlessly moving between the contraries. If there is not only a Dot in *The Cricket on the Hearth* but also a May, it is because at least two women are required for the distribution of needs, one to cool and one to burn. Unable to settle on a single outcome, the fiction must generate more possibilities, more women, but then what else are families for?

Among other things, they are for showing that the choices are not of equal standing. Yes, youth has its rights, desire its demands, but *A Cricket on the Hearth* is unambiguous in giving pride of place to undemanding Dot, leaving May to be passionate in the wings. Dot is Tom Pinch's complement, his sister in self-denial, in heroic sublimation. But there is of course a difference. The abstaining male—think ahead again of Jarndyce—keeps himself apart from marriage and gives off a glow of benevolent bachelorhood, while the young woman abstains her way into marriage. Giving, not taking, she doesn't tax the older husband. What makes her a fit mate is that even as the lively daughter/ wife she has learned how to be quiet; she knows how to distribute her pleasures throughout the household miscellany. Rattling her keys, she tends and bustles and brightens, finding her satisfaction in the many little tasks rather than in the great romantic embrace.

Dickens knows what psychic athleticism is involved in all these acts, male and female, of disavowing, chastening, sublimating. When John is in the midst of his misery, the cricket comes down from the title and conjures a voice, a presence, and a swarm of fairies, who crowd the stage of home.

> From the hearthstone, from the chimney; from the clock, the pipe, the kettle, and the cradle; from the floor, the walls, the ceiling, and the stairs; from the cart with-out, and the cupboard within, and the household implements; from every thing and every place with which she had ever been familiar, and with which she had ever entwined one recollection of herself in her unhappy husband's mind; Fairies came trooping forth. Not to stand beside him as the Cricket did, but to busy and bestir themselves. To do all honor to her image. To pull him by the skirts, and point to it when it appeared. To cluster round it, and embrace it, and strew flowers for it to tread on. To try to crown its fair head with their tiny hands. To show that they were fond of it and loved it; and that there was not one ugly, wicked, or accusatory creature to claim knowledge of it—none but their playful and ap-proving selves. (91)

In *The Cricket on the Hearth* where there might have been sex there is a cricket and his fairies. Dickens teaches that the answer to the fearful visual tableau— the wayward, sensuous wife seen by the decent, tired husband—is a rival pleni-tude. Here is the other, overwrought spectacle of intimacy, not the thrill of scandal (Caroline Norton and the prime minister found by the footman), but the revelation of buzzing *Heimlichkeit*. The story brings these two sensations illuminatingly close. But even when they are prised apart, elsewhere in the corpus and the culture, they will keep memories of one another. What better way to hide the flagrant body than beneath a cloud of chirping crickets?

Within a different context, that last question has another revealing answer. When Dickens met the wealthy philanthropist Angela Burdett-Coutts, he and she pondered how to spend her money wisely, which meant in practice how to spend it within the frame of the Dickensian domestic vision. The result at the end of the 1840s was the founding of Urania House, a home for fallen women, dedicated to reclaiming lost female virtue.

The prostitute was to the forties what the coquette was to the twenties and thirties, the visible sign of sexual insurrection. As such, she is the inevitable conclusion to a decade of Dickens's brooding on publicity and sexuality, much as fallen Little Emily in *David Copperfield* is the result of all those earlier plots dancing close to the edge of female transgression. We have been arguing that the will to popularity and the upsurge of desire meet in Dickens to create a thrusting outward of domestic inwardness, and that the consoling replacement for sexual need is the chaste buzz of public regard. The secrets of private life must be on display; desire compels it; and so do the conditions of publishing. The task is not to suppress personal trouble but to invent an anodyne publicity, the good publicity of a Christmas story or a house of good repute.

The prostitute appears, like Sim Tappertit, as one who has been transformed from a "private individual" into a "public character." The mission of Urania House will be to reverse the movement. In his prospectus for the house, Dickens attributes to Baroness Coutts a digest of his own compacted thought.

> She has resolved to open at her own expense a place of refuge near London for a small number of females, who without such hope are lost forever, and to make a HOME for them. In this home they will be taught all household work that would be useful to them in a home of their own and enable them to make it comfortable and happy. . . . And because it is not this lady's wish that these young women should be shut out from the world after they have repented and learned to do their duty there, and because it is her wish and object that they may be restored to society—a comfort to themselves and it—they will be supplied with every means, when some time shall have elapsed and their conduct shall have fully proved their earnestness and reformation, to go abroad, where in a distant country they may become the faithful wives of honest men, and live and die in peace.[27]

Among the many startling effects in this passage is the simultaneous double gesture of invitation and exclusion. Come in, farewell. The stained woman is to be welcomed, is to be reformed within the moral laboratory of home life, but then, as though Dickens suddenly remembers that home is a sacred ground, this second impulse erupts, the impulse to banish her, to expel the never fully reclaimable soul—not just to some safe elsewhere, but to a "distant country," and not only for quite some time, but to the very end of life, until death finally cancels the stain.

The project of Urania House was a complement and a culmination to the fiction of the 1840s. The streetwalker solicited to a domestic career serves as a figure, an alluring and troubling figure, for the new conditions of Dickensian narrative. The attempt to absorb her within the zone of marriage and housework forces an acknowledgment of what she represents. Urania House was an assertion of domestic will. But it also contained a recognition that the campaign for "HOME" would have to construct the hearth out of "impure" materials and that it would have to issue its call for privacy out there in the public world.

PART THREE

Was That an Angel in the House?

Chapter Five

LOVE AFTER DEATH: THE DECEASED
WIFE'S SISTER BILL

1

During a richly sentimental tableau set in the middle of *The Cricket on the Hearth*, we read of the two female friends that

> May's face set off Dot's, and Dot's face set off May's, so naturally and agreeably, that, as John Peerybingle was very near saying when he came into the room, they ought to have been born sisters: which was the only improvement you could have suggested.[1]

And why? why would it have been an improvement if the two had been sisters? Well, because nearer is better, and nothing is nearer, nothing is better, than family relation. In its full Dickensian splendor, the flourishing family creates its satisfactions from within, and where you might have been forced to look outward for a friend, now you can look inward to a sister. In fact, when in the following year Dickens came to write his next Christmas story, *The Battle of Life*, he made that one improvement: he made his two young women sisters, and it will be important to indicate their fate, at once so rosy and so challenging.

The Battle of Life seems to have dropped almost entirely from cultural memory. Partly, this must be due to the rhetorical awkwardness of the story, the strain in its governing tones, the sentimentality, which immediately struck even so partisan a supporter as John Forster.[2] But the awkwardness has further causes of its own. *The Battle of Life* has the strangeness of a secret too intimate to reveal. The story turns on the love of the two sisters for the same man, for Alfred, who spent his childhood as the ward of the family. Grace, the elder sister, is "home-adorning" and "self-denying"; Marion is a dazzling beauty.[3] Alfred chooses beauty, leaving poor self-mortifying Grace to keep her love to herself. But Marion knows; even as she accepts Alfred's love, she understands Grace's secret and suffers the delicious agony of knowing that her gain is her sister's loss. Such a situation repeats often in Dickens; it disturbs and excites him; and in *The Battle of Life* it impels him toward some wild, but revealing, improbabilities.

On the very day when she was to seal her engagement with Alfred—on that sort of raging winter day when home is "doubly home" (279)—the beautiful Marion runs off with a dissolute, weakly Byronic scamp and stays away for the next six years, not sending a single message back to the scene of family devastation. What's the deserted Alfred to do? Naturally, he is to fall in love with the remaining sister, with earnest Grace. Thrown together in their sorrow, they mourn their way into devotion and weep themselves into marriage. Then, in the story's unlikely miracle, Marion returns, and her secret is revealed: it was all a ruse, her running off with the scamp, a pretense to get the others to give her up, to treat her as if she were dead. "I am still your maiden sister," exults Marion, "unmarried, unbetrothed" (307). The elaborately staged spectacle of her fall was the only way she could give Alfred to "home-adorning" sister Grace. And here Grace reveals to Alfred her own secret: that on that terrible night six years before, Marion had written her a farewell letter, "praying and beseeching me, as I loved her, and I loved you, not to reject the affection she believed (she knew, she said) you would transfer to me when the new wound was healed, but to encourage and return it" (303).

This is the shuddering act that will open a next phase in our account: this transfer of love, the relocation of affection from one sister to another, performed with all the resources of Dickensian sentiment. They cling, and cry, in high emotional transport, almost as if all that moisture were necessary in order to wash them toward this small but momentous change: the unsettling displacement of affection from one to the other. We propose this gesture as a controlling fantasy not only in Dickens but in the culture that he inhabits, assimilates, and helps to reinvent: the fantasy that a husband will always have a second choice, a second sister, waiting nearby in domestic reserve.

In *Martin Chuzzlewit* this same displacement had been enacted in the low comic, rather than high sentimental, mode. The villainous Jonas Chuzzlewit pretends to love Charity Pecksniff, the hypocritical self-deceiving daughter of a hypocritical self-deceiving father. But in fact Jonas courts Charity on his cunning way to her sister Mercy. When the three are out together, "Mr. Jonas being in the middle, and having a cousin on each arm, sometimes squeezed the wrong one."[4] He habitually calls Mercy "the other one," and at the very moment of the expected proposal to Charity, he clasps each around the waist and reveals the dastardly trick. It's not Charity he wants, it's Mercy; and so begins the frightful marriage built on violence and brutality.

What *Martin Chuzzlewit* puts harshly, and what *The Battle of Life* puts in tones of rapturous sentiment, is the uncanny existence of "the other one," the other sister, the second object of affection. What one might call official Victorian moral sentiment, official in the sense that it undergirded public debate and parliamentary legislation, relied on the picture of marriage as an exclusive tie, adorned but not challenged by the children it bred. Yet, Dickens's work of the middle 1840s builds a rival picture of the household as a crowded enclosure of mobile desire, a Gothic domesticity in which objects of affection can be changed and in which the stability of married love has to contend with challenges near at hand. That this is no mere Dickensian idiosyncrasy but a diffuse domestic topos can be seen through a turn to a contemporaneous episode that might be regarded as the parliamentary counterpart to *The Battle of Life*.

2

In 1835, in a very particular set of circumstances, Parliament approved legislation known as Lord Lyndhurst's Act, which attempted to put an end to the centuries-old confusion of marriage within the prohibited degrees.[5] Long before, the question had come to prominence during the cataclysms of Henry VIII's married lives, which had led to Archbishop Parker's Table of Kindred and Affinity, rigorously laying out the forbidden zones of marriage.[6] Initially, the ecclesiastical courts considered all such taboo marriages as null and void. But during the reign of James I the courts of common law intervened and devised a gentler way of dealing with the prohibition. Marriages within the forbidden degrees of affinity were not void, only "voidable"; they were permissible as long as they were not successfully challenged during the time of the marriage; and if no action were taken against the couple during their lifetimes, then the question could not be raised after their deaths. The great significance of the new convention was that after the death of the parents, the legitimacy of the children was secured, and their right to inheritance could not be contested.

This is where matters largely stood, until Lord Lyndhurst's Act of 1835.[7] The stated aim of the legislation was to end the uncertainty disrupting the lives of those within "voidable" ties, who in principle might discover at any moment that neither their living marriage nor their children's claim to property had any legal standing. Notoriously, the act moved in two contrary directions. On the one hand, it legitimized all existing marriages within the prohibited degrees; on the other hand, it forbade any new transgressions. After 1835 marriages to any legally forbidden mate were not ambiguously "voidable," but definitively "void." They would be disallowed from the start; there would be no uncertainty, because there would be no legal marriage, nor the possibility of inheritance. As an early stroke in the ambitious nineteenth-century attempt to rationalize domestic law, the motive was to rid marriage of some old and terrible unclarities.[8] With one stroke a stained marital past was forgiven, and a tainted future abolished.

Such was the legal dream. But according to whatever measure one prefers, it's clear that after the passing of the bill, and in the face of its harsh legal rigor, the prohibited marriages to the wife's sister nevertheless continued to take place. If they did not number in the many thousands, as some claimed, they were frequent enough to create a shadowy constituency agitating for change. Some couples went to Hamburg to take their vows, some to Denmark, some simply lied before the authorities. Others hadn't yet taken the step, but longed to do so.

Near the end of 1846 a group of these guilt-tempting individuals joined together to investigate whether they were alone in marrying, or in seeking to marry, the sisters of their dead wives. Hiring investigators to conduct interviews in five districts of England, they assembled the findings into a report purporting to show that despite the illegal character of such marriages, they were widespread, and perhaps ineradicable. (Within its limited field the investigation counted 1,364 transgressions of the approved degrees, of which nine-tenths were said to be marriages with the deceased wife's sister.) On the basis of this report, a parliamentary commission was appointed to investigate the state of the law of marriage "as relating to the prohibited degrees of affinity,"[9] a purview that quickly narrowed to the question of marriage with a deceased wife's sister.

During its work in 1847 and 1848, the commission sent queries around the country; it consulted authorities, religious and civil; most strikingly it conducted interviews with a number of men who had married a deceased wife's sister. To read the transcripts of those interviews now is to peer through the keyhole of history, as these men, almost all from the middle classes, step forward, one after the other, in obvious embarrassment, desperate to turn what is now a sexual crime back toward respectability. Repeatedly, almost obsessively, they refer to model citizens who have also transgressed with their sisters-in-law: the distinguished surgeon, the "man of large fortune," the "warm supporter of the Bible Society" (*Commissioners*, 65, 68). They insist that their friends and neighbors fully accept their decision, and they yearn for a legal sanction to their private life.

Much of what that yearning conveys is the desire never to have to leave home: the longing of these widowed husbands to be allowed to stay within the domestic circle, not to be forced to look outside for a second wife but to find her here, already, the familiar sister.[10] So, for instance, one of the anonymous witnesses before the commission, who has lost his wife, now asks helplessly, "What was to become of me and my family?"

> I am a man who has lived all my life in retirement. My whole course of life and my enjoyments of every kind are entirely domestic and literary. To take a stranger into my family is in itself really a visitation. . . . I most earnestly protest against what I feel to be a most heavy personal visitation. It would be repugnant to my feeling to displace old associations, and to seek marriage elsewhere; I could not do it. My wife's sister disturbs nothing; she is already in the place of my wife. (64, 66)

To such soft pleading, the commission listened with evident sympathy, sharing the view of the private inquiry that the statute of 1835 had not attained its object: "It has not prevented marriage with the sister, or niece, of a deceased

wife from taking place in numerous instances," a failure that the commissioners see as "a great and continually increasing evil" (ix).

From our historical standpoint, two great social pressures can be seen as
creating the conditions for domestic "transgression."[11] On the one side was
the growing isolation and detachment of the middle-class home. With the separation of the family from the workplace and the rise of suburbia,[12] the household became a place apart, less easily given to the commingling of private and
public relations. One can hardly be surprised to read of the shy unwillingness
to venture beyond the cozy hearth in order to find a new wife and, often more
pressing, a new mother for the children, nor can one be surprised that these
more securely enclosed domestic spaces would yield "temptations and opportunities" (*Commissioners*, 29) not always resisted. The second historical pressure was the massification of urban society. Where once a parish priest who
called the banns would know the couple well enough to preserve the workings
of the law, now individuals were able to guard their private lives, including
their private legal infractions. As one clergyman testified, "In large towns the
population is all on the move. It would be idle to require that we should ascer-
tain really the relationship of the parties in the case of banns; it would be
impossible to do it" (97). At the same time the new right (as of 1835) to marry
outside the church simply through the sanction of the registrar compounded
the difficulty of moral surveillance. In the view of another clerical witness,
"The power of marrying at the Registrar's office is a source of irregular marriages of every kind that is bad to a degree of which the British public cannot
have the slightest conception" (61). Taken together, these historical conditions
that had ripened by the 1840s—the increasing privacy of domestic life and the
impersonal massification of society—create the double solicitation of opportunity and obscurity.

Within such contexts, marriage with a deceased wife's sister quickly presents itself as a difficulty for the middle classes but also an occasion for defining the norms of middle-class domestic life. Those in higher stations are not
so confined to the family circle; their expansive households are "less closely
domestic and private" (*Commissioners*, xi). For those of more modest means,
when the wife falls ill, the family naturally looks to her sister, who often assumes an indispensable role. On the other hand, the wealthy can turn to private
nurses, to governesses, or to an elite corps of domestic servants. As for the
poor, the commission and its clerical interviewees see the lower classes as
habitually given to loose "concubinage" that resists moral regulation.[13]
Scarcely attending to the law to guide their own behavior, they are portrayed
as willing to invoke it in order to discredit middle-class claims to respectability.
The Reverend John Garbett testifies that when they are upbraided for their
loose morals, some among the "common people" will point to a "respectable"
man now married to his wife's sister and will say that "Such a one . . . is no

more married than I am, according to the law of the land" (96). Just such
an accusation lay behind the nervous deliberations of 1847–50—the dread
insinuation that respectable members of the middle class were themselves not
only legally suspect but guilty of sexual immorality that placed them on the
level of the erotically swarming poor.

The agitation for reform became then an assertion of a middle-class right to
enjoy its domestic self-enclosure and to avoid the sexual openness and affective mobility that paradoxically linked the very rich and the very poor. In
pursuit of the aim, the proponents of the bill relied on the rhetoric of enlightenment, on a progressive critical consciousness that would overcome a tangled,
burdensome legal inheritance.[14] Indeed solicitors were in the forefront of the
effort to rationalize the law of marriage, many of them signing an early petition
that affirmed that, given the large number of marriages celebrated in defiance
of the law, the current legal condition was "calculated to create doubts as to
the legitimacy of children . . . and to place the titles of numerous estates upon
an insecure footing."[15] The fact that the current narrative could be traced back
so easily to the machinations of Henry VIII allowed opponents to see Lord
Lyndhurst's Act as the residue of "tyrannical purposes" (Wharncliffe, 3), the
product of an incoherent tradition emanating from a corrupt source.

At the same time liberal clergyman pointed to the weakness of the biblical
foundation, the overinterpreted passage from the eighteenth chapter of Leviticus: "Neither shalt thou take a wife to her sister, to vex her, to uncover her
nakedness, beside the other in her life time." Opponents of Lyndhurst waved
the banner of the last prepositional phrase, which seems to imply so clearly
that after the wife's death marriage is permitted with the surviving sister. The
reforming clergy willingly admitted that the taboo had a long tradition in the
church, but argued that this was because "very few of the clergy, indeed, have
looked into it." If only the subject were "once well weighed and thoroughly
digested in the minds of the body of the clergy," then, suggests the Reverend
John Hatchard, the opposition to reform would disappear (*Commissioners*, 63).
His colleague John Garbett puts the point in still more severe terms, telling
the commission that he believes

> that Lord Lyndhurst's bill has put the law upon a ground upon which it cannot
> stand; it has enforced a more searching inquiry as to the real basis on which it
> rests. So long as the thing was allowed to go on as it did before, nobody ever went
> into it much, but I think that since that time the question has been much more
> discussed, and the scriptural and moral grounds more rigidly examined. (98)

Certainly, much of the historical resonance of the controversy was that it became the occasion for strenuous reflection on the very foundation, the "real
basis," of domestic life. To the progressive, critical reformers, so confident of
success, the task was simply to lay bare the inconsistency, the contradiction,
and the groundlessness of the current law. This could be most persuasively

done by showing the true conditions of middle-class family affection. The result was that much of the reformist discourse was a modernizing portrait of the family that emphasized a reading of motives and circumstances, an interpretation that depended on a psychology and a sociology, rather than a morality and a theology. Accordingly, in their summary of the evidence, the commissioners claim that the contested relationships "spring out of a peculiar combination of circumstances, which, when they do occur, give rise to feelings naturally leading to marriage" (x). Or, as Abraham Hayward put it, "the strictest law made by a single state, in opposition to the general feeling, would have no moral influence at all."[16]

Again we see—as we have seen with Caroline Norton, Queen Victoria, and the characters of Dickens—that the claims of private feeling now appear strong enough to contest a public tradition. Richard Sennett has argued that private life "gradually became a yardstick with which to measure the public realm": "Privacy and stability appeared to be united in the family; against this ideal order the legitimacy of the public order was thrown into question."[17] In the campaign for the Deceased Wife's Sister Bill, the reformers' goal was to bring the law into conformity with natural feelings, real circumstances, and ineradicable motives.

A man's wife falls ill; her sister arrives to support the family in its need. The children see their mother languish and come to depend on their aunt, much as the husband in his grief looks to the affection of his sister-in-law. After the death, this sister becomes more indispensable than ever. She is not only a source of emotional succor; she is a familiar face. Where there might have been a cold stranger, there is instead a dear, well-known intimate, already a member of the domestic circle. In the hour of need, what could be more natural, more inevitable, indeed more beautiful, than that husband and children would transfer their love to this domestic redeemer?

Such was the logic of a progressive domesticity, eager to show that the attempt to legislate against family affection was doomed to failure. One of the witnesses, a stockbroker, testified that he "was led [to marry his wife's sister] by a chain of circumstances which were almost irresistible" (*Commissioners*, 24), and the burden of the commission's report was to emphasize the resistless pressure of such natural sentiments. Indeed, as the constituency for change grew—as the archbishop of Dublin gave his frank support, as six hundred other members of the clergy joined the cause, as seventy-six firms of leading London solicitors signed a petition, as three thousand Manchester merchants signed another—the success of reform seemed assured. Leviticus would be read with open eyes, the burden of Henry VIII would no longer weigh on the present, the law would conform to real motives and actual circumstances, and those who now lived embarrassed and guilty lives would recover the sanction of respectability.

But even as James Stuart Wortley introduced his bill to Parliament, the opposing party was organizing its resistance. Polemic sharpened, and tempers flared. In Edinburgh an enthusiastic London barrister named William Campbell Sleigh attended a public meeting of Wortley's opponents and tried to introduce an amendment to the effect that "It is the opinion of this meeting that marriage with the sister of a deceased wife is not prohibited by the Word of God, nor repugnant to the laws of nature"[18]—whereupon he was ejected from the meeting by the police, tried at the police court, and fined two guineas. In a rival meeting two days later, Sleigh, now a partisan hero, exuberantly described the findings of the parliamentary commission. He claimed that there were no fewer than thirty thousand marriages in violation of Lyndhurst's Act, affecting upward of one hundred thousand people, and by portraying the law as merely answering the "private ends of a few members of the aristocracy" (*Edinburgh*, 23), Sleigh heightened the class character of the struggle over domesticity.

On the other side of the dispute, the attempt to make law conform to feeling was taken as the sign of a decadent modernity; in the words of E. B. Pusey, who became the leading voice among the traditionalists, such a "reform" was merely "preparing the way for the coming of Antichrist."[19] People may recklessly discard the age-old Levitical laws, but then "What authority have they wherewith to supply their place?" From a reinterpretation of the Bible, it is only a short step to the abandonment of the church, which "in its purer days" also prohibited those marriages. "Where, then, is this to end?" asks Pusey. "If the first dams be broken down, where is our guarantee that the flood of incest shall be stayed?" (9–10).

This last remark crystallizes the fear that rouses Wortley's enemies, the terror that home will become a sexual laboratory, in which husbands would be forever contemplating marriage with the woman who stood next in line. Every fond cheerful sister of every doting wife would become a possible sexual successor. Alexander Beresford Hope, a leading parliamentary opponent of the bill, gleefully quoted testimony from one of the commission's own field researchers, "I saw one woman, who was the third sister the man had married, and her expression to me was, 'that if she died, she believed her husband would have the fourth'; that was in Sheffield."[20] Opponents railed against the sexualizing of the family circle, which would indelibly stain the cherished image of a grieving husband consoled by the warmth of the sister-in-law. An excited essay in the *Quarterly Review* brooded heavily on the threat.

> In the actual state of public feeling and of the law, a man looks upon the sisters of his wife as upon his own sisters; and the wife brings into her new abode her own sisters as having such an interest in her husband's affection and attentions as his own sisters by blood. In life they are united as one family. . . . But if the wife be to feel that her sister may become her rival and her successor, she will pause before she hazards the interruption to her own peace which the introduction of

such an inmate may occasion. In the existing constitution of the law and of the feelings it sanctions, the husband . . . sees his wife's sister as he sees his own, with a freedom which is pure to the pure; and which we are confident is indulged in by thousands and tens of thousands with no other emotion than that which is felt by the same men towards their own sisters; —the idea of any other affection never for an instant rising in the minds of either party. . . . But change the sister of a wife into a young marriageable stranger, and the attentions which are now offered by the husband and received by and witnessed by the wife, with purity, with delicacy, and with confidence, become insults alike to both females . . . the relation of brother-in-law to sister-in-law will cease to exist . . . while the wife will be deprived of that support and comfort which she now derives from the presence of the sister of her youth.[21]

In Pusey's more condensed formulation, the catastrophe occurs when "affection is sacrificed to passion" (A Letter, 13). The angry archdeacon of London, William Hale Hale, asserts that English society is "the purest in the world with regard to marriage," and that the existing law has caused this happy innocence by working "to check incest and to produce purity." English marriage now allows for "a real brotherhood and sisterhood," which would be quickly destroyed by a law permitting these long forbidden marriages (116–17).

And yet it would be wrong to say that the language of purity belonged only to those standing against Wortley's marriage reform. Those hopeful widowers, ardent parliamentarians, and tolerant clergyman also sketched an image of domestic innocence. What could be more chaste, they asked, than the simple delight of welcoming the familiar, already beloved sister-in-law into the household as wife and mother? Did anyone believe that it would be better for the grieving husband to leave the family circle in pursuit of unknown love?

Still, however the case was turned, whether toward innocent marriage or pure sisterhood, the leading fact about the episode was its sheer indelicate visibility. Suddenly, the "arcana of family affections"[22] were in full view, creating intense consciousness that changed the very problem under review. Some began to argue that the widespread new awareness of the 1835 law roused the desires it had been designed to suppress. The North British Review tartly dismissed such a claim—"It is almost like the schoolboy's excuse, that he would not have thought of such a piece of mischief if the master's prohibition had not put it in his head"[23]—and yet other opponents fretted over the power of public consciousness to create transgressive desire. "So corrupt is our nature," intones the archdeacon of London, "that the very fact of a thing being prohibited makes people desire to do that which they would not otherwise have dared to do" (Commissioners, 118).[24] And having been asked whether he is surprised by the many marriages contracted in defiance of Lord Lyndhurst's Act, he replies, "I am not at all surprised at that result; because on this point so many intelligent men have actually combined to persuade people not to obey that law. The question of the fitness of marriage with a deceased wife's sister has been brought before the public mind in a manner calculated almost to create the sin of disobedience" (116).

What Hale Hale recognized bitterly and the reformist John Garbett cheerfully was that consciousness could not be returned to the box. During the last years of the 1840s petitions accumulated, statistics clashed, newspapers published, positions crystallized, and rhetoric heightened. Although this intensifying consciousness was itself a defeat for traditionalists, it was their only defeat on the issue. Wortley's bill failed, and for the rest of the century (and until 1907) similar bills failed and failed again. The cause would become a standing parliamentary joke, but at this moment of high concentration, it was pursued with earnest and humorless purpose. The controversy became a discursive forcing house, thrusting awkward questions into public circulation. How far should family affection reach? Was affection itself a passion? Should one, could one, legislate desire? Was family life a deep essential innocence or a preparation for corruption? Was domestic virtue a relic of tradition to be preserved, or a triumph of modernity, still to be invented? No one could claim that the debates created the disturbance, which surely lay within the complex intersection of demographic change, legal aspiration, family delight, and the enigma of sexuality, but whatever the causes, the result was a conspicuous image of a domestic nest in which a serpent curled.

3

And the deceased husband's brother? Where was he in the cauldron of polemic? The logic of symmetry demanded that the husband considering marriage with his dead wife's sister should be mirrored by the wife pondering a future with her brother-in-law. But no sooner was the issue raised than it was quickly set aside. Biology was definitive; the symmetry was an illusion.[25] If the wife became the body in common between two men, then their blood would incestuously, immorally mingle, and this presumably because the wife was a vessel, while the husband was a dry stick, into which no fluids could dangerously penetrate.

Then, of course, apart from the bodily fixation, there were the usual entrenchments of masculine agency and female passivity. The act of choice involved in picking a next sister fit naturally within the domain of male prerogative. Indeed to many women the Wortley proposal seemed to endorse an extraordinary broadening of a man's sexual agency. Petitions from women against the change became one of the emblems of resistance to reform.[26] Speaking on behalf of such women, the earl of Albemarle asked "who would be 'relieved' by this measure?" and caustically answered:

A few men who attached themselves to a *forbidden* object. And the interests of those few are to outweigh those of the wives, widowers, spinsters and children which will be affected. For the interests of those men, loving sisters are to be changed into possible wives, affectionate brothers into possible suitors.[27]

Certainly, the leading scenario for intrafamilial remarriage displayed men conducting a sexual opera, in which, through a mere nod of preference, the waiting sister would step into the role of wife.[28] Yet there remained one curious opportunity for women to exercise agency within this constrained scenario. As the moment of death approached, the wife could plead for that very marriage which so many saw as the cruellest affront to her memory. In their final summary the parliamentary commissioners refer to the "many cases where the wife on her death-bed, has declared her anxious desire that her husband should contract marriage with her sister" (*Commissioners*, x). A man from Manchester struggled to explain how he came to marry his sister-in-law.

> It was on her death-bed that my former wife expressed a very strong desire that, if I married again, I should marry her sister, provided such a marriage was not contrary to the Scriptures. I felt myself peculiarly placed at the time, having three young children under five years of age, and the youngest under one year, and having received from my former wife the very earnest injunction I have stated, she knowing the very deep interest which her sister took in the children, and also the strong affection which the children appeared to have for her. Of course I remembered the dying injunction; but it was not until some months after that I became acquainted with the fact that, unknown to me, my former wife had also expressed to her sister that if she married she should marry me, if such a marriage was legal; so that, in point of fact, we were both, it might be said, doubly tied up. (67)

In his contribution to the pamphlet wars, the earl of Albemarle had turned to *David Copperfield* as a trophy of antireformism, taking the married life of Tom Traddles as the ideal instance of a husband's chaste relation to his sisters-in-law. This argument, so representative of conservative opinion, also deserves to be heard in its full rotundity.

> Consider the delightful Traddles protecting Sophy's nine sisters; how happily Sophy crams five of them in to the rooms only just large enough for themselves; how joyous they all are, hanging about him "with an amount of kissing such as I never saw inflicted before on any mortal head," and remark how this continued into Traddles's prosperity, which was shared (thanks to prohibitory law) by the whole family—how "they were always a crowd, somehow, in the large house, all pretty, a perfect nest of roses," running to meet the parental brother-in-law, "handing him about to be kissed, till he is out of breath"; and the unlucky Beauty, with her orphan child, taking up her abode here; now, besides that, Sophy was the eldest

of these roses—a little older than her husband, too; does not one see at once, that not only innocence, but the most absolute and unquestionable security is indispensable to this happy state of things? (*A Parent's Appeal*, 6–7)

The earl relishes Dickens's picture of the unassuming Traddles rolling about in the shower of kisses, and it seems fair enough to see Dickens as relying on the barriers to transgression—not just the wall of the law but also the fact that Sophy is alive and adored—in order to release the domestic carnival of touch and tickle. But how far can the tickles go? As a longtime bachelor, Traddles finds it all "positively delicious": "I hide the girls in the day-time, and make merry with them in the evening."[29] Only a cad would accuse Traddles of lusting after those merry sisters, but can it really be that "law" and "innocence" will allow limitless indulgence in the kissing, hugging, squeezing, tousling? The core assumption of the antireformists was indeed that the legal regime could create, or at least preserve, familial innocence, but it requires the high-minded purity of our pamphleteer to look past the polymorphous sensuality of the romping sisters. Certainly, if one turns from Traddles back to his famous friend, the novel's lessons lose any reassuring simplicity.

"She in whom I might have inspired a dearer love, I had taught to be my sister" (ch. 59)—this is David's sigh of resignation at the beginning of his romantic crisis with Agnes. Without sighing, he has made this claim before: "Agnes is a sister to me" (ch. 18); "Agnes was my sister" (ch. 24). But David is not the only one who makes her the cherished female sibling. The wedding celebration of chapter forty-three becomes a festival of sisterliness between the two young women, "Agnes taking care of Dora," Dora "always clasping Agnes by the hand," and "Dora being so fond of Agnes that she will not be separated from her" (ch. 43). All of this prepares carefully for David's late realization that he has been tied nearly as tightly as the man from Manchester, and tied in such a way as to make clear that through its final phases *David Copperfield* reveals itself as a deceased wife's sister novel. At the moment when David can no longer suppress his longing to wed a second time, when he speaks out his ardent hope that Agnes Wickfield will marry him, he looks into her eyes and sees that "the spirit of my child-wife [Dora] looked upon me, saying it was well" (ch. 62). Then when the engagement is sealed, we learn from Agnes that Dora had followed all those dying women in uttering a final awful plea. She had summoned Agnes to her bedside; she had asked that no one else be near; and then, as Agnes now reveals,

> "She told me that she made a last request to me, and left me a last charge."
> "And it was—"
> "That only I would occupy this vacant place."
> And Agnes laid her head upon my breast, and wept; and I wept with her, though
>   we were so happy. (ch. 62)

Dickens was neither prepared nor inclined to represent an open challenge to the now celebrated transgressive marriage. Still, we know not only from *The Battle of Life* but also from the battle of his own life that the dream of the sisters was never far from the current of his reverie. Dickens did not love his dead wife's sister, but he unabashedly loved the dead sister of his living wife; he loved Mary Hogarth, whose sudden death devastated him (he later said that he "dreamed of her every night for many months" after she died). We recall his growing impatience with his wife, his obsession with the memory of Mary, and then, remarkably, his devotion to Mary's successor, the next sister, Georgina, who replaces her in the house and through whom he believes that the dead sister's "spirit shines out" again.[30]

This biographical opera has no special cultural authority but, together with *The Battle of Life* and the other fictional instances, makes clear that, like the men who testified in 1847, Dickens pondered long over the conundrum of the sisters.[31] In listening to the witnesses who came before Wortley, one often feels that these stammering men had read *The Battle of Life* the year before; so perhaps they had; and by the time he reaches the conclusion of *David Copperfield*, it's as if Dickens had worried the problem as exhaustively as any parliamentary commissioner. Both in the leading of his life and the public play of his fiction, Dickens staged what E. B. Pusey, John Keble, and William Hale Hale had desperately feared: the coursing of domestic desire in twisting streams that will carry away the reassuring simplicities of home life.

When David first feels the stirring of a different desire for Agnes, he thrusts it down. In struggling to affirm that their "long-subsisting relation must be undisturbed" (ch. 58), he occupies just the agitated situation of all those wistful men who looked at the surviving visitor and asked, Could this too be? In deciding that it could not, David aligns himself with the opponents of Wortley's bill, and to that extent the earl of Albemarle enjoyed the novelist's support. Dickens invests the purity of the sister with all the sacred innocence that any antireformist polemicist could demand. Of Agnes's long-standing fondness for her "brother," David braces himself to write,

> It was for me to guard this sisterly affection with religious care. It was all that I had left myself, and it was a treasure. If I once shook the foundations of the sacred confidence and usage, in virtue of which it was given to me, it was lost, and could never be recovered. I set this steadily before myself. The better I loved her, the more it behoved me never to forget it. (ch. 60)

What more could E. B. Pusey want? And yet, having constructed the relationship in impeccably canonical terms—the sister as the inviolate companion, never the wedded successor—David Copperfield crosses his own meticulously drawn threshold. Desire, even high-minded desire, will not stay down. Tremulously, David will ask if he might call Agnes "something more than Sister, widely different from Sister!" (ch. 62) In that last, long-deferred turn, the novel violently breaks with the earl of Albemarle and offers a richly compelling image of love between "sister" and "brother," while the dead wife looks on with sweet approval.

Is *David Copperfield*, then, finally a partisan novel? In addition to everything else, is it a long pamphlet in support of Stuart Wortley? What makes this implausible is that Dickens so clearly shares and so lushly represents the vision that animates the conservatives; he manifestly values the innocence of home and the existence of a dispassionate affection, which becomes all the stronger by refusing sexual expression. Tom Pinch before David Copperfield and John Jarndyce after him are assertions of the rival principle: that the failure to marry can yield a heightened domestic glow, without which marriage itself risks a coarsening. It seems best to see Dickens as living on the cusp of erotic indecision: nothing is better than the innocent sensuousness of sisters and brothers, unless perhaps its conversion into the experience of married joy. Finally, *David Copperfield* can offer little reassurance to the earl, because if Sophy should die, even Traddles might someday ask the Beauty to be "something more than sister."

4

There remains one further implication in the hectic emotions at the end of the novel. It concerns the asymmetry between the two sisterly wives tied to the same man. The great moral labor assigned to David Copperfield is the overcoming of fantasy and immature desire, a labor cast in terms of the transfer of love. A manifest struggle for the novel is to explain and to justify what, on the plane of narrative invention, amounts to the murder of one woman for the sake of another. The keynote of the justification is Annie Strong's phrase that we considered earlier: "the first mistaken impulse of an undisciplined heart" (ch. 48). But it is one thing to identify the moral task as the correcting of a mistake, the tutoring of an impulse and the disciplining of a heart; it is another to relieve that process of its cruelty.

In this connection a signal feature of David's romance with Dora is that, short though it is, it comes to seem interminable. This is in part because the history of the marriage is so often told in narrative summary, and in part because almost as soon as he is married, David begins to grow moodily retrospective. "All this time," begins chapter 33, "I had gone on loving Dora, harder than ever." The effect, here, as throughout, is to throw emphasis on the long *durée* of the short marriage. When Dora begins to fail and her toy dog Jip with her, she remarks that Jip is growing "slow and lazy," to which Aunt Betsey responds that "he has a worse disorder than that. Age, Dora" (ch. 48). Dora's own illness is so vague that we might as well say that she dies of aging desire— David's aging desire, which cannot protect itself from fatigue. She has been the great fetish object in his swooning adolescent love: "I was steeped in Dora. I was not merely head over ears in love with her, but I was saturated through and through. Enough love might have been wrung out of me, metaphorically speaking, to drown anybody in" (ch. 33) and so on. The novel allows David to spin and to reel, but then it sternly suggests that a life built on dizzy desire can satisfy for only so long.

When Dora obligingly dies and when a chastened David makes his way back to Agnes, the novel suggests that this is more than a transfer of love from one object to the next. As no reader of the novel is allowed to forget, David is correcting his mistake through his second chance. He is rising from the lure of fantasy into a moral maturity. Where Dora was the self-confessed "child-wife," Agnes is "modest," "orderly," and "placid"; her upwardly pointing finger at the end of the novel is not only a spiritual gesture; it is a sign for the narrative geometry that the novel seeks for itself. A strong upward curve, beyond pleasure and toward earnest duty, is the shape drawn by that movement from Dora to Agnes. In this respect *David Copperfield* seeks a congruity between the conventions of *Bildungsroman* and the conventions of the marriage plot.

During the parliamentary hearings a recurrent emphasis of the men who had married, or who longed to marry, the sisters of their wives was the need to save a disintegrating household. The death of the wife had left the home without a manager; the children are without a guide; all domestic virtue was now at risk; and here was the saving angel, if only Parliament allowed. What is consistently missing through the testimony is any allusion to love for the sister-in-law. Partly, of course, this is explained by the reticence encouraged by the committee room, but partly it seems due to the recognition displayed in *David Copperfield*: that the second marriage represents a change in the character of affection. Where once there was the quickening of desire, now there is the slow rhythm of gratitude. The novel, like the law, can only see these two states as terms in a sequence, a life of eager appetite giving way to the life of trust, respect, and acknowledgment.

But a deeper fantasy can sometimes be glimpsed. It appears in Traddles's winsome confession, "The society of girls is a very delightful thing" (ch. 59), revealing that for all his chaste humility, even Tommy fancies a domestic kingdom. In giving two wives to David and permitting the added spice of dalliance with Emily and Rosa Dartle, the novel surrounds its protagonist with women. In the linear time of narrative, one gives way to the next, but in the simultaneity of readerly memory, they all continue to hover, fluttering like Sophy's many sisters.[32] In Margaret Oliphant's *Miss Marjoribanks* the complaisant Mr. Cavendish will find it impossible to choose between two women, leading the narrator to observe that "If such a thing had been permissible in England as that a man might marry one wife for his liking and another for his interests, the matter might have been compromised by proposing to them both."[33] Such a thought hovers everywhere in the background of this strange episode, which changed the aspect of those sisters close at hand. Whatever their own inclinations and preferences, they came to signify an invitation to the erotic wandering of mobile male affection: at least two wives, one for youthful pleasure, and one for the management of home.

THE TRANSVESTITE, THE BLOOMER,
AND THE NIGHTINGALE

1

Queen Victoria, Caroline Norton, and Sarah Stickney Ellis make a complex triad within which to locate the quizzical poetic oddity that is Tennyson's *The Princess*, a poem that will serve us, as it served many of its contemporary readers, as a fantastic gateway into a scene of domestic transformation. Composed and revised between 1839 and 1847, *The Princess* absorbs a decade of vision and ridicule on the eve of a resurgent feminism. The result is a notoriously tremulous achievement, but all the more interesting for that.

As a product of Tennyson's determination to write verse confronting the here and now, *The Princess* might well have been expected to address the "here" of class conflict and the "now" of Chartism. In fact, the first verse chapter of the poem stands as an anodyne refraction of social unease.[1] There on the "broad lawns" of the stately house, the whole local population—the landed aristocrat, his family, his tenants, the working population of the borough—can mingle freely inside the sedate festival. The philanthropic institute, of which Sir Walter Vivian is the patron, charms and disarms his public, soothing those who might have uttered first groans and then demands. *The Princess*, in effect, puts to sleep the disruptions of the hungry 1840s, as if this were the condition for approaching the here of modern marriage and the now of intractable sexuality.

Much of the difficulty of *The Princess* is that, as in many other places, Tennyson writes not as a social thinker, committed to diagnosis, judgment, and proposal, but as a social *sensitive*. Alert to the pressure of history, he responds with the freedom of fantasy. Some time ago, John Killham argued that the poem grew out of the angry debates circulating around Caroline Norton.[2] The abusive personal attacks on Norton, the controversy over the Infant Custody Bill, and the sharp exchanges over women's colleges—Killham places these within the frame of utopian thought on sexual relations, in order to show that the work was no anomaly. And yet, the salient feature of Tennyson's poem is that it wildly exceeds the events that inspire it.

Certainly, since the publication of Mary Wollstonecraft's *Vindication* (1792), the concept of a feminist transformation had a persistent life in the culture. But in part because of the stain on Wollstonecraft's reputation, and even more because of the solidifying conventions of separate spheres, "equal-

ity between the sexes" was not yet the energizing proposal of a social movement but still an erratically floating idea, typically invoked as the example of
an absurdity. Recall that into the 1850s, Caroline Norton was still measuring
her distance from "the absurd claim of equality" between the sexes.[3] There on
the eve of a new sexual agon, confronted with images of woman's freedom
just on the point of becoming political ideas, Tennyson occupied a peculiar
historical position. It gave him literary stimulus without practical constraint.
The eerily prophetic character of *The Princess*—prophetic of feminist demand
and masculinist refusal—is a product of its suspended moment.

Killham was right. The polemics around Norton and infant custody in 1839
make an important context, but they should not divert attention from a grander
figure of the same moment. After all, 1839 also saw Queen Victoria's assertion
during the Bedchamber Crisis, when the proud young queen refused to allow
men to disrupt her private society of women; it was also the year of Prince
Albert's successful engagement visit, arranged like that of Tennyson's Prince
in order to gauge the hopes for a marriage laid before him since childhood.[4]
Caroline Norton was a nimble insurrectionist in the early campaigns for wom-
en's domestic rights, but the queen represented the sovereign female power
that the poem will nervously put into its testing space.

Thus in the prologue when the young men prepare to invent their story and
the aunt concedes that it needn't be ancient, grave, and solemn, young Walter
thinks of his strong-willed sister: "Take Lilia, then, for heroine, clamour'd he /
And make her some great Princess, six feet high / Grand, epic, homicidal."[5]
These lines are strange and revealing. At its moment of resolve, when the
poem decides to face modernity, it immediately thinks of women, and thinks
in particular of the strong woman, the woman of authority, as a kind of giant-
ess—tall, murderous. In this image Tennyson releases a mass of confusion and
anxiety that it requires the whole poem to relieve, if indeed it ever gets relieved.[6] The poem is called "The Princess," not "The Queen," but in every way
it shudders in the face of queenly authority.

What sharpens the challenge is that it will not stop with the single authoritative woman. In the old chronicle found by the narrator at Vivian-place, a story
is told of a warrior lady, the "miracle of noble womanhood" who refused to
yield in battle. She returns later in the prologue, this "feudal warrior lady-
clad," and when our narrator praises her nobleness, Walter pats Lilia's head
and asks where "lives there such a woman now?" Lilia retorts that: "There are
thousands now / Such women, but convention beats them down" (*Princess*,
prologue, 119, 127–28). Here is the logic of a worried phantasmagoria, the
concern that there will be not one warrior lady but hundreds, and beyond them
thousands, enough to fill a college, woman not as a wonderful anomaly, a
magnificent exception, but a social torrent, a geyser of female multitudes.[7]

The writings of Sarah Ellis have shown that the production of the doctrine
of separate spheres was an active process, even an improvisation, frequently

The son, on the other hand, is the softest of princes: Tennyson spoke tellingly of his "comparative want of power."[8] His frequent withdrawal into a land of imaginary shadows, his indifference to military glory, and, most notably, his transvestism mark him as a failed successor to the growling patriarch.[9] The decision to assume "female gear" (1.196) has a simple narrative explanation: the prince and his friends need to disguise themselves in order to enter the "she-society" of the princess's mountain college. But this motivation allows for the release of a different fantasy, the young prince as himself another princess, this as the figural truth of his failure to be "hard." When he first approaches Ida in his disguise and evokes the desperate romantic infatuation of the prince he is pretending not to be, her response is: "Methinks he seems no better than a girl" (3.202). Later, when the ruse is exposed, she will remark that "you look well too in your woman's dress" (4.508), and when he makes his bedraggled way back to the military camp, a warrior snipes that "The woman's garment hid the woman's heart" (5.295). Certainly no scene in the poem is more uncanny than the prince's love song ("O Swallow, Swallow"), performed not only in his rustling "maiden plumes" (1.199) but in the "maidenlike" (4.73) voice that conceals his maleness. In a poem that continually invites a reading aloud here is a dizzying sexual disenfranchisement. His "treble" is a surrender of the style of masculinity, within which the symbology of voice—deep, decided, and resonant—has always played a leading role.

In all these respects, the romantic career of the prince seems to give unruly, even unconscious, secrets away. When the reader is busy looking after the heroine, the prince strays off in "mincing mimicry" (2.403). Thrilling to the abandonment of the prerogatives of manliness, he becomes "disprinced" (5.29). He dotes on Ida's superb self-possession, her beautiful arrogance, her mastery. In a disorienting figure, he will say that he "desire[s] you more / Than growing boys their manhood" (4.436–37).

Surely what allows this risky androgyny is the portrait of manliness as a stupidity and a violence. To the extent that the "hard old king" and Arac, the "genial giant" (5.264), are brutal, witless boors, the poem constructs a stage on which the prince can mince without affront. Moreover, the king, who wants to "crush [Ida's] pretty maiden fancies dead / In iron gauntlets" (1.87–88), is not only a relic of the past; he is also the partisan of a recognizably nineteenth-century doctrine of separate spheres:

> Man for the field and woman for the hearth:
> Man for the sword and for the needle she:
> Man with the head and woman with the heart:
> Man to command and woman to obey;
> All else confusion.
>
> (5.437–41)

This big father with his predatory solution to the ence—"Man is the hunter; woman is his game. . . . ride them down" (5.147, 150)—misapprehends th princess. Furious patriarchy will never vanquish bawls, but what defeats the visionary is the prince see me fall" (5.506), he thinks, as he rides forw mighty Arac. Only from this point, when the prin Dishelm'd and mute, and motionlessly pale" (6.8. sympathy.[10]

The narrative goes on to correct for the indulge now soften and accept the searing humiliation. dress; he will return to a man's vocation. As he betrothed Ida,

> Accomplish thou my manhood
> Lay thy sweet hands in mine an

But as decisive as is the plotting of defeat, w should not also be read nonnarratively, in defia of event. Why should we assume that the las all, regrets over Ida's fall begin as early as the yielded" says young Walter (conclusion, 5). beginning is not canceled by the pale ending

Then, too, even within the terms offered by more than the trouncing of Ida. Her chasten of the brutal king-father: the poem enacts a a supersession of hard patriarchy. The prin the "woman's cause is the man's" (7.243) the now imaginable future when man and

> Sit side by side, full-summ'
> Dispensing harvest, sowing
> Self-reverent each and reve
> Distinct in individualities,
> But like each other even a

This could be read as an uninspired ref already performed his sexual revision. H impure and narratively compromised w yny—unfolding through the years until (7.264)—the poem can no more erase forget Ida's blazing invention of "sh sliding forward and then backsliding

changing its images and its force. We have suggested that within this labor of persuasion home accumulated so much symbolic density that Ellis could imagine it as its own society. *The Princess* can be seen as an elaboration of this insight, as if Tennyson recognized that the pressure of separation might transform the domestic realm. For what if the sexual contrast were cast not only in the terms of home and firm? What if the female space were not a site of "protected" dependence but instead the chosen theater of autonomy? Home would then become a preparation for college—college in its most radical character, as a utopic self-sufficiency, what Ida calls a "fold" (5.380) a collective place apart where women might teach themselves, might indeed feed and amuse and govern themselves.

The reach of Ida's feminism and its clattering fall seize the foreground and the reader's memory. No one can doubt that the narrative offered its respectable readers the reassurance of a revolution not merely defeated but self-defeating. By the time the prince and his friends arrive, the fissures within solidarity have opened wide. Cold Lady Blanche resents Ida's fondness for warm Lady Psyche, creating such vulnerability that the men can bring down a visionary enterprise with a few rude claps of the hand. Prideful women left to themselves will turn self against self. Even Ida's loyal brother recoils from the dissension: "the woman is so hard / Upon the woman" (6.205–6). As the protective fold of womanhood shrinks and withers, Ida's hundreds desert her, in favor of the "swarms of men / Darkening her female field" (7.18–19). Where once men had been forbidden to walk, now

> Love in the sacred halls
> Held carnival at will, and flying struck
> With showers of random sweet on maid and man.

> (7.69–71)

Abandoned, Ida softens like the rest: "Her iron will was broken in her mind; / Her noble heart was molten in her breast" (6.102–3). She wakes from "the foolish work / Of Fancy" (6.100–101). The poem trounces the "theoretical" mind that would suppress instinct in the name of a visionary politics.

Yet the very sensation of the Princess's fall makes possible other maneuvers conducted in the shadows. Ida's career is both the poem's central text and its most convenient pretext—a pretext for the revision of maleness that unfolds even when the poem is in active flight from its "feminism." The story of the princess has the simplicity of revolution and recantation, while the surprise of the poem, its special strangeness, is her husband-after-all, the prince. He is such a reluctant dragon of a prince that he scarcely seems to belong to the same species as those gigantic warriors who surround him: the "fresh young captains" and the "huge blue-bearded Barons" who "heaved and blew" (5.20). Then, rising beyond these men, there looms the prince's roaring father, the "hard old king" (5.456).

The son, on the other hand, is the softest of princes: Tennyson spoke tellingly of his "comparative want of power."[8] His frequent withdrawal into a land of imaginary shadows, his indifference to military glory, and, most notably, his transvestism mark him as a failed successor to the growling patriarch.[9] The decision to assume "female gear" (1.196) has a simple narrative explanation: the prince and his friends need to disguise themselves in order to enter the "she-society" of the princess's mountain college. But this motivation allows for the release of a different fantasy, the young prince as himself another princess, this as the figural truth of his failure to be "hard." When he first approaches Ida in his disguise and evokes the desperate romantic infatuation of the prince he is pretending not to be, her response is: "Methinks he seems no better than a girl" (3.202). Later, when the ruse is exposed, she will remark that "you look well too in your woman's dress" (4.508), and when he makes his bedraggled way back to the military camp, a warrior snipes that "The woman's garment hid the woman's heart" (5.295). Certainly no scene in the poem is more uncanny than the prince's love song ("O Swallow, Swallow"), performed not only in his rustling "maiden plumes" (1.199) but in the "maidenlike" (4.73) voice that conceals his maleness. In a poem that continually invites a reading aloud here is a dizzying sexual disenfranchisement. His "treble" is a surrender of the style of masculinity, within which the symbology of voice—deep, decided, and resonant—has always played a leading role.

In all these respects, the romantic career of the prince seems to give unruly, even unconscious, secrets away. When the reader is busy looking after the heroine, the prince strays off in "mincing mimicry" (2.403). Thrilling to the abandonment of the prerogatives of manliness, he becomes "disprinced" (5.29). He dotes on Ida's superb self-possession, her beautiful arrogance, her mastery. In a disorienting figure, he will say that he "desire[s] you more / Than growing boys their manhood" (4.436–37).

Surely what allows this risky androgyny is the portrait of manliness as a stupidity and a violence. To the extent that the "hard old king" and Arac, the "genial giant" (5.264), are brutal, witless boors, the poem constructs a stage on which the prince can mince without affront. Moreover, the king, who wants to "crush [Ida's] pretty maiden fancies dead / In iron gauntlets" (1.87–88), is not only a relic of the past; he is also the partisan of a recognizably nineteenth-century doctrine of separate spheres:

> Man for the field and woman for the hearth:
> Man for the sword and for the needle she:
> Man with the head and woman with the heart:
> Man to command and woman to obey;
> All else confusion.
>
> (5.437–41)

This big father with his predatory solution to the problem of sexual differ-ence—"Man is the hunter; woman is his game. . . . They love us for it, and we ride them down" (5.147, 150)—misapprehends the modern difficulty of the princess. Furious patriarchy will never vanquish Ida. The king blusters and bawls, but what defeats the visionary is the prince's final collapse. "[L]et her see me fall" (5.506), he thinks, as he rides forward to be shattered by the mighty Arac. Only from this point, when the princess sees him "lying stark, / Dishelm'd and mute, and motionlessly pale" (6.84–85), does she feel the fatal sympathy.[10]

The narrative goes on to correct for the indulgence of its daydream. Ida will now soften and accept the searing humiliation. The prince will take off his dress; he will return to a man's vocation. As he says in his last speech to the betrothed Ida,

> Accomplish thou my manhood and thyself;
> Lay thy sweet hands in mine and trust to me.

(7.344–45)

But as decisive as is the plotting of defeat, we might ask whether the poem should not also be read nonnarratively, in defiance of the accommodating logic of event. Why should we assume that the last truth is the fullest truth? After all, regrets over Ida's fall begin as early as the poem itself: "I wish she had not yielded" says young Walter (conclusion, 5). The memory of the triumphant beginning is not canceled by the pale ending.

Then, too, even within the terms offered by the narrative, we have something more than the trouncing of Ida. Her chastening accompanies the obsolescence of the brutal king-father: the poem enacts at once the failures of feminism and a supersession of hard patriarchy. The prince promises his mortified bride that the "woman's cause is the man's" (7.243) and that their marriage will point to the now imaginable future when man and woman will

> Sit side by side, full-summ'd in all their powers,
> Dispensing harvest, sowing the To-be,
> Self-reverent each and reverencing each,
> Distinct in individualities,
> But like each other even as those who love.

(7.272–76)

This could be read as an uninspired reformism, were it not that the prince has already performed his sexual revision. He has minced and trebled, and however impure and narratively compromised we find the vision of progressive androg-yny—unfolding through the years until "man be more of woman, she of man" (7.264)—the poem can no more erase his cross-dressing theatrics than it can forget Ida's blazing invention of "she-society" (prologue, 158). Nervously sliding forward and then backsliding, *The Princess* intimates the terms of a

Grand Bargain, which will hover around the midcentury conversation. Suppose women give up their "absurd" excesses of she-society, and suppose that men give up their "hard" domination. What then stands in the way of domestic utopia? The answer, of course, is quite a lot.

2

In the aftermath of that epoch-making event, the Great International Exhibition of 1851, the American delegation left behind one particular relic of its stay, the bloomer, which quickly became a fashion sensation on the streets of London. To read through the vaporings of the press in the latter part of the exhibition year is to see a sudden declension from the mood of national pride and to witness in its place the growth of a popular fixation: an obsession with the provoking spectacle of women in bloomer costume. If these strolling women seem to create a tonal shudder, coming so close beside Tennyson's gender warriors in heroic dress, then we must learn to live with the shudder, because in the early 1850s the vexations of sexual dyadism begin to tremble everywhere in the culture. What could it be for a man to marry a bloomer?

In the United States, the wearing of bloomers and the demands of an early feminism were securely linked. But what is striking in the British context is that at a moment just before the emergence of a coherent feminist program into general public discourse, Bloomerism appeared merely as an astonishing affront to the proprieties of appearance. Disregarded as a deliberate counterpart to a political campaign, it released anxieties and dreads likely to be suppressed in the more formal abstraction of political debate. Here, first of all, is an excited squib from *Bentley's Miscellany* that saw Bloomerism as the culminating episode of Amazon insurgency.

> Their [women's] progress was slow and insinuating, until the Bloomers rushed into the contest with full ardour, determined to strike a great blow at once. It will have been remarked that the attacks hitherto made had been entirely from the waist upwards; the Bloomers, however, with the spirit of true Amazons, resolve upon "going the whole animal," and the reform takes its foundation from the ground, and attacks the entire figure.[11]

What was once only "above the waist" now includes the "whole animal," inviting leering readers to imagine what remains when "above" is subtracted from "whole." Predictably the effigy of Lady Macbeth is paraded as a sign for the "the bold, the resolute, the uncompromising" demeanor of women who would show the shape of their legs. The *Lancet* repudiated bloomers in favor of the petticoat, which "is the garment that is the most in harmony with the mental qualities that Nature has implanted in the female sex."[12] And when Lord Ashley, now the earl of Shaftesbury, looks to compliment Caroline Chisholm for her splendid work on female emigration, he can't resist joining the attack on

Bloomerism, which he does by defining the true bloomer. "Mrs. Chisholm," he intones, "had attained the highest order of Bloomerism: she had the heart of a woman, and the understanding of a man."[13] Whatever else this remark means, it indicates the strain placed by bloomers upon the male imagination of the female body. The instinctive response is to create strange bodily hybrids composed out of the combination of male and female parts, as in Shaftesbury's picture of womanly heart joined to manly head—the head here substituting for the male garments worn down below.

Shaftesbury releases only a gentle arrow, but all through the press, one finds a teasing, taunting derision, nowhere more compulsively performed than in the pages of *Punch*. For several months in 1851, scarcely an issue goes by without several swipes of the broad comic brush. Bloomers become an invitation to endless cartoon creativity, and to follow the many pages of satire is to see how the bloomer craze touched off a male sexual panic, stirred by the thought that if women can wear men's clothes, then no marital convention is safe.

The pages that follow contain only a few specimens of *Punch* cartoon satire (Figures 3 and 4), but they demonstrate the obsessive fascination. In one scene after another the *Punch* cartoonists visualize the transfer of power to women, and once begun the device has no apparent end. The dream vision "Bloomeriana" registers the nightmare dread of women's authority—female carriage drivers, female soldiers, female jockeys, women to the left of them, women to the right of them. And one does well to remember that this uncomfortable and harsh satire of women's authority comes at a moment when a queen sits heavily on the British throne.

Between the end of his work on *David Copperfield* and the beginning of *Bleak House*, Dickens too felt a quivering antibloomer rage, releasing his anger in a disturbing essay called "Sucking Pigs." Here he conjures a wife, names her Julia Bellows, gives her bloomers, and addresses her in plaintive irony.

> Apple of our eye, we will freely admit your inalienable right to step out of your domestic path into any phase of public appearance and palaver that pleases you best; but . . . should we love our Julia better, if she were a Member of Parliament? . . . Do we not, on the contrary, rather seek in the society of our Julia, a haven of refuge? . . . Is not the home-voice of our Julia as the song of a bird, after considerable bow-wowing out of doors?

Dickens's satire is relentless, leading to the lumbering barnyard joke that the problem with sucking pigs is that, like their cousins the whole hogs, they always go too far. So that,

> even if Mrs. Bellows chooses to become, of her own free will and liking, a Bloomer, that won't do. She must agitate, agitate, agitate. She must take to the little table and water-bottle. She must go in to be a public character. She must

ONE OF THE DELIGHTFUL RESULTS OF BLOOMERISM.—THE LADIES WILL
POP THE QUESTION.

Superior Creature. "SAY! OH, SAY, DEAREST! WILL YOU BE MINE?" &c., &c.

Figure 3. From *Punch* 21 (1851).

work away at a Mission. . . . She must discharge herself of a vast amount of words,
she must enlist into an Army composed entirely of Trumpeters, she must come
(with the Misses Bellows) into a resounding Spartan Hall for the purpose.[14]

A few years earlier Dickens had been an ardent supporter of the campaigns of
just such public women. Privately and publicly, he had boosted the causes of
Caroline Chisholm, especially her plans for female emigration. And yet as
he begins writing *Bleak House*, Chisholm transmutes into Mrs. Jellyby, the
notorious "agitating" woman, who leaves her family in a domestic swamp,
while she pursues the distant cause of Borrioboola-Gha. What had happened
between the support of 1850 and the satire of 1852? In a word, Bloomerism.
For Dickens, as for others, the shock of the bloomer seems to have been elec-
tric, creating a violent recoil from those brazen women who leave the household and parade in public. The fallen women of the lower classes can be con-

BLOOMERIANA. A DREAM.

Figure 4. From *Punch* 21 (1851).

fronted and sent away, but when those women of the respectable classes refuse their husband's authority and make themselves into a fashion spectacle, then there is panic in the hearth.

What is only implied in Dickens's sour satire is emphasized elsewhere: that the aggression of Bloomerism, the female appropriation of a male fashion convention, involves not only a "monstrous" change for women but at least as horrifying a transformation in men. Bloomerism generates a remorseless logic of gender reversal. Week after week, the cartoonists work out the nightmare of an exchange of roles. Suppose she asks *him* to dance; suppose she proposes; suppose she wears the trousers in the household. Every vision of a militant step for a woman brings with it an image of the retreating man.

A boisterous essay in *Blackwood's* called "Husbands, Wives, Fathers, Mothers" describes the costume as "indecent." And why? "Because, simply, it removes the separation wall, as it were, between the sexes." It creates a "new order of masculi-femininity," and while the result is unattractive in women it is catastrophic for men: "where man and woman are, so to say, confused in dress, so will they be to a great extent in mind. The masculine must become feminine, as the feminine masculine; and from a congenital confusion of ideas, a man, when he sees his wife after dinner cross her legs, put her feet on the fender and smoke a cigar, will have to say the least, sensations of doubt."[15] The essay in *Bentley's* had amused itself with reports of men, sympathetic to the cause, who are forced to prove that they themselves are not female bloomers, and *Blackwood's* takes the conceit still further, describing a scene at a recent public meeting:

> Behind the lady we observed what we supposed must be characterised as the male of the species "Bloomer." He wore a silken cassock with sleeves, deep cuffs, and ruffles embroidered round the throat; had his collars turned down à la Byron, and his cravat tied outside his coat, the bows jutting out from each side in the modern fashion of Cheapside, and the ends falling down in a cataract of silk to about half over his manly bosom. We could not see his nether extremities, to define what alteration had been there effected; but his cheeks were fringed with a thin whisker . . . his countenance, on the whole, wearing that chastened aspect which so well befits the husband of a species, the female of which talks so much and so well. (84)

With such "doubtful masculinities" abroad (80), it is likely that "manhood will soon be at a discount" (85).

The prepolitical character of the short-lived bloomer episode invited the sexual phantasmagoria displayed before the eye of the reading public. Treated as a great joke, all winks and elbows and "Har-har-har," it allowed the enactment of roles within an absurdist drama of gender revolution. Like the caricatures of women in command, the figures of cross-dressing men belong with Tennyson's transvestite prince as fantasy constructions that point toward otherwise unimaginable transformations. So far were the critics from engaging serious discussion that they diverted themselves and their readers by elaborating the future for a world of parading women. *Bentley's* refers to a vaudeville in Paris called "1851 et 1951" which is said to present the fulfillment of *Punch's* caricatures, and Mr. Punch himself, in an involuntary prophecy of an imminent feminism, conjures the image of an insurrection that will bring women out of the angelic home into the public sphere.

> Are men to yield all? asks Mr. Punch, may we not suggest half-and-half: For instance, may not the House of Lords be enlarged into the House of Lords and Ladies?
>
> May not the House of Commons divide with the women?[16]

Much of what passed for side-splitting humor would before long become part of a familiar program of demands: why not women in the professions, or why not in Parliament?

Indeed there is good reason to suspect that the visible buffoonery excited by Bloomerism brought into circulation ideas and images that were then appropriated by women and recast in very different tones. In this respect the excitement inadvertently stimulated a debate on issues that from the mid-1850s would dominate feminist engagement with Victorian domestic norms.

Yet, if she successfully invited men to imagine issues on which earnest debate would soon be joined, the bloomer remained a figure of ridicule. Stigmatized as a monster, a sucking pig, an Amazon, a Lady Macbeth, she stood in the place long occupied by Mary Wollstonecraft, as the scandalous object of respectable scorn. Like the "lady doctor" at the end of the decade, the bloomer was used to discredit the seriousness of early feminism, though here it needs to be said that not only stubborn traditionalists but also moderate reformers used such "monsters" for purposes of their own. One striking illustration occurs in Caroline Norton's *English Laws for Women*, a work that would prove so important to the reform of family law. Even as her personal narrative widens to include all women, Norton cannot resist the prevailing language of monstrosity. Writing of her loathed husband's sister, she remarks, "I pleaded that her eccentricities prevented my friends from inviting her; that she dressed differently from other ladies; wearing a sort of Bloomer costume, a short dress with trowsers, and her hair cropped like a man's; and altogether affected masculine singularities, which astonished and repelled persons who had the usual habits of society" (*English Laws*, 36).

Vulnerable to attack on every side, the bloomer nevertheless made inescapable the question of wives in public, women awkwardly visible. Even when the bloomer went out, there would be no putting her back in. But what was she to do? What was the unchastened, unprotected woman to do when she crossed the threshold and strolled down the street?

3

Tennyson's Princess Ida arrives at her moment of domestic revelation when she descends to the battlefield, approaches the cross-dressing prince now lying badly wounded, and immediately decides to nurse his broken body. From this point, the resolution of the poem is assured. In the work of Sarah Ellis nursing also assumes a privilege, because the opportunity to tend the sick husband or the sick children gave inspiring grandeur to the woman-wife-daughter. As a nurse the "woman of England" is able to assume fully the responsibilities of her central position in home life, or as Ellis puts it: "a high-minded and intellectual woman is never more truly great than when willingly and judiciously performing kind offices for the sick."[17] Such images of benevolence, of delicate condescension, appear in the context of personal affection, confirming already existing ties. To care for him (husband, fiancé) in times of unusual need, indeed to touch him in an unusual way, is to achieve an apotheosis of intimacy. The specter of the professional nurse, harshly caricatured in Dickens's Sairey Gamp, is countered by the alluring figure of the nursing amateur, the wife or daughterly wife-to-be, who requires no training and demands no payment, but who simply relies on the instinct of affection.[18]

Among the multitude of artifacts excited into being by the cultural episode we know as "Florence Nightingale" was an anonymous pamphlet called *Notes on Nurses*, which seized on the new fireside vision suggested by the glory of the Crimea.

One of our most popular novelists, in alluding to the common education of young ladies, says, with truth, that a man does not want a singing wife, or a playing wife, a dancing wife or a painting wife—but a *talking* wife. By most men it would be considered an advantage to have a *nursing* wife—a wife who understood how to tend him in sickness, how to administer effectually to the little patients of the nursery; one who understood and could relieve the minor ailments of her children, and who could in more dangerous illnesses, carry out intelligently the directions of the doctor.[19]

Much of the mobile connotative power of "nursing" comes into this fervent paragraph. Instead of singing, dancing, or even talking, the wife will nurse her husband, becoming a new and cherished prop in the domestic tableau. She will serve not merely as another sign of the foundational inferiority of woman, but also as an occasion for a male reverie luxuriating in the wife's adoration displayed through prim efficiency. The practical advantages of the medically adept wife is enlivened by the eroticism of bodily attention. Indeed the sexualization of household management excited by the image of the nursing wife culminates the eroticopractical fantasy long secreted within the domestic narrative. The stylized, ritualized, eroticized aspects of housekeeping so visible in Dickens's heroines unfold in the sacred ceremonies of nursing, when it is not merely a question of shaking the housekeys or bustling (so charmingly) over an aromatic supper, but of solemnly applying the prescribed remedies to a feverish body thrashing beneath the sheets.

Nightingale's little book of 1860, *Notes on Nursing*, strongly confirms the domestic interpretation of her example. If, as her preface tells us, "every woman is a nurse,"[20] then nursing can represent the splendid enhancement of the responsibilities of the housewife or the daughter.[21] In this respect Nightingale is in accord with the anonymous author, whose tract she kept in her possession. Even as she prepares for the keen extension of professionalism in her training institute, she, too, looks to a new epoch of *nursing wives*. No longer a special occasion for devotion, nursing becomes a continuous vocation, the foundation of a properly flourishing household life. Early in the work she asks,

Do you ever go into the bed-rooms of any persons of any class, whether they contain one, two, or twenty people, whether they hold sick or well, at night, or before the windows are opened in the morning, and ever find the air anything but unwholesomely close and foul? And why should it be so? And of how much importance is it that it should not be so? During sleep, the human body, even when in health, is far more injured by the influence of foul air than when awake. Why can't you keep the air all night, then, as pure as the air without in the rooms you sleep in? But for this, you must have sufficient outlet for the impure air you make yourselves to go out; sufficient inlet for the pure air from without to come in. You must have open chimneys, open windows, or ventilators; no close curtains round your beds; no shutters or curtains to your windows, none of the contrivances by which you undermine your own health or destroy the chances of recovery of your sick. (*Notes on Nursing*, 10)

As Nightingale develops a picture of the home, it becomes just such an intricate mechanism, upon whose functioning depends the life or death of its inhabitants. Windows and doors, smoky chimneys and open sinks, bodily fluids and poisonous vapors—the house is an organism perpetually confronted with threats to its existence. It falls then to the housewife as nurse, or the daughter as nurse, or any other household female as nurse, to maintain the vigilance necessary to defeat unseen villains.

We recall that what invested dignity in the housewife for Ellis was the sense of perpetual domestic drama. If "every passing event, however insignificant to the eye of the world, has its crisis, every occurrence its emergency," then in the epoch of Nightingale, the stakes are still greater, and the "eye of the world" can no longer mistake their significance. The threat that beguiled Ellis—"the machinery of household comfort . . . thrown into disorder"—transforms into an assault on the preservation of health. The role of the housewife now far exceeds that of the nurturing fond source of maternal cheer: the performance of the role is seen as the condition of survival. Home becomes something like the living shell of the human body—if it is not tended with the utmost care, then disaster will follow.

In all these respects, it's clear enough how the picture that emerges from *Notes on Nursing* ratifies the virtues of home life. Nightingale is represented as the radiant mother, the self-sacrificing female Christ, the Lady with the Lamp who makes a home out of a bloody hospital ward.[22] But here we might recall a joke, told by Florence Nightingale, who from the midst of her difficult work in the Crimea writes to her friends, the Bracebridges, that "The greatest compliment I have had paid to me was by the Vice-consul . . . who said that Lord Raglan was dead which was bad—but that Miss Nightingale was going to be married, which was worse."[23]

A brief history of the Crimean War lies within that half-daring battlefield joke: the military disappointment, the shock to British national pride, which is relieved triumphantly, by the Lady with a Lamp. It's not hard to see why in the darkly comic disposition of those enduring the hardship of the war, the death of a roundly criticized general would be called merely "bad." But more important is to consider what is at stake in that *worse* condition—the marriage of Nightingale, the dread event that she managed to forestall. That marriage would be the death of her legendary mission: it's not too much to say that this recognition would alter the terms of the Victorian domestic reverie.[24]

Before she even returned to Britain, when she was still a newspaper sensation caressed into celebrity by the *Times*, Nightingale had erupted into the discourse of womanhood. She arrived at a moment of instability, and therefore opportunity. On one side, the side of the fireside imagination always looking for new tropes of the daughterly, motherly, housewife, Nightingale excited the daydream of the caretaker, whose coolly accomplished hand rests on the burning forehead of husband and children. But if the hearth was one receptive context for her spectacular fame, it was not the only one. The anxiety over women in public that had erupted during the bloomer episode reached an impasse by the mid-1850s. In the figure of the strolling bloomer gathered all the dense, unruly images of the "unprotected female," the superfluous woman, the sister in reserve, one of the half million who could not be secured within the marriage tie and who therefore threatened, in Dickens's words, "to agitate, agitate, agitate." By the time Nightingale was home in Britain, "agitation" had taken on political form as a demand for new laws on married woman's property and divorce. The Nightingale sensation descended at just the moment when the demands for parliamentary action on these issues had grown clamorous, and, to a culture frantically trying to tell an acceptable story for the unattached woman, the life of Florence Nightingale appeared as a solution to the broken narrative.

In 1848 Anna Jameson published a startling pamphlet under the bland title *The Relative Position of Mothers and Governesses*, a work that exposed the misery attending the life of a governess. The problem, writes Jameson, is one that the nineteenth century has made for itself: "It is within the last fifty years, since marriage has become more and more difficult—forced celibacy with all its melancholy and demoralizing consequences, more and more general—that we find that governesses have become a class, and a class so numerous, that the supply has, in numbers at least, exceeded the demand."[25]

Political economy thus combines with moral outrage to compel a response. Even as the male educator has assumed more importance and dignity, the woman in a comparable position has nothing to look forward to "but a broken constitution, and a lonely, unblessed old age" (*Mothers and Governesses*, 5). The bleakness of the picture is unrelieved: ever increasing numbers of young women look to become governesses, without training, with little compatibility with their employers, and with meager hopes of securing themselves against an uncertain future. We learn that in 1846 sixty-five candidates applied to the Governesses' Benevolent Institution, hoping to receive one of two pensions of fifteen pounds a year.

In the same year that Jameson's pamphlet appeared, F. D. Maurice and his sister Mary took their own steps to help by opening Queen's college, Harley

Street. The first public institution for the higher education of women, it was conceived with the mission of training those who worked as, or sought work, as governesses, but it quickly extended its student population in acknowledgment that no one could predict when a family crisis would require a young woman to seek the position. Girls as young as twelve were received into the college, while Maurice recruited friends and political allies to his faculty.

Maurice anticipated the criticisms, which he would soon receive, and in his own pamphlet of 1848 he imagines the challenge in revealing terms. Evoking a harsh skeptic, he envisions these questions put to his plan for the new college:

> Is not this a practical confession that you have some new project of Education; that you desire to wage war with all our habitual notions; that you would set up a College not so magnificent as the one which a great poet of our day has lately made us acquainted, but scarcely less extravagant in its scheme and pretensions?

> I believe we can, with a safe conscience, plead Not Guilty to these charges. We should indeed rejoice to profit in this, or any undertaking, by the deep wisdom which the author of the "Princess" has concealed under a veil of exquisite grace and lightness; we should not wish to think less nobly than his Royal heroine does of the rights and powers of her sex; but we should be more inclined to acquiesce in the conclusions of her matured experience, than to restore—upon a miserably feeble and reduced scale, not without some fatal deviations from the original statutes—her splendid but transitory foundation.[26]

At this founding moment in the history of women's education Tennyson's poem is precedent and guide. For all the unsettled character of the princess's example—shown in Maurice's defense of the "the rights and powers of her sex," even as hairs are split between the "splendid" but "transitory" original vision and the mature (that is, chastened) later view—the passage leaves no doubt that the strange poem of 1847 was seen as confirming the plans for a woman's college. Maurice, who recognized that controversy over Queen's College was inescapable, understood his "feminist" provocation in terms of the dialectic of extremism and reformism drawn from *The Princess*.

Queen's College was a blunt response to the insufficiencies of the domestic orthodoxy, rudely specifying the failures that haunted the fireside dream. As Jameson puts it elsewhere, the fallacy is the assumption that a woman is "always protected, always under tutelage, always within the precincts of a home; finding there her work, her interest. We know that it is altogether false. There are thousands of women who have no protection, no guide, no help, no home."[27] Indeed, *hundreds of thousands* of women were unassimilated by the marital norm, and the hope of the educators was to train some among them for life outside marriage. But what could that life be? The governess stood out as the genteel example, inspiring Maurice's efforts and arousing wide sympathy. Yet neither Jameson nor Maurice exhibits confidence that even a well-trained governess will achieve dignity, or even safety. Jameson wrote that for "the woman who either has no home, or is exiled from that which she has, —the occupation of governess is sought merely through necessity, as the *only* means by which a woman not born in the servile classes *can* earn the means of subsistence" (*Mothers and Governesses*, 6). She concludes her pamphlet by recording the annotated biographies compiled by the Governesses' Benevolent Institute.

"It is very possible," insists Jameson, "that the necessity of having private governesses, except in particular cases, may at some future time be done away with by a systematic and generally accessible education for women of all classes and that some other means of earning a subsistence may be opened to the earnest woman, willing and able to work" (*Mothers and Governesses*, 13). But like so many others Jameson had no examples to suggest of those "other means" of earning a living.

In 1853, Maurice published *Theological Essays*, which attracted new charges of heterodoxy and led to his dismissal from King's College, where he had held professorships since 1840. He carried on at Queen's College and in 1854 he founded the Working Men's College in Red Lion Square. Though the plan had been to admit only men to the new college, early in the following year the decision was reversed. Maurice had assembled a corps of committed faculty both at Queen's and at Working Men's College, and when women joined the second project in the spring of 1855 the group offered and then published a series of *Lectures for Ladies*, so successful that a second edition appeared soon after. In the book as in the lecture hall, one male expert after another came forward and offered instruction: in district visiting, in sanitary policy, in family law. Here indeed is the world of the "mature" princess, with women no longer training and teaching themselves, but firmly under the tutelage of professional men. And yet even in the context of a male patronage bestowed on a weaker sex, the consciousness of struggle is pervasive. In his opening lecture Maurice refers to "the daily vexations of domestic life."[28]

What runs as a thrill through Maurice's presentation of 1855 is the tone of revelation, the sense that a veil has dropped; Florence Nightingale has appeared. Suddenly, he admits, the college has a coherence and a purpose: it will prepare women to be nurses; it will instruct them in law, religion, and social policy, stirred by the confidence that a genuine vocation will be the goal of the labor. One can scarcely overstate the giddiness that the idea brings. There had been an impasse; now there was a Nightingale. The Reverend J. S. Brewer, in his lecture on "District Visiting," expresses the surge of elation, declaring that "Extravagant as the assertion may appear, as new a region has been laid open to female labour in the cause of humanity by Miss Nightingale, as if she had discovered some *terra incognita*, and with results, I believe, that are scarcely less important to her own sex than to ours" (*Lectures for Ladies*, 286).

Earlier in 1855, Jameson had published her *Sisters of Charity*, a work that Maurice acknowledges as inspiration to his own. Whether or not she felt that terra incognita had been found, Jameson also saw Nightingale's example as nothing short of monumental, as marking the start of a new epoch in the relations between men and women. She quotes a long passage from Brontë's *Shirley* concerning the need for single women to have "more to do" and reports showing it to two men, one of whom suggested that such a woman "ought to emigrate" and the other that "The girl ought to be married"(16). Now at last, declares Jameson, an alternative has shown itself. The resigned critic of 1848, who had seen the position of the governess as the only reasonable employment for women of the middle classes, exults that "all the unemployed and superfluous women in England cannot be sempstresses, governesses, and artists" (*Sisters of Charity*, 101). For Jameson, as for Maurice, the reinvention of nursing in the Crimea means that it is possible to imagine a vocation that is not a long career of indignity or degradation. The movement from 1848 to 1855 is among other things a movement from the governess to the nurse. The arc of the transformation appears not only as a change from a disagreeable necessity to a noble vocation, but also as a passage from the interior life of home to the dramatically public realm of the hospital.

True enough that the nursing topos emanated from the ideology of home and reaffirmed the sanctities of private life; but it is no less true that at a moment of disarray in the public life of gender, a disarray produced by anxieties over too many women in too many awkward situations—too many sisters, too many needleworkers, too many prostitutes, too many bloomers, too many governesses—Florence Nightingale suggested a solution that lay not within the home circle but beyond it.[29] To Jameson's pointed question, "How shall we employ this superfluity of the 'feminine element' in society, how turn it to good and useful purposes, instead of allowing it to run to waste?" (*Sisters of Charity*, 61), there seemed an answer, unimaginable before, that combined respectability and exteriority, dignity and publicity.

The astonishment at the panorama of Nightingale in the Crimea, so geographically spectacular, must have stimulated thoughts of a movement across the threshold toward distant lands. But more telling in the longer term were the images of nursing that simply pointed beyond the walls of home. Mary Poovey has incisively distinguished two narratives within nursing, what she calls the "domestic" and the "military" narratives,[30] and if we recast that distinction as a contrast between a "myth of care" and a "myth of administration," then we have the emphasis we need. All through the domestic manuals these two myths had competed and clashed. Was the foundational act of domesticity the tending of moral character and the immortal soul, or was it the efficient management of routine, the workaday struggle just to keep the household running? Sarah Ellis had been vigilant in opposing the latter view, warning women away from the barren rituals of housekeeping, and encouraging them to tend the flame of personhood. Nightingale's *Notes on Nursing* stands on the other side of the balance, not by repudiating the soul, but simply by attending so remorselessly to the body.

The picture of domesticity that emerges in *Notes on Nursing* is that of the supremely administered household, the household prospering under a domestic management that perpetually arranges windows and doors, establishes precise routines, delegates responsibilities, hums with the brisk noise of the efficient machine. In her review of the book, Harriet Martineau mentions that it has been called "querulous" and "severe." Martineau denies that it is querulous but insists that it must be severe. Nightingale, she writes, shows the needs of the sick "in a sharp, clear, epigrammatic style, without calling names or making fine invocations."[31] The central chapter in the book, "Petty Management," is an unsentimental rendering of the regimen of home. It is not, of course, that the myth of care disappears. On the contrary it is surely enhanced by the trope of the sweet Nightingale. But *Notes on Nursing* suggests that care is the after-effect, the tender reward earned through the triumph of administration.

The 1850s were the great decade of administration.[32] From the Crystal Palace to the professions, great pleasure was taken in demonstrations of efficiency, order, and discipline. In this respect, the supremely administered home arranged by Nightingale became a homology for the administrative activity in the public world, and it's not difficult to see how she could move so easily from plans for reforming the British army or devising a training institute for professional nurses to the household advice contained in her famous pamphlet. If "every woman is a nurse" (preface), then the home can stand as a microcosm of the hospital, and the power of the administrative homology suggests that household efficiency can be a preparation for a professional career. While never understating the demands of professionalization, *Notes on Nursing* excites the thought that home can be a training for an escape from home.

Martineau extends the reach of the image when she argues that Nightingale treats the conditions of health and sickness as "radically distinct," and that the "Nurse represents the sound, and the Invalid the sick." She then goes on:

> What then is to be done if there is this impassable gulf between the experience of the sick and the well? It is a great thing to have brought complacent persons to this point—of inquiring what can be done. It is clear that there is something—that there is everything to be done by the healthy for the sick. The lives saved that have been despaired of, the alleviating of suffering which astonishes the sufferer himself, the ingenuity in resource which at once delights and amuses the patient, the intensity of gratitude which makes the sick man kiss the passing shadow of his nurse upon his pillow, the success which follows the ministrations of individuals in private homes and in hospitals, all indicate the truth that, though the sensations of health and sickness are insuperably different, no difficulties from this cause need be insuperable. (402)

Under the spell of Nightingale, Martineau projects a social universe that divides between agents and patients and redraws the boundaries between private and public domains. The "well" and the "sick" can be located anywhere and on any scale, "in private homes and in hospitals," a phrase that bounds across the separation of spheres. Are the sick preeminently characters in a domestic drama, or do they belong to the theater of social crisis? The spirited answer is, Both.

Alongside the productive confusions of homology stimulated by the administrative imagination there stands another pressure, material rather than figural, toward the erosion of the entrenched barriers. This is the pressure of an environmental causality, vigorously promulgated in Nightingale's work. The flourishing of a body occurs only within a healthy milieu: to improve the milieu is to prepare the recovery of the ailing patient. Here is the aphoristic foundation of Nightingale's influential therapy. Disease is seen as a disruption of the environment, as the product of foul air and dangerous vapors. And while this obliges the "nursing wife" to keep an eye on the secret dangers of the household—the accumulation of stale air, the circulation of dangerous drafts—the unremitting wariness cannot stop at the threshold. Because toxic vapors and foul air respect no laws of property, attention cannot be restricted to the physical space of the home: the need is for cleanliness "within and without" the house (16). *Notes on Nursing* warns of the poisonous atmosphere outside the home, emanating from the sewers or from dung heaps, and it becomes clear that a healthy house can only exist within a healthy outer space, a healthy city, a healthy London. The robust environmentalism of the nursing mission offers another call for a crossing of thresholds and a breaking of the domestic enclosure. In principle every conscientious housekeeper needs also to be a social reformer.

The anonymous pamphlet *Notes on Nurses* not only anticipates the exchange of "talking wives" for "nursing wives"; it also exults in the prospect of work for women who would otherwise languish at home.

> Of all the changes anticipated, we cannot regard any one as of greater importance than the opening of a new field for the employment of the energies of our unoccupied or perhaps ill-occupied women, whose social state places them above the need of working for their bread, but whom public opinion in England has hitherto condemned to expend all their energies on works of no or at least of doubtful utility.

And further:

> [W]hen we consider the vast amount of female energy which is at present lying fallow in England, or which is not employed in the most useful manner, but frittered away on works of what is termed by courtesy ornamental art, or exhausted in spasmodic and desultory visiting among the poor; when we look at the enforced

inaction of so many of our intelligent and energetic ladies—we believe numbers
will hail with delight the prospect of a new and useful career.

Which is it to be, then, *a nurse* or *a nursing wife*? The writer of the pamphlet
wants it all ways: nursing will be a source of employment for all those superfluous women, and it will also be the supreme enhancement of the married
woman—much as Harriet Martineau looks for the Well to minister to the Sick
"in private homes and in hospitals." Here, as elsewhere, Florence Nightingale
figured not only as a woman of gifts and resources: she was a stimulus to labor
on both sides of the chasm. The deepening of responsibility thrust upon the
housewife, the opening of work for middle-class women, both were confirmed
by the mobile Nightingale.

Moreover, through a strange spatial logic, as the private and public lives of
women swell in implication, they come ever closer to one another. The act of
writing *Notes on Nursing* constitutes Nightingale's refusal to opt for the exclusive professionalism that was attractive to her in many moods: there at the
end of the 1850s she simultaneously worked to ensure that nurses would be
professionally trained and that "every woman is a nurse." For others, the opportunities for nurses created a nervousness even among those most eager to promote its value. In the same lecture in which he celebrates the solution to the
impasse of women's work, Maurice reassures the ladies that if they choose to
study public nursing, "all this time you are only studying what you may prac-
tise with infinite advantage at home, if sick relations should confine you to it,
and your labours among the poor should be suspended" (*Lectures*, 18) and
invokes Jameson's judgment that "every home duty demands the same spirit
of sacrifice as the hospital work at Scutari" (16). But the circuit of implication
works both ways. If home life can seem as heroic as Scutari, then so may
Scutari appear as "familiar" as home.

The ambidexterity of the Nightingale cannot be reduced to a figurine beckoning from one part or other of the divided terrain. In her severe song, as in
her hybrid example, home and hospital ripen together; private and public domains both glow with urgency. But in the midst of this doubleness, at least one
thing is clear: there can be no rest in the peace of home or the equilibrium of
public life. Train, work, manage, delegate, ventilate, circulate—more than any
proposal or policy, it was Nightingale's call to action that echoed in the cacoph-
ony, the rousing of woman's will on both sides of any threshold.

PART FOUR

The Architecture of Comfort and Ruin

Chapter Seven

ON THE PARAPETS OF PRIVACY: WALLS OF
WEALTH AND DISPOSSESSION

IN THIS NEXT SECTION of the study we adjust the emphasis to consider the material environment of domestic life. The ambitions of the midcentury family, its longing for privacy and its fear of exposure, were not only enacted through image, idea, and emotion; they were performed in rooms, among objects, near streets. As we first suggested in our reading of Dickens, Victorian domesticity was as much a spatial as an affective obsession. Increasingly, to imagine a flourishing private life was to articulate space, to secure boundaries, and to distribute bodies. Nightingale's dictum—"Windows are made to be open, doors are made to be shut"—is a brisk reminder that home is a system of compartments, something not only felt but built.[1]

Within our ongoing concern to interpret the public life of the family, its fall into visibility, we concentrate in this section on the effort to keep the public world at bay, the attempt to forestall the invasions of spectacle. To create material defenses against exposure and to design the interior of the household as a series of safe boxes were architectural imperatives prompted by a cultural longing. And yet, as we show in what follows, the demand for the self-enclosures of privacy remained uncomfortably aware of its antitype. As the privileged classes found intricate new ways to fold back upon themselves, they were transfixed by the outfolding poor.

Most immediately, the subject of this chapter is the social force of the wall. It divides street and house; it conceals and inspires the invention of a household universe; it stirs the fantasies of those locked outside in physical and social separation. Our introduction spoke of the image guiding the 1851 census: the bounded household, which achieves "the exclusive command of the entrance-hall and stairs—and the possession of the free space between the ground and sky." The wall represents a barrier that separates privilege from dispossession, and privacy from public life. It converts free space into a series of domestic parcels, and while it stands within a complex array of social meanings—legal, economic, symbolic—it also stands as a conspicuous physical object, which signifies through its heavy materiality.

1

In the final movements of *Our Mutual Friend*, Dickens allows John and Bella Harmon to enjoy their belated reward. Accepting the rich inheritance of the cruel father, John carries his astonished wife out of their cottage in Blackheath and leads her north and west through London. There they enter the precincts of urban privilege, arriving at a townhouse which the reader has known as the "eminently aristocratic family mansion." The building has most recently belonged to the Boffins, the old Harmon servants, but it had entered the novel as the special claim of the corrupt street vendor Silas Wegg. As Wegg sits at his stall on the public thoroughfare, he gazes possessively on the walls of the building which he has never entered but calls "our house" and which he populates with a family of his own fantastic invention: Miss Elizabeth, Master George, Aunt Jane, Uncle Parker.[2] In the punishing critique of Wegg the street-dwelling domestic fantasist, close cousin to Wegg the blackmailer, Dickens enforces the power of the wall to act as the shroud of privacy. Here is a barrier resistant to the intrusions of a cunning predator, a wall strong enough, blank enough, to condemn the enemy to harmless dreams of an unseen interior—and what kind of wall is that?

Identified as "a corner house not far from Cavendish Square," the house falls within London's great expanse of Georgian home architecture, the stout legacy of an eighteenth century whose values could be abandoned more quickly than its buildings. The square-edged townhouse, with its unrepentant uniformity, its brick in neutral tones of gray or brown, and its facade often adorned by nothing more than the repetitive pattern of rectangular windows, was for Dickens, as for many of his contemporaries, an architectural monstrosity. The dully staring house was the counterpart of a staring bourgeois respectability. The stolid Georgian brick front was the face of a cold privilege.

When Bella Harmon (née Wilfer) finally crosses the threshold of the aristocratic mansion, the novel penetrates the wall to find a living core. What the street seller could only desperately imagine now appears as a vivid domestic phantasmagoria, replete with ormolu clock, ivory casket, a nursery, and even an aviary with tropical birds flying above "gold and silver fish, and mosses, and water-lilies, and a fountain, and all manner of wonders" (bk. 4, ch. 12). The figure of the pleasure garden behind impassive walls stands as one luminous icon of midcentury domestic desire. By the time John Harmon is finished with refurbishment, the old dingy mansion has become a "dainty house," as if to prove that the most unprepossessing facade can be redeemed by a household visionary (bk. 4, ch. 14). The fish, the birds, and the fountain create the extravagance of a private carnival, but Dickens knows himself to be pursuing an excess that lives within the emergent norm. That even grim walls can contain a dainty interior is a first principle of Victorian domestic ambition in a gray climate.

The brick simplicity of the Georgian facade encourages the picture of a flat plane marking the boundary between two realms, a plane appearing both solid and eerily sheer. One instant you are in the social domain, the theater of visibility; in the next, you turn a key, or the butler opens a latch, and you discover the blanket of intimacy. Indeed it may well have been the sense of flush proximity between the Georgian house wall and the neighboring street that encouraged more aggressive flourishing of the household edge. When John Nash undertook his urban renovation for the prince regent, he lavished stucco on the palatial park terraces built for grandees. After the dull brick of the previous century, the creamy paste not only brightened the colors of the city, but it also invited a lordly elaboration of the forward wall of home. Given the notorious malleability of stucco, which could be smoothly molded atop a coarse underpinning, proud aristocrats, prosperous merchants, and successful professionals could adorn their homes with columns, pediments, and window treatments, converting the front of the townhouse into a commanding declaration of privilege.

The mid-Victorians would come to revile the "fakery" of Nash's material, which concealed the "truth" of structure beneath the pretense of classical dignity. And yet there could be no turning back to the plainness of the Georgian surface. When the "Queen Anne" style emerged in the second half of the century, it replaced the creamy building paste with its own vision of a prosperous facade: red brick, sash windows, prominent gables, and high chimneys. But for all their stylistic differences, what "Queen Anne" shared with Nash's stucco was an ambitious construal of household physiognomy, a refusal of gray brick blandness in favor of the assertions of an articulate wall. The color and the ornament were one indication of house pride, but the most conspicuous sign was the brazenly protruding doorway, extended through muscular columns or, as the century wore on, through elaborate iron or glass awnings, stretching toward public space as if they were the advance guard of a militant privacy. This elaboration of the house front, not only as a single proprietorial wall but as one in a commanding line along the street, represents the material precipitate of a social victory: the extension of privilege from aristocracy and gentry to the middle classes. In a district such as Cubitt's Belgravia, old and new types of family distinction met and mingled, and in the high-shouldered presentation of their facades they announced, even as they securely hid, the existence of pleasures out of sight.

2

Kept outside though he is, Dickens's Wegg manages to pitch his stall "over against" the wall of the town mansion, resembling "a leech on the house that had 'taken' wonderfully" (bk. 1, ch. 5). When the Harmons take residence and Wegg's schemes are blown apart, he is told never to come "outside these windows" again (bk. 1, ch. 14), as if possession of the house brought control wherever the wall cast its shadow. Then in a last indignity he is flung into a scavenger's cart on the corner. The novel conducts this sequence in vengeful tones representing the standpoint of the wealthy middle-class householder, and yet through all its harsh presentation of the rights of privacy, it continually acknowledges the street tumult beyond the brick curtain. Wegg at his stall and the scavenger beside his cart belong to the ceaseless parade through the public thoroughfare. Here is how the scene appears outside the "blank house" of Dickens's Dombey, who had lived in the same West End district.

> The summer sun was never on the street, but in the morning about breakfast-time, when it came with the water-carts and the old-clothes men, and the people with geraniums, and the umbrella-mender, and the man who trilled the little bell of the Dutch clock as he went along. It was soon gone again to return no more that day; and the bands of music and the straggling Punch's shows going after it, left it a prey to the most dismal of organs, and white mice; with now and then a porcupine, to vary the entertainments; until the butlers whose families were dining out, began to stand at the house-doors in the twilight, and the lamp-lighter made his nightly failure in attempting to brighten up the street with gas.[3]

"Uproar" is Dickens's frequent term for street life, and, as the work of Henry Mayhew showed those who had been too blind to see, the streets outside the home were swarming with the poor, the plaintive, the cagy, the cold, the hungry. To cross the threshold and to enter the street was typically to meet not only the street seller in a stall, but also the crossing sweeper eager to clear the way of horse droppings, the groom tending the carriage, and the inevitable mob of boys. "Leech" is Dickens's cruel name that nevertheless evokes the social life on that threshold between home and street, where privilege draws the veil, while dispossession lives in need.

Among those who held social power and the power of the word, it was an article of complacent faith that the millions of poor who streamed through the cities had failed to comprehend the resources of the wall. They were radically external creatures, whose exposure to open space, especially open urban space, deprived them of the indispensable pedagogy of home. In his exhaustive study of urban poverty, Henry Mayhew at once discovered a counterworld and confirmed a prejudice. The costermongers who hawked their wares in the street were "the Nomades of England, neither knowing nor caring for the enjoyments of home. The hearth, which is so sacred a symbol to all civilized races as being the spot where the virtues of each succeeding generation are taught and encouraged, has no charms to them."[4] The young girl who lives in the streets will resist the attempts to reclaim her; she suffers from a "muscular irritability" that "makes her unable to rest for any time in one place." The poor appear as a great fluid or current, seeping past foundations and enclosures, enduring and then enjoying an escape from the boundedness so central to the prevailing definitions of home. As George Godwin tersely put it in *London Shadows*, "the health and morals of the people are regulated by their dwellings."[5] The loss of the physical delimitations of the house incited a release of mobile appetite and rootless passion. Poverty was in its essence an antidomesticity.

Nevertheless, there remains an undercurrent within the new urban journalism that suggests another way of construing the unwalled poor. Mayhew himself, for all his emphasis on the savage repudiation of home, gives fascinated attention to the persistence of family life. Under the most appalling conditions of deprivation, parents and children cling together as microeconomies, improvising to eke out subsistence. Children "are sent out by their parents in the evening to sell nuts, oranges, &c." (Mayhew, 24). Mayhew praises those loyal girls without whose help the family would be sent to the workhouse, and in a summative mood he notes, "When, as is the case with many of the costermongers, and with the Irish fruit-sellers, the parents and children follow the same calling, they form one household, and work, as it were, 'into one another's hands' " (479). He is silent on the apparent contradiction between the refusal of home and the persistence of these intimate personal ties, but his own evidence suggests the need for a sharp conceptual distinction between "domesticity" and "family." The poor may live on the streets without the protections and solicitations of the cozy middle-class fireside; they may prefer the beer shop or the penny gaff, warmed by the presence of many other bodies, to the damp of a bare room. But it is clear that forms of familial webbing remain decisive for many of Mayhew's poor, who must be understood as antidomestic families, families without walls.

If so many Victorian newspaper readers refused to acknowledge family life on the boisterous streets, this must surely be due to the assumption that the definition of a family was architectural as well as biological. We recall the opinion of the registrar-general of the census, who held that it was "in the order of nature that a family should live in a separate house." The very idea of a houseless family comes to appear a methodological anomaly and a national disgrace. If the poor move in hordes through the streets, it must be because the precious vessel has broken, spilling privacy into the open streets, where it can only wither and rot. The failure of the poor to enact the "isolation of families" is what brands them as savages.

But the challenge to walled isolation came not merely through the long day's swarming through the streets in search of a small sale, an odd job, or a wily cadging. The poor slept somewhere. At the point of exhaustion they too sought walls and a roof. Commonly, however, the architecture of poverty was not the self-contained house, but the corner of a room within a house in a court. Growing at such an extraordinary rate through the nineteenth century, the cities of Britain were ill-prepared to absorb the vast numbers. Old family houses were broken up into separate lodgings; new buildings crouched behind old buildings. The effect of the filling of rooms and the infilling of space was to create diverse systems of infamous courts, with hundreds of families squeezed together, facing one another across a narrow lane. "As by a fatal attraction," observes Thomas Beames, "opposite houses grow together at the top, seem to nod against one another, conspiring to shut out the little air which would pierce through for the relief of those beneath."[6]

In Scotland and the north of England, a familiar pattern was the arrangement of working-class housing into the notorious pattern of back-to-backs: two contiguous, parallel ranks sharing rear walls. Except at the end of rows each house would thus have common partitions with three others, leaving only the front exposed to any light and air; the walls were sometimes just a half-brick (4½ inches) thick; and to increase the density, the double rows would be matched with others, so that the one open side would face onto a narrow court.[7]

In 1847 the *Quarterly Review* recounted the scandalous narrative of a young person arriving in London, who is directed to Duck Lane, St. Giles's, Saffron Hill, Spitalfields, or Whitechapel, and then obliged to pass "through tight avenues of glittering fish and rotten vegetables, with doorways or alleys gaping on either side—which, if they be not choked with squalid garments or sickly children, lead the eye through an almost interminable vista of filth and distress."[8] The rookeries of the major cities were the moral and social counterparts to the great country mansions; in their most sprawling and intricate arrangements, they became a monstrous inversion of the fortified castle.

Within this new system of walls, then, is a second, more deeply disturbing, provocation of the poor. Although they affront the norms of enclosed domesticity by coursing so visibly through the streets or attaching themselves like leeches to the facades of respectable homes, they are all the more offensive when they recede from view behind walls of their own. Godwin remarks that "If there were no courts and blind alleys, there would be less immorality and physical suffering. The means of escaping from public view which they afford, generate evil habits" (Godwin, 10). The physical enclosure for the poor is not the individual household, providing that "exclusive command" of family space; it is rather the widely encompassing public barrier that surrounds the inhuman density of bodies and stirs images of a den, a nest, or a lair.

Within the pervasive decay of these wandering mazes, there were special nodes of degradation, the lodging houses of the great cities, temporary dwellings for masses of the poor, who would fall together in the ill-tended rooms, crowded, filthy, verminous. Mayhew made the lodging houses a focus for his outrage and sorrow, and in parliamentary debates of 1851 Lord Ashley, soon to be the earl of Shaftesbury, compelled the other honorable gentlemen in the room to listen to tales of horror. Ashley's premise was that "nothing produced so evil an effect upon the sanitary conditions of the population as overcrowding within limited spaces; and if people were in a low sanitary condition, it was absolutely impossible to raise them to a just moral elevation" (*Hansard*, April 8, 1851, col. 1259–60). From this high-minded principle he moved to a chilling exposé, quoting the town clerk of Morpeth, who had described lodging houses that

> have no beds, but their occupiers are packed upon the floor, in rows, the head of one being close to the feet of another. Each body is placed so close to its neighbour as not to leave sufficient space upon which to set a foot. The occupants are entirely naked, except rugs drawn up as far as the waist; and when to this is added that the doors and windows are carefully closed, and that there is not the least distinction of sex, but men, women, and children lie indiscriminately side by side, some faint idea may be formed of the state of these places, and their effect upon health, morals, and decency. (col. 1263)

Such tales became almost routine at midcentury, leading to the passage of two acts sponsored by Ashley in 1851, the first direct legislation on the problem of working-class housing. One requirement of the new laws was that the commissioner of police had to register each lodging house and ensure the "well ordering" of the building and "the separation of the sexes therein."[9] This involved ongoing inspection—an institutional resolve not fully appreciated by the targets of benevolence. For if, from the standpoint of privileged respectability the courts and their lodging houses were little more than "fever factories,"[10] from the perspective of inhabitants they were living communities vulnerable not only to fever but to the assaults of the authorities. Philanthropists who built model houses—cleaner, better equipped, fully supervised, and with higher rents—failed to see why their bounty was often refused, not calculating the psychic cost of moral surveillance. Mayhew himself, despite being a harsh critic of the moral degradation of court life, discloses much evidence of the social formations created by these forcing houses of collectivity. He records the case of a boy who had kicked at a policeman in a scuffle, noting that "The whole of the court where the lad resided, sympathized with the boy" (Mayhew, 16). A young coster tells him that "all as lives in a court is neighbours" (40), and frequently the reader hears of the daily social ceremonies in the shared space between the clustered rooms: the gathering of men and women at the mouth of the alley, where they meet for a chat and a smoke. Martin Daunton has observed that the physical arrangement of the court—the simple undifferentiated rooms so close beside one another, the narrow lane, and the common use of privies and water supply—brought about a "sharing of facilities in the private domain, a cellular quality of space in the public domain, and a threshold between public and private which was ambiguous and permeable."[11] Within such a social topography, the most significant walls were the outer boundaries of the court, penetrated by a narrow entrance opening into a world where meager accommodation (including the flimsy party walls) created a common life almost unimaginable to those of any substantial means.

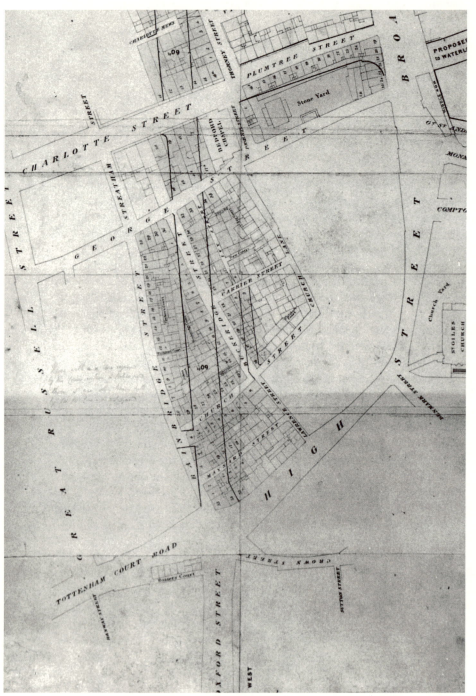

Figure 5. Detail from the plan for the cutting of New Oxford Street. By permission of The British Library, MAPS 3495 (54).

3

Insofar as the genteel imagination gave itself to pictures of life behind the court walls, these were almost always pictures of foul blight, urgently demanding inspection if not eradication. One of the most significant urban reconstructions of the first half of the century was the cutting of London's New Oxford Street through the notorious rookeries of St. Giles's (see Figure 5). The street becomes a broad sword slashing through the collective interior of the courts in a gesture widely hailed as a triumph of urban hygiene. Daunton has suggested, however, that it was also a defeat for solidarity. The effect of the sustained clearance was to redraw the relationship of private and public spheres, repudiating the rich ambiguity in favor of a stern differentiation between the dwelling and the mere "connective tissue" of the street. The political result "was to 'open up' the city in order to make it visible for inspection" (Daunton, 204). In fact, all through the century the cutting of new streets was as much an exercise in social engineering as a development in the lines of transport. When John Nash undertook the massive renovation of London, he saw the course of the triumphal Regent's Street as an opportunity to divide luxury from need: "my purpose was, that the new street, should cross the Eastern Entrance to all the streets occupied by the higher classes, and to leave out to the East all those bad streets."[12] As with later projects, the street was seen as at once a thoroughfare and a wall, a means of facilitating movement along its length, but also obstructing once easy movement across its width.

Still, no matter how wide the boulevard, how imposing the stucco or brick facade, how well managed the servants, there remain conspicuous signs of anxiety that the middle-class fortress of home remains vulnerable. In the early 1860s a great furor erupted on the subject of street music. The Italian organ grinder became a figure of violent loathing for a large section of the professional classes, which defined their seriousness and their status in opposition to the tumult outside the window. Spurred by the anger of such figures as Dickens, Tennyson, and Charles Babbage, the MP Michael Bass took up the cause, editing a volume of documents called *Street Music in the Metropolis*—at the center of which were the splenetic outcries of a cultural elite that saw the constant distractions in the thoroughfare as dangerously corrosive to privacy, putting physical health and intellectual vocation at serious risk. As part of the packet of evidence, Dickens contributed a letter of outrage that reads in part as follows:

> Your correspondents are, all, professors and practitioners of one or other of the arts or sciences. In their devotion to their pursuits—tending to the peace and comfort of mankind—they are daily interrupted, harassed, worried, wearied, driven nearly mad, by street musicians. They are even made especial objects of persecution by brazen performers on brazen instruments, beaters of drums, grinders of organs,

bangers of banjos, clashers of cymbals, worriers of fiddles, and bellowers of ballads; for, no sooner does it become known to those producers of horrible sounds that any of your correspondents have particular need of quiet in their own houses, than the said houses are beleaguered by discordant hosts seeking to be bought off.[13]

Here is one sign of the pathos of the "respectable" household wall: that no matter how impenetrable to the petitioning "leeches," it would always be vulnerable to sound. Indeed, an irony of the household narrative is that the repeal of the window tax in 1851 had created a boom in the production of glass and had led to a brightening of the street wall with larger-paned windows, but this architectural improvement only exposed the home dwellers more directly to the commotion on the street. The passage of Bass's act made it easier to bring legal remedies against such noisemakers, but as long as the cities of Britain continued their steep growth in population and as they throbbed with the clamor of industry, no parliamentary act could ensure velvet domestic serenity.

When a new sewage system and interior plumbing become common features of middle-class social life, a terror of sewer gas disturbed domestic calm. Waves of panic circulated through the press, and the fear of a sudden backup of poisonous gas, which could kill in instants, became a visible marker of the weakness of walls, even those with the most arrogantly jutting chins.

Still more frightening were the outbreaks of cholera in the middle decades of the century, especially the wave of illness in 1854, which in its attack on the parish of St. James destroyed the comforting mythology of the immunities of wealth.[14] Death on one side, Florence Nightingale on the other, made clear that attention to domestic hygiene could not stop at the threshold—because toxic vapors and foul air respect no laws of property. The hazards of poor drainage, open sewers, and exposed dung heaps can creep beneath the thickest walls; there can be no healthy house in a diseased neighborhood.

Was there to be no peace anywhere for the ascending middle classes? The aristocrats, the great gentry, and the barons of industry could enjoy the sanctuary of their country houses, perfectly intact at the end of long rural roads. Their walls were as close to inviolable as the castles they imitated. But for the middle classes, who were growing in wealth and numbers—where might they hear the birds sing without the din of urbanism? The answer, of course, was in the suburbs. Beginning after the Napoleonic Wars and consolidating in the middle decades of the century, suburbanization offered a radical solution to the struggle between private and public domains. On the one hand, it allowed for the construction of a still more self-enclosed household space, either in the form of semidetached or fully detached villas, which broke out of the linear patterns of urban terraced housing and offered the promise of walls surrounded on at least three sides by the pleasures of a garden. On the other hand, it secured a physical distance, becoming ever greater as railways confirmed the suburban boom, between the garden villa and urban pandemonium. In significant respects, the household wall was now stretched as wide as the train journey into the city.

4

Merely to watch the transformation of walls through the nineteenth century—the turn from Georgian gray and brown to creamy stucco and then Queen Anne's red brick, the internal partition into rooms and compartments, the infilling of urban space and the development of the maze of courts, the cutting of streets through those same offending courts, the march of walls into the green fields on the edge of town—is to follow a mobile topographical narrative, in which space is continually carved and molded, closed and opened. Then to restore people to the architectural scene is to recover a social drama of movement and barriers. The century of walls was a long disentangling of social mixtures. Architects devised ways to divide the house into male and female domains and to keep the family from its servants; city planners drove streets through the inner mysteries of poverty; building speculators developed suburban estates. As prosperous commercial titans joined the world of the country house, many middle-class professionals rode the trains to the suburbs. The most fortunate of working-class families reached the dignity of terrace houses, but rising rents kept the poorest in cramped, dirty, and porous spaces.

From one perspective, the disposition of walls achieves the sharp clarity of articulated social space: the wealthy in the country, the middle classes in the suburbs, the artisans in their terraces, and the poor squeezed into their single rooms. But apart from those who enjoyed the astonishing privileges of the country house, the ordering of the social strata was an impure process, forever caught in forms of spatial snarl. The large urban centers continued to grow, and though many members of the middle class left on the suburban trains, others rose to take their place within the cities and found the same challenges to the life of household privacy. The movement of the laboring poor from courts and cellars into terraces was made unsteady by precarious economic conditions, so that any proudly rented house could break apart into the divisions of subletting: first a floor, then a room, then a corner of the room.

In Gustave Doré's engraving "Over London—By Rail" can be seen a richly complex display of the unsurpassable ambiguities of a partitioned society (Figure 6). Here are the poor who have escaped the lodging house abyss: they have achieved gardens and garden walls, those conventional tokens of what the registrar-general calls "free space." But plainly this image marks a painfully incomplete emancipation for those struggling into the kingdom of privacy. Within those much-valued walls, signifiers of domestic individuality, the two-storied houses are each crammed thick with more than one family, and the parallel row of terraces shows just how easily "free space" can revert to the

Figure 6. "Over London—By Rail." From Blanche Jerrold and Gustave Doré, *London: A Pilgrimage* (New York: Harper, 1872).

squalor and crowding of the court. In the background and above, a train steams onward, presumably carrying middle-class commuters to their less compromised gardens. And yet even for those seeking refuge in the suburbs, history had ironies in store. What appeared in one decade as the safe distance from the vortex of the street was likely in the next to have been absorbed by the ooze of urbanism. Overly ambitious building speculators often had to lower the price on untenanted houses, giving the middle-class arrivals the surprise of working-class neighbors.[15] In erratic slow pursuit the artisans followed the clerks out of town, and the clerks, in fleeing to the next train junction, chased away the doctors and solicitors.

The dream of impenetrable walls was the dream of an orderly society, tidily distributed according to function and fortune. No doubt for some—especially those wealthy few immured in rural settings—it must have seemed that the street was permanently distant and that the infolding of private virtue was triumphantly achieved. And yet, an abiding feature of the middle-class desire for enclosure, so widely embraced by other classes, is that after the scream of the railway, the spread of infectious disease, or the news of a violent crime, the act of self-containment must begin again. A house remains an object in social space, inevitably exposed to the winds of public life, and walls designed to keep inside and outside apart only sealed them in intimate antagonism.

Chapter Eight

ROBERT KERR: *THE GENTLEMAN'S HOUSE* AND
THE ONE-ROOM SOLUTION

1

The ordinary eight or ten-roomed house, inhabited by
decent middle-class folk, is a gruesome sight. What a huddlement
of male and female.
—George Gissing[1]

"Do you call it managing this establishment, Madam," said
Mr Dombey, "to leave a person like this at liberty to come and
talk to *me*! A gentleman—in his own house—in his own room—
assailed with the impertinencies of women-servants!"
—Charles Dickens[2]

Robert Kerr has only just survived in historical memory, the author of a few
works of documentary interest, which appear briefly in the breathless surveys
of architectural historians and are then forgotten along with the rest of him.
But he lived, walked, worried, wanted, rejoiced, and resented, all without any
genius, but with the accidental dignity of an exemplary figure who was also a
concretely willful human being. His concerns as an architect emerged out of
the web of issues developed in the preceding chapter, and his career gives us
a shape for diffuse cultural pressures. Kerr aimed to build a private world of
such strength and intricacy that it could resist both pressures from outside and
pressures from within. But as we show at the end of this chapter, he couldn't
resist the temptation to turn his study of genteel privacy into lessons for the
urban poor. Another enemy of spectacle, he couldn't resist looking at what he
loathed.

   In the fall of 1861 Kerr, aged forty, applied for the newly vacant professorship of the arts of construction at King's College, London, and having been
evaluated against two competitors, one of them being Charles Percy Shelley,
Kerr was favored for the position. Even as it made its recommendation, however, the selection committee noted that Kerr appeared to be a member of the
Presbyterian Church, which if true—it was—would challenge the doctrinal
commitments of King's. The Reverend Richard William Jelf, the principal of
King's, visited Kerr to discuss the difficulty, and out of their meeting came a
letter from the candidate.

I beg to state that I am quite prepared to give my adhesion to the Church of England
in any way which may be proper under the following circumstances.

Being of Scotch birth and education, I was brought up in the Presbyterian practice;
and at present I hold sittings in the Scotch church in Regent's Square, which happens to be near my house. But during a long residence in various parts of England
I have attended, always occasionally and sometimes regularly, the service of the
Established Church; my children, being of English birth, I have caused to be bap-
tized into the Established Church; and I have thought it right to encourage in their
case such a course of education as may give them a leaning towards that communion. Upon removing to my present house, if it had not been for the convenient
position of the Scotch church in Regent Square I certainly should have given great
weight to a desire I then had, in pursuance of the above policy, to attach myself
to one of the English churches in the neighbourhood; and sooner or later, indepen-
dently of all other considerations, it seems plain that I must do so.[3]

The conversation and the letter must have satisfied the Reverend Jelf, who
reported that "Mr. Kerr had stated explicitly that he was very glad of taking
the present opportunity for becoming, as he had long anticipated, a regular
attendant upon the Church of England."[4] This obstacle removed, the professorship came to Kerr at the salary of one pound one shilling per annum for each
matriculated student in his course of study—seventy students being the stated
average in the college advertisement for the position.[5]

The episode makes an emblem in the history of Kerr's professionalism, and
it is as the consummate professional that he attracts the attention of this study.
The bland willingness to undergo religious conversion is a token of Kerr's
acceptance of institutional norms, even when they obliterate something as intimate as the religious habits of a lifetime. During the decade of the 1860s he
positioned himself in a variety of professional roles, which taken together gave
him a privileged authority to speak out on domestic issues dominating public
discussion much as they dominate this phase of our own history. As the author
of one successful book and one forgotten lecture, Kerr brought the technical
language of architecture into the general conversation. How to design the ideal
house? Kerr's career shows how around the questions of comfort, convenience,
room size, and style collect issues of privacy, chastity, pleasure, and status.
Because he was a man of no sentimentality, he let inconvenient subjects float
to the surface.

During the same year in which he took the professorship at King's College
Kerr became a member of the Council of the Royal Institute of British Architects, a body that since the granting of its charter in 1834 had overseen the
gradual acceptance of architects as respectable professionals. Kerr was the
perfect institute man.[6] He faithfully attended meetings, both select and general;
he made his modest contributions to the institute subscriptions; he lectured

more frequently than any other member; and surviving transcripts show that at the lectures of others he could always be counted on to raise discussion from the floor.[7]

A third appointment during this period of professional ascent brought Kerr the district surveyorship for St. James, Westminster, in 1862. When the Local Government Act finally created a central authority for London, the Metropolitan Board of Works, it provided for a corps of surveyors to superintend the construction and renovation of buildings. These positions seem to have been welcome sinecures, especially in the case of an assignment like Kerr's to one of the wealthiest areas of London (including New Bond Street, the Burlington Arcade, and Pall Mall), which he held for the next forty years, until just two years before his death. Sinecure or not, the role of district surveyor gave Kerr an official forum during a time of extraordinarily intense building in the metropolis.

As professor of the arts of construction at King's College, as council member of the Royal Institute of British Architects, as district surveyor for the Metropolitan Board of Works, Kerr embodied the social consolidation of architectural expertise which by the sixties had become academically respectable, institutionally secure, and legally sanctioned. It was precisely within the context of a consolidated professionalism that Kerr composed and published his large and successful book, *The Gentleman's House* (1864), which brought him his two most important commissions: from John Walter III, owner of the *Times*, and then soon after John T. Delane, editor of the *Times*. It is fitting that the principal powers at the *Times*, the great organ of the professional middle class, should turn to Kerr, the apostle of a new architectural expertise.[8] The third edition of *The Gentleman's House* proudly displays Kerr's designs for these houses, one of which, Bear Wood, will catch any eye on the watch for architectural spectacle. In the words of its owner, Bear Wood stands as "the second palace of Berkshire." "My house painfully impresses me," wrote Walter III, "with the belief that it will survive every Institution of this country, except perhaps the Press."[9]

2

The Gentleman's House presents itself in the tones of a definitive treatise, but it possesses a rich imaginative life that can tell us much about dreams of the ideal home. Written without literary pretensions (Kerr would wait another fifteen years before composing his three-decker novel), it nevertheless stands as an intricately constructed text, rich with emotional investments and social anxieties. This work, so full of sketches, charts, designs, and diagrams, becomes itself a diagram of middle-class self-understanding at a particularly fragile moment in its history, when distinctions of sex, class, and property, all under pressure, twisted within one another's arms for comfort. Beneath its tone of boundless complacency, professional authority, and national pride, it is a nervously stammering text that unwillingly reveals the secrets of the fantasies it looks to support.

Kerr defines what he means by his title, and his definition gives a useful place to begin. A gentleman's house, he writes, is "a convenient and comfortable English residence of the better sort, on whatever scale."[10] This description is already a formidable polemical act. In these last two prepositional phrases—"of the better sort, on whatever scale"—Kerr makes one crude and one subtle social observation. With a first stroke, "of the better sort," he separates English society into better and worse, higher and lower. And having made that sharp stroke, Kerr peremptorily banishes the lesser sort, the lower toiling classes and their dwellings, from his concern.

But if the first phrase makes a brisk class distinction, the second—"on whatever scale"—deftly suppresses one. All through *The Gentleman's House* the architectural notion of "scale" serves complex purposes, and in its first use here it has nothing to do with charting relative room size. It works instead to mute the many tensions between those middling classes ascending the slope of social power and those high-born holders of land, title, and pedigree, reluctant to descend to meet them. The subtitle of the book is "How to Plan English Residences, from the Parsonage to the Palace." Such a slogan not only elides variations within the "middle" orders but also any opposition between "middle" and "high." When Kerr defines the gentleman's house as a house of the better sort *on whatever scale*, he is in effect suppressing the differences within the middle class and between it and the gentry and aristocracy. The idea of a gentleman's house absorbs such distinctions, even as it preserves and heightens the contrast between better and lower orders.

According to Kerr the modest middle-class home falls into the same category as the aristocratic mansion, because the concept of the gentleman's house includes "an entire class of dwellings, in which it will be found, *notwithstanding infinite variety of scale*, that the elements of accommodation and arrangement are always the same; being based, in fact, upon what is in a certain sense unvarying throughout the British Islands, namely, the domestic habits of refined persons" (*Gentleman's House*, 63, emphasis added). Kerr's "infinite" is of course disingenuous. We already know that the varieties of scale halt abruptly at the lower boundaries of the better sort—Kerr bluntly announces that he will not "deal in any way with inferior dwellings" (63). But, having thrust inferior dwellings to one side, he posits an underlying domestic solidarity between the humble shopkeeper retired to a small suburban villa and the young aristocratic blade riding to hounds across a great estate that has been in the family for centuries.

As a first point, then, one might say that the ideal of the Victorian home proposed by Kerr represented a way to organize class relationships, in particular a way to divorce in one stroke the "labouring classes" from the ideal of gentility and then, in a second stroke, to marry blood with money. But Kerr's position is more complex than that, just as the wider domestic mythology is more complex.

3

For *The Gentleman's House* the career of intimacy cannot prosper on its own. It must be the gift of expertise, provided by the systematic methods of modern architecture,

> a science of delightful intricacy, which, when duly applied, even on the smallest scale, constitutes the edifice a thing of complete organisation, in which every part is assigned its special function, and is found to be contrived for that and no other; the express purpose of the whole being that exquisite result which is signified by our scarcely translatable phrase—*home comfort*. (12)

"Comfort" is how intimacy shows itself to Kerr, as the product of expert management. But the first thing to be noticed about Kerr's comfort is that it names a negative virtue. Within a society that was beginning to pay the emotional costs of industrialism, comfort was associated with the absence of noise, the effacement of unsightly objects, the freedom from sudden disruption, the impregnability of a private space. In short, "home comfort" connotes a reduction of personal anxiety and an easing of interpersonal tension, signifying rest, peace, stasis. Kerr describes it as a condition of being "at ease," as an essentially "passive" state (71).

This celebration of home comfort secures a further effect. Within the historical picture sketched by the book, it ensures that the Victorian gentleman's house does not simply *belong to* a venerable aristocratic tradition, but that it *culminates* that tradition. Earlier epochs in home life had pursued ornament, magnificence, and grandeur and, in doing so, they had sacrificed the comforts of home.

Comfort, that is, becomes a polemical weapon with which to defend the preeminence of Victorian domesticity. The comparative modesty of the Victorian home, its sobriety, its managed intimacy, becomes a mark of distinction. Economy, not extravagance; modesty, not grandeur; comfort, not luxury— these are the measures of architectural maturity.

If part of Kerr's project, then, is to establish continuity between the middle-class gentleman and his aristocratic precursors, he is equally vigorous in seeking to depict bourgeois domestic life as an ideal that the English nobility never quite achieved. When the good citizen of nineteenth-century London returns to his "substantial economical, common, good house," he can enjoy pleasures that were impossible within a cold and solemn palace, a draughty manor house, a luxurious neoclassical villa. The Victorian home is not only the heir to these achievements; it is the *realization* of values that earlier structures only gropingly expressed. For Kerr, the Victorian gentleman's house has become more than his castle; it is what his castle had tried and failed to be.

In trying to explain why it has taken so long to attain domestic fulfillment, Kerr invokes the triumph of modern science. The problem of domesticity is a problem of techniques. The varying demands of hospitality, ornament, cooking habits, family temperament: "All such cases furnish problems to the architect, which it is his pride to solve" (*Gentleman's House*, 73). The superior value of a comfortable home deserves the exaction of the "utmost scientific pains" (72), and science has made comfort possible.

This last proposition, on which Kerr leans so heavily, itself represents a telling convergence within mid-Victorian thought. It brings together the twin ideals of rationality and pleasure and, what is more, rationality in the service of pleasure. A powerful fantasy in the imaginative life of the mid-Victorians, especially those mid-Victorians like Kerr who were in such harmony with their age, was that the result of the painstaking application of reason would be a release into much-deserved ease.

The science of architecture has at last made it possible to devise a space in which the maid can always be prompt, the water closets handy, the corridors unobstructed, and the food hot. It has often been noticed that the Victorians relied on the image of the garden as a metaphor for the satisfactions of home. But the machine was just as prominent an image, and Kerr shows how these two figures become entangled with one another. The smooth running of the household apparatus yields the passive sensations of home comfort; the scientific machine blooms into a fertile garden.

4

Kerr's book opens with a historical survey that traces the ancestry of the gentleman's house from the eleventh-century Saxon hall, which is identified not only as the origin of English architecture but also as the lowest depth of the domestic sensibility. What disturbs the moralizing architect is that the hall comprised just one room, one shared space for men and women, the high-born and the low-born, adults and children, people and animals, and all private functions of the body.

> When our Saxon ancestor and his household dwelt in a primitive Hall, the one only apartment they possessed for eating, cooking, sleeping, dressing, and altogether undressing, indiscriminately, we may be said to [be] as near the bottom of the ladder as imagination would approve. (*Gentleman's House*, 27)

This is Kerr's lurid spectacle of intimacy; it serves as the grotesque antitype of his architectural ideal, and for reasons that will become clear, the Saxon hall exerts a constant pressure on his thought.

Within the long history, the gentleman's house gradually emerges from its rudimentary, scarcely imaginable beginnings, and begins a painfully slow development. Writing as Darwin's close contemporary, Kerr becomes the evolutionist of domestic life, who records the halting movement from the protozoan Saxon to the Victorian vertebrate. He traces the "origin of separate bedrooms" and the "germ of the Parlour" (21). Rooms appear as species, multiplying, dividing, some becoming extinct, others flourishing. In a great advance for the twelfth century a second story is added to the house, and in the fourteenth, the hall itself reaches perfection—although, notes Kerr, it "has still to be remembered, that when the feast was done the bulk of the company, of both sexes alike, passed the night upon the floor" (29). Finally, there occurs that notable event which Kerr celebrates under the heading, "Privacy Introduced."

"It is hard to believe nowadays," writes Kerr, "that female privacy was of such slow growth as we shall find it to have been" (10). Here he makes a rare approach to a joke, in the form of a historical riddle. "What member of the family first obtained an absolutely private room?" The answer, the priest, is meant to underscore the fact that "the fastidiousness of the lady was all undeveloped" (27).

Indeed, Kerr's history enacts an elaborate narrative, a narrative without characters, in which the setting alone plays out the drama: the struggle of privacy to escape the Saxon hall, to find a second room, and then a second story, to escape down a corridor, past an inner door, behind a partition, until, after this long flight through the centuries it finds a place that will suit the fastidious Victorian lady when she makes her belated nineteenth-century arrival.

5

When she does finally appear in Kerr's story, the Victorian woman sexualizes the space in which she dwells. The gentleman's house takes on the aspect of a human body, especially a woman's body. It should display "delicacy," "simple grace," and "repose" (*Gentleman's House*, 86). It should be "fairly adorned" and "ought to exhibit a reasonable amount of intellectual liberality, faithfully keeping on the side of simplicity and moderation . . . but avoiding that poverty of dress which is not self-denial but inhospitality" (90). The gentleman's well-dressed house fuses with his well-adorned wife. They even share a manner. "*Elegance*, therefore, unassuming and unelaborated, touching in no way the essentials of home comfort, never suggesting affectation and pride, moderated by unimpassioned refinement, and subdued even to modesty, will invariably be accepted in England" (87).

The sex of home, however, takes on further nuance, which emerges when Kerr addresses the controversy over contemporary architectural style. For in defending the rights of Gothic within the battle of the styles, Kerr adjusts the gender of his metaphors. The revival of medieval style has brought back "hon-est," "masculine simplicity," and even an affection "for the Ugly, because, however odd, it has at least not the weakness of being feminine" (368-69). But this sympathy for male Gothic must be chastened: in a representative midcen-tury response, whose consequences still affront the eye, he defends "Eclecti-cism" as the only historically defensible position.

Modern architecture must accept the claims of both Gothic and classical traditions, both their stylistic principles and their sexual connotations. Not only is Gothic male, but the classical is female. Furthermore, in comparing French and English architects, Kerr reserves "masculine power" for the latter, while he assigns to their French rivals a "feminine grace." The risk with English Gothic is that it will be "clumsy and crude," and with French classicism that it will be "too finical" (363). Hence Kerr refuses to choose between them, calling for a reconciliation between the styles, which is at the same time an architectural union of the sexes.

If the house as a whole regularly appears as a distinguished woman—mod-est, graceful, subdued—the various domestic regions divide both male and female identities, with the result that the household becomes a concise geogra-phy of sexual relations. Mark Girouard has described the sexual articulation of space in Victorian architecture, and Kerr occupies the point where a propen-sity turns into a fixation.[11] The dining room, notes Kerr, must be "massive and simple" if it is to attain "masculine importance" (*Gentleman's House*, 94), while the drawing room should be cheerful, delicate, elegant, and light—in short, "if the expression may be used, it should be entirely ladylike" (107). Accordingly, an ever discreet Kerr discourages a door connecting the two rooms. The library is male; the morning room is female; leading to the observa-tion that "One advantage . . . of a door of intercommunication between Morn-ing-room and Drawing-room is that it provides for the ladies what is called *escape* in a manner the most legitimate of all" (105). In the example of Kerr's own Gothic design (Figure 7), the house divides cleanly along a vertical axis that bisects domestic space, running from the saloon through the fountain to the garden thoroughfare. With one significant exception to which we'll turn in a moment, everything to the right of that imaginary line is male, everything to the left female, and the gentleman's house thus achieves that rational differenti-ation of the sexes to which it had long aspired.

6

Quiet comfort for his family and guests, —
Thorough convenience for his domestics, —
Elegance and importance without ostentation.

(*Gentleman's House*, 66)

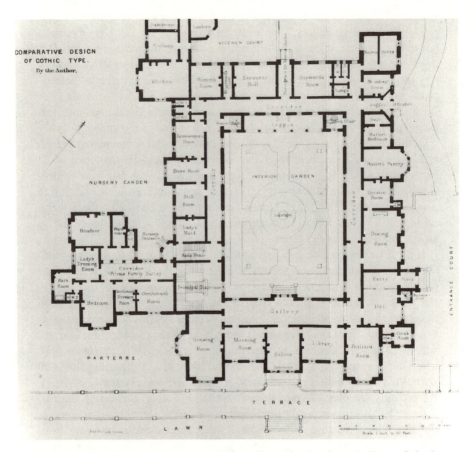

Figure 7. The Gothic solution. From Robert Kerr, *The Gentleman's House*, 3rd ed. (London: John Murray, 1871).

The third phrase quoted here, uniting female elegance and male importance, gives another example of the architectural nuptial conducted all through this treatise. But the first two mottoes suggest something else, indicating first of all how Kerr's two supreme values, "comfort" and "convenience," separate along class lines. In the household world this means a separation between family and domestic staff.

The household divides into a realm of production and a realm of consumption; indeed it becomes a scale model of the Victorian economy. The increasing rationalization of the work process, epitomized in Kerr's notion of convenience, exists in order to promote the "passive" delights of comfort. At the rear of the house is a model factory ("with a place for everything and everything in its place, —with no deficiency, no superfluity, no awkwardness, no doubtfulness, —with one obvious way of accomplishing an object, and that the right way"; *Gentleman's House*, 71), a domestic factory that vibrates with the hum of modern industry but which must never disturb those who sit in the garden and consume the fruits of the machine.

Notably, the gentleman's house at once withdraws from the new industrialism and contains it. The spirit of manufacture, from which home is to be a refuge, enters the house in a disciplined squad of modern domestics, whose role is to protect home life from the disruptions they exemplify. Our earlier question of walled protection changes when the issue is no longer how to construct a barrier against the roaring streets, but how to arrange a pattern of rooms, corridors, and staircases in order to manage those household workers, who confuse the boundary between inner and outer. Home and street, it is clear, must be seen as two great systems, topographically as well as socially, linked not only in their opposition but in their mutual dependency. The well-to-do felt anxiety to repel the indigent, but also to choose carefully among them, in order to assemble the corps of servants within, who will become allies against the petitioners seen through the window.

The success of this complex operation requires its own rigorous spatial logic. Whatever the size of the house, notes Kerr, "Let the family have free passageway without encountering the servants unexpectedly; and let the servants have access to all their duties without coming unexpectedly upon the family and visitors" (68). The family must never catch sight of the scullery and the kitchen; the outer walks must be kept free from the servants' view.

Kerr's Gothic design is an effort to satisfy this spatial demand. Just as a vertical axis separates the male and female regions, so a horizontal axis, passing again almost exactly through the fountain and with another revealing exception, marks the dividing line between the two classes inhabiting this one dwelling.[12] The starkness of this arrangement accords with the "foremost of all maxims," namely "that what passes on either side of the boundary shall be both invisible and inaudible on the other" (*Gentleman's House*, 67).

With one axis separating the sexes and another the classes, Kerr's gentleman's house divides into quadrants, so that every room has a gender and a social station. Not only is it essential to keep the servants in their own "department," they are also to be segregated by sex. Kerr recommends (and shows in his Gothic design) that the servants' hall marks the point of sexual division: "with the domain of the butler on one side and that of the housekeeper on the other and as little necessity as possible on either side to pass the boundary" (67).

This brings us to the two exceptions to Kerr's rigid household geometry. The first concerns the assignment of the gentleman's bedroom, the husband's bedroom, to the female side of the house. Given the nature of marriage, such a "transgression" was bound to occur; and it stands as an exception only because the sexual frontiers are otherwise impermeable. But it does suggest that married life belonged to no third realm where the two sexes could meet, but that marriage was conceived as falling within the wife's domain—that at night a husband crosses an invisible border and dwells among the ladies.

The second exception involves the strategic placing of the lady's maid. Her room is the only one that violates the horizontal division of the classes, and there is no mystery as to why. If she is to attend faithfully the mistress of the house, then she must always be close at hand (by contrast, the butler's bedroom stands at the greatest possible distance from its sexual and social opposite: the boudoir). But notice that in bringing the lady's maid just across the line into the family region, Kerr cuts her communication with the rest of the servants' department. The only door from her room opens away from the other servants, from whom she is separated by a wall, a flight of stairs, and two storerooms. At the same time she is separated from the family rooms by the stairwell, an entranceway, and a corridor. Placed in household limbo, Kerr's lady's maid experiences all the ambiguity of the domestic social order: the family's intimate dependence upon a group of people with whom there must be no intimacy.

Kerr is not simply concerned to segregate two kinds of household activity in line with an abstract social principle. More urgent is the desire to protect the family from the *sensory* provocations of the servants. He enjoins his fellow architects to ensure that "the sight, sound, and we must add, smell of the servants' working apartments are perfectly shut out."[13]

> How objectionable it is we need scarcely say, when a thin partition transmits the sounds of the Scullery or Coal-Cellar to the Dining-room or Study; or when a Kitchen window in summer weather forms a trap to catch the conversation at the casement of the Drawing-room; or when a Kitchen doorway in the Vestibule or Staircase exposes to the view of everyone the dresser or the cooking-range, or fills the house with unwelcome odours. (*Gentleman's House*, 67–68)

Odors, indeed, furnish a leading theme of *The Gentleman's House*, and in a maxim that might have crowned a Victorian copybook, Kerr observes that "every place that is likely to have in any way an unwelcome odour must be either placed apart, or associated with others of its own kind" (79).[14] One consolation remains. Because the "servants are not so sensitive to low temperature as their superiors" (202), the ventilation of their rooms can be pursued more aggressively.

Every house is both a map of urban society, which represents the topography of class, and a map of the human body, which diagrams its pleasures, its needs, its fears, its humiliations. Kerr's preoccupation with the sights, sounds, and smells of the servants' quarters suggests that he not only identifies the domestics as the lower social orders but that he associates them with the lower bodily parts. Furthermore, it is difficult to avoid the suspicion that behind his discouragement of any sensory encounter with the servants lies the scarcely suppressed fear of the mistress of the house turning a corner only to find the cook and the butler locked in a passionate embrace.

The obsession with boundaries may be seen as a rejoinder to that ancestral image of the Saxon hall with its agglomeration of both sexes and all classes in a single grotesque space. As Kerr puts it, "The family constitute one community: the servants another. Whatever may be their mutual regard and confidence as dwellers under the same roof, each class is entitled to shut its door upon the other and be alone" (68). In its broadest implication Kerr's book constitutes a punctilious attempt to differentiate space in order to differentiate classes and sexes, architectural styles and parts of the body, activity and passivity, business and pleasure. And yet the extravagant exercise in difference is in the service of reconciliation. Characteristically, Kerr writes that "the family must have privacy and the servants commodiousness, and the whole dwelling must display an unassuming grace" (66). The controlling idea is that, if distinctions are upheld, then unity will follow. What Kerr offers his many readers, in effect was a myth of national reconciliation, in which master and servant, man and woman, classic and Gothic, comfort and convenience will move in perfect harmony—as long as they are perfectly distinct.

7

The great expansion of the middle classes in the middle of the century meant that *gentility* had become a more accessible cultural ideal even as it created strains for those dedicated to its pursuit. Not only had more families become aspirants to "home comfort," but the house itself contained more: more children, more servants, more artifacts. If its importance as a refuge from society increased, so too did its mimicry of the social world.

The common notion of a "complete household" required a minimum of three servants, and when we add the five or six children of the average family, we can easily appreciate that the standard "middle dwelling" contained a small crowd within its walls, a crowd that needed to be carefully arranged if the values of comfort, quiet, and passivity were to achieve their cozy realization. In the aristocratic mansions of an earlier period this was not a pressing issue; the great size of the buildings meant that the odors of cooking, the sight of servants, and the noise of children could be accommodated without strain. But with the extension of the domestic ideal to the burgeoning numbers of professionals, industrialists, shopkeepers, and clerical workers, the need to organize household space became a leading concern and a vexing difficulty. Kerr's design of the comfortable house—with its many compartments, its carefully arranged corridors, and its impassable boundaries—expresses the urge to gain control over the accumulations of home life, things as well as people, which a rising standard of living now brought within reach.

And yet, the achievement of a complete household was always an ambiguous victory. To keep servants was the surest mark of ascendancy into the respectable orders—families were ranked according to the number they kept—but in the very act by which the newly genteel classes ratified their triumph in the social arena, their supremacy over the laboring masses who could not aspire to such domestic heights, they brought the daughters and sons of laborers into their home.

Imagine a successful clerk in the City, a beneficiary of midcentury prosperity, who is able to afford the gentleman's house that his parents could not, and who finds that the gesture that will ensure his social standing is to hire three servants from the class he is trying to escape. Then, like Robert Kerr, he will puzzle deeply over how to maintain distance from those he brought so close. The ambiguity is captured in a spatial-social paradox that one might call the paradox of the staircase. In *A Small Country House* Kerr advises that the servant stairway and the family stairway should be placed *near* to one another. And why?—because if they are near, then the servants will never be tempted to use any stairs but their own. Throughout *The Gentleman's House* such architectural solutions express the fragility of an arrangement in which two communities are brought near, so as to remain more distinctly apart.

For a house the size of Kerr's Gothic design, the trick could be easily managed. Men and women, adults and children, family and servants, classic balance and Gothic irregularity could each be given their own domain, and if one is as punctilious in planning as Kerr, one could live for months in passive comfort without ever encountering the sights and smells of active convenience.

But here the concept of scale resumes its strategic labors. Kerr, we know, prides himself on the wide application of his principles of design, "whatever the scale" and at the end of his book he attempts to show the great range of domestic possibilities from a "very modest establishment" to a "very stately one" (381). "Very stately" is accurate. Kerr enumerates the dimensions of the 197 rooms (100 for the family, 97 for the servants) which 40,000 pounds will buy in 1864. Such a house, with its shoe room, its two beer cellars, its gun room, its school room, and its oddroom, easily achieves that longed-for articulation of classes, sexes, generations, functions, and pleasures.

As one proceeds downward through his financial scale, however, the amenities erode. At 10,000 pounds one surrenders the gun room; at 5,000 pounds the billiard room disappears; at 2,500, the morning room goes; and at 1,250 pounds, the "very modest" bottom of Kerr's scale, both family and servants must make do with thirteen rooms each. At each lower rung in the ladder of gentility, the risk grows that children will be heard and servants seen and that female privacy will be rudely assailed. In a passage that recalls Edgar Allan Poe, Kerr entertains the vision of Comfort's Catastrophe:

There are many otherwise good houses in which the sense of contractedness is positively oppressive; you experience a constant fear of overturning something, a sense of being in somebody's way; you speak in a subdued voice, lest you should be heard outside, or upstairs, or in the kitchen; you breathe as if the place were musty; you instinctively stoop to pass through a doorway; you sit contractedly in your chair, and begin even to lie contractedly in bed; and to step out into the open garden, or even upon the footpath of a street, seems an act of leaping into free space! (*Gentleman's House*, 74)

The question, of course, is what happens when one descends still further down Kerr's scale? What happens when one carries through the logic of his own graphs and charts and diagrams, when one passes beneath the arbitrary limit of a thousand pounds?

Kerr neglects to ask this question, but to extrapolate from his scalar calculations is to recognize the fate of the house when income dwindles. By the force of Kerr's own argument, home comfort depends on elaborate and precise distinctions within household space, and if the distinctions cannot be maintained, then the cataclysm of home life must inexorably follow: the smell in the library, the sharp cry piercing the parlor walls, the collision with the servants.

The Gentleman's House maintains its unbroken silence on the question of the "inferior dwellings" of the "inferior orders"—a silence that speaks volumes in the context of the domestic crisis of mid-Victorian industrialism. One need not rely on Engels's description of the slums of Manchester, or even Dickens's angry evocation of the crowded hovels of London. The pages of the *Builder*, the journal of the architectural profession of which Kerr was so honored a member, were full of hand-wringing over the wretched housing conditions of the poor. In an article almost exactly contemporaneous with *The Gentleman's House*, a *Builder* correspondent records the plight of families in the "tenemented dwellings" of London.

There is the feeling of a want of privacy, which is painful; there is an incessant wandering of feet, from early morning till late at night, up and down the uncarpeted and noisy wooden stairs common to several families; there is the thundering noise of children, &c., in the rooms above or below: a fender or a chair cannot be moved in one family without making a certain amount of annoyance to other families; the noise of the children seems never to cease, the voices of the women, well exercised in attempts to preserve order, are generally loud and shrill.[15]

This scene, it is clear, is just what Kerr dreads, and just what inspires his fastidious planning. What is illuminating, however, is the way this spectacle of modern domestic misery mirrors Kerr's representation of Saxon barbarism. The mass of bodies crowding together, the failure to segregate by sex and by age, the rude manners, the assault on the senses—these are precisely the features Kerr had found in the primitive Saxon hall and which he considered "as near the bottom of the ladder as imagination would approve." The historical account in *The Gentleman's House* suggests that physical and moral disorder belongs to a precivilized past that has grown steadily more remote. But it requires only a carriage ride from any gentleman's house to discover that the Saxon past is waiting around the bend in the river.

It should be clear what Kerr has done. He has projected a contemporary problem onto a temporal axis, and instead of locating the crisis across the city, he has located it across centuries. This allows him to preserve a myth of architectural progress, indeed a myth of moral progress, which culminates when aristocratic pleasures and bourgeois rationality meet in the modern gentleman's house. Within his fable, anyone whose income falls below a thousand pounds falls out of the rank of gentleman and into Saxon brutality. In this context the squalor of tenement living appears only as a nagging remnant of the feudal past, instead of what it is, a shameful product of the present.

It is a fragile machine, this gentleman's house, which builds walls against the inferior orders and then hires them to cook and clean and nurse; which brings together men and women, children and adults, and then pursues distance at close quarters; which gathers enough people to constitute a small community and then arranges them to further the cause of privacy. Good architecture can suppress the spectacle of family awkwardness. It can manage sight lines, control movements, and distribute bodies. Through a network of channels and impasses, it can create the poise of a community arrayed against publicity.

The fountain at the center of Kerr's Gothic design stands at the point where the imaginary lines dividing men from women and masters from servants meet. It has a fine geometric necessity, and it invites us to imagine a mild summer evening when it becomes a gathering point for those who dwell together—the soft plash of water summoning the husband from the library, the wife from the drawing room, the butler from the pantry, the housekeeper from the store room, the children from the nursery, the bachelor from the billiard room, the cook from the kitchen, the lady's maid from her tight corner. But that is a meeting which the house works to prevent, even as it conjures the possibility. The gentleman's house, like the society it reenacts, seeks unity through many strong partitions.

8

An astonishing coda followed the success of *The Gentleman's House*. At the end of 1866, when Robert Kerr was enjoying the high tide of his professional apotheosis—with his book appearing in a second edition, with his design for the country house Bear Wood for John Walter III proceeding apace, with his professorship at King's College secured, and with his sinecure at the Metropolitan Board of Works comfortably established—he decided to make an aggressive intervention into the debates over urban housing so studiously ignored in his long treatise. On the evening of December 3, he delivered a paper at the Royal Institute of British Architects entitled "On the Problem of Providing Dwellings for the Poor in Towns."[16] Everything in its tone suggests that Kerr was speaking in the warm flush of his success. Having attained a metropolitan eminence, he was prepared to take on a problem that had come to seem intractable.

Philanthropy has failed. This is the premise for Kerr's brazen rhetorical sally. After more than a quarter century of noble effort, the philanthropic mission has had its run and now has precious little to show.[17] Admittedly, a number of associations with grand-sounding titles—The Metropolitan Association for Improving the Dwellings of the Industrious Classes, the Labourers' Friend Society, the Marylebone Association—had won the support of benevolent individuals and attracted the attention of the press. At the time of the Great Exhibition, the prince consort had lent his name to the model houses placed on display. The generosity of Angela Burdett-Coutts and George Peabody had led to diverse housing projects in London. And yet, asks Kerr, what have these efforts really produced, when set against the rapid population growth of London and the conspicuous domestic catastrophe of the poor? He quotes Alderman Sydney Waterlow, a leading figure in the housing movement, as affirming that all the model housing efforts of the past twenty-five years are "only a drop in the bucket compared with the ordinary progress of population" ("Dwellings," 60).[18]

Kerr looks with barely disguised contempt on the compounded failures: rents too high, returns too low, the wrong population accommodated. He identifies the difficulty as the failure of technical experts to engage the problem, with the result that it has been left to the sentimentalists, those given to "virtuous declamation or passionate description" (46). The time has come to set emotion aside and to recognize the problem as one "to be solved by professional architects" (38). Kerr's address represents the effort of a newly confident professional to extend the status of his institution, but what distinguishes his speech is the extent of its willingness to challenge moral orthodoxy from the standpoint of expertise.

"The dogma of the three bed rooms"—this is what Kerr takes as the disabling assumption that has so badly constrained the housing movement. He recalls a recent speech by Lord Shaftesbury, in which the nation's leading philanthropist had put the dogma "in words to this effect—'that no decent family could possibly be accommodated with fewer than three bed rooms,—one for the parents, one for the boys, and one for the girls' " ("Dwellings," 40).[19] With such a guiding principle for model housing, the result has been that the poor, the truly poor, never live in such houses at all. This is the bitter irony marking the social failure.

Why has this happened? —because the house of three bedrooms is both beyond the requirements of the poor and beyond their means. Kerr gives a catalog of the "excesses" built into the model home:

> I will pass by what I call *extravagances*: for instance, the idea that a colony of these dwellings should possess general wash-houses and drying apparatus; the notion of having baths, sometimes even private baths; the idea of a general lavatory; and that of a playground for the children: I pass all these by. I take the simplest form of the mere home itself. This gives us a living room, a special scullery, perhaps a coal closet or a pantry, often a private water closet, a cooking range, a copper, a sink, water supply of course, and a dust shoot, with, lastly, separate and special bed rooms, three as the basis of the design, and two or one in exceptional cases. (41)

All these are very well, but as the poor cannot afford them, they must go. Philanthropy, which has sought to relieve poverty, has misidentified its object.

Here Kerr offers a sketch of urban poverty, which depends on a distinction that will become a familiar resource to those who manufacture discourse and influence public policy. The noble visionaries speak of helping the "poor," but two radically distinct classes are hidden within that name, and they are separated by "a distinct line of demarcation" (38). Kerr, who as a district surveyor has walked the high and the low regions of Westminster, invites his audience to imagine two streets in London. On the first, a "modest street—say in Islington, or Camden Town"—one will find "the houses comparatively tidy in appearance, the street doors, as a rule, kept closed, and the children (who are obliged to use the street as their only playground) comfortably clad and creditable in appearance." The houses are let in floors: one floor, usually with two rooms, is taken by each family, who will share the backyard and its conveniences. The inhabitants of such houses on such streets are journeyman mechanics, small masters, or small dealers, homeworkers and pieceworkers, and single-women workers, who make reasonably good earnings and are content with their accommodation. They are the "superior class of the working population in towns" (39), who should not be identified as the poor, the groaning, suffering poor whose needs have brought London to crisis.

Walk, please, down another street, requests Kerr, where the houses are a little smaller, the street doors not always closed, the children more numerous and less well clad. The difference, the "radical distinction," is that on this street each family has not a floor in a house, but a single room, and as Kerr solemnly intones, "To live in two rooms is quite a different state of things from living in one room." Here is the "inferior class" of the poor, those who are the real objects of need, but who have been so disregarded by a quarter century of philanthropy. Their income is far too low for the rent demanded by the model houses, with the result that the noisy domestic benevolence has almost entirely

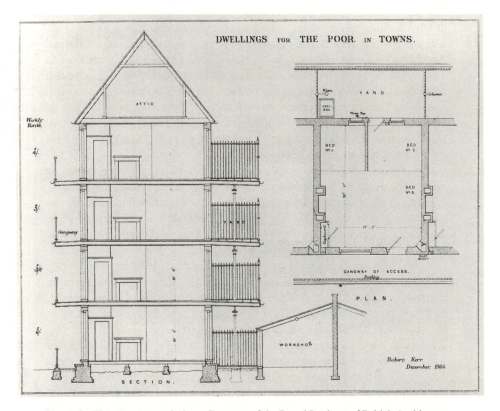

Figure 8. The one-room solution. Courtesy of the Royal Institute of British Architects.

passed them by. If they are to be accommodated in decent dwellings, some other solution must be found.

"WHAT IS REALLY WANTED? WHY NOT SINGLE-ROOM ACCOMMODATION" reads the heading of the climactic section of Kerr's paper. Now that we know who the poor are, how they live, and what they can afford, we can at last emancipate ourselves from the dogma of the three bedrooms and find a practical answer to a domestic disaster. The answer is to accept the fact that the poor only "require" one room and that if architects will just tax their ingenuity, they will be able to find a one-room solution to the present crisis (Figure 8 shows Kerr's proposed design). This "may be somewhat startling at first sight," admits Kerr; "it may well appear strange for an architect to stand here and propose that English families should be confined to the system of single rooms" (41); but he asks forbearance.

By living in single rooms, the poor have shown that this is all they "require": now it is for the architectural scientist to provide it in well-engineered form. Furthermore, once the radical step is taken, and the dogma repudiated, then housing for the poor can at last be made to pay. The spare enclosure, repeated through building after building on the same austere plan, demands little in the way of material, and almost nothing in the way of technical improvisation. According to Kerr's computation, each room can be built at a prime cost of seventy pounds; rents could be under four shillings a week, while still leaving investors a return of 9 percent on their money.[20] It would no longer be necessary to defy the "natural laws of every-day commerce" in the name of an ineffectual philanthropy. Now the resources of the poor would converge with the investment needs of the wealthy, meeting in those single rooms that could be built by the thousands all across London.

Part of what makes the proposal shocking is that it flies against the strenuous mythology that Kerr had developed in *The Gentleman's House*, the ideology of privacy, of compartmentalization, of the articulation of domestic life according to gender, age, and bodily function. The history of the family written into Kerr's book is a tale of the overcoming of the moral depths of the single room, the hall, great or small, within which the saving distinctions are obliterated. When he stands before his colleagues at the Royal Institute, Kerr plainly has his historical scheme in mind, but the occasion of the present housing crisis encourages a marked rhetorical change. Gone is the attitude of moral scandal; now Kerr invokes the medieval hall in soft tones, reminding his audience that one room was "the average *house* of even the gentry of this country up to the fifteenth century . . . where the honoured guest was placed at mid-day at the right hand of the lord at the table, in the evening sate by my lady's ear at a snug corner of the ingle, and for the night was awarded some other comfortable corner, where he could lie down on the straw of rushes which covered the floor, with his feet to the fire" ("Dwellings," 42). Kerr goes on to point out that "single room accommodation" continued to flourish among the yeoman and has not disappeared even in the present day. This man, who had recently published an ambitious narrative of emancipation from the hall, now asks why architects should despise such a time-honored tradition.

Kerr's proposal can only be read as a further act of aggressive professionalism. Beyond their role as domestic servants, the poor had not figured in his book; they had occupied the unspoken space below a thousand pounds, where the table of accommodation reaches its bottom limit. Below that limit, walls disappear and distinctions fail. But what had been the monstrous antitype in the gentleman's house now becomes the basis of social policy.

The immediate audience response to the proposal was bafflement: the design calls for a large room; why leave it so provokingly open to dangerous view? During the two formal discussions held at the Royal Institute of British Architects on December 17 and January 14, the oddity was repeatedly challenged. As one architectural fellow was quick to point out, in an area of 20 by 17 feet, "there was as much surface as was required for a good three-roomed house."[21] Unimpressed by Kerr's historical lineage, T. Chatfield Clark could only exclaim, "Consider what it must be to eat, drink, and sleep in the same room!" ("Discussion," 51). Kerr was accused of seeking to perpetuate "a debased state of society" described in a trade journal as "pigging together in one room" (62).

In asking why he held so fast to single rooms in the face of such obvious objections, we need only look to the theory of class stratification underlying his entire project. If his colleagues were outraged, it may be because they were less willing to draw conclusions from their social practice. Kerr dared to say what the others could not admit they believed. He recognized, and was prepared to affirm, that the present distribution of family housing tended to divide the population into groups so differently endowed that they seemed to become not just separate classes but different species.[22] The poor have wants and capacities that should not be confused with the pleasures of gentility. He speaks of the absurdity "of our most advanced appliances and conveniences when forced upon those who do not happen to want them." You may quiver and protest, but "I only say as a fact they are content to occupy single rooms." Kerr reduces the argument to an aphorism: "Simple folk, simple dwellings" ("Discussion," 61). On the basis of what the poor have been made to bear, he tells us what they require and what architects must provide, which is "the expediency of keeping to the very lowest standard" (80).

Brightly visible behind the discomfort of his critics is the scandal of exposed sexuality, the parents clutching and moaning, with no wall to separate them from attentive children. Eating and drinking and sleeping together—this image creates a shudder among the architects, but Kerr knows that a deeper shudder comes from the unuttered thought of what takes place between drinking and sleeping. Eager to play the plain speaker to his fastidious colleagues, Kerr makes the dangerous allusions. Introducing the single-room plan, he insists that "the only objection is on the score of *delicacy*," and then characteristically asks, "do we not assume too much with regard to the violation of the principles of delicacy in the homes of the poor?" ("Dwellings," 42). True, his plan places limits on privacy, but "as regards the non-transmission of sound from one compartment to the other, which is in a great measure the real question of delicacy, the brick partition would be, I think, sufficient" (45). He appeals to his experience as a district surveyor to suggest that even in difficult cases, adult "contrivance, and especially feminine contrivance (which is chiefly concerned)" will not fail (42). After all, there are "degrees of delicacy," and he warns his colleagues not to "jump to the conclusion that [the poor] are positively degraded, when the fact is that they are only negatively unrefined" (42).[23]

Through all these leering, insinuating passages Kerr avails himself of his recently won stature in a transparent bid to astonish the cramped sensibilities of the moralists. He flourishes scandalous images before half-closed eyes, insisting that no dogma can conceal the alternative moral life found just a few streets away. When his colleagues weakly call for some gesture of "progress" or "improvement," Kerr is unrepentant: "let us deal with the world of to-day, and leave to-morrow till it comes; let us take our poor brethren at their own poor standard" ("Discussion," 78). He offers no moral consolation, only the satisfactions of professional frankness. That frankness indeed seems not just his method but his goal.

During the course of the three gatherings during December 1866 and January 1867 Kerr continued to display his provoking opinions, even as he disarmingly suggested that his plan was but an "experiment," an exercise of dispassionate thought, well prepared to have its ideas challenged and reformed. "I represent," said Kerr, "nothing more exalted, but nothing less severe, than scientific curiosity." Having had no connection with the "social movement" for better housing, he has taken up the question of dwellings for the poor "merely incidentally": "I stumbled upon what I considered to be an interesting question of *domestic plan* (none the less interesting because so humble); I am known to be a student of domestic plan; and it is in this capacity alone that I have ventured to set on foot a discussion intended to be professional no more" ("Discussion," 75). What this disclaimer of interest allowed was the uncovering of an important consensus behind the nervous fret over sexual delicacy and moral scandal. The rhetoric of "frankness" served as a basis for recovering an independent professional identity from a confused public discourse.

If his colleagues resisted the one-room solution, they enthusiastically affirmed the ideology of professionalism.[24] The domestic emergency must be put before the "opinion of experts" ("Discussion," 75); it "is a problem to be solved by professional architects" ("Dwellings," 30)—this is the welcome affirmation reasserted time and again. Kerr derides the search for "some Utopian state of things which is, to say the least, unattainable" (47); he satirizes the "excess of good intention" ("Discussion," 76) that has led to all the dogmas and superfluities of the philanthropic mission: "For when Mr. Peabody lays down his hundreds of thousands, and Miss Coutts and others display almost equal profusion in their liberality, they take no responsibility upon themselves as to the mode in which their money is to be laid out" (61). These strong words are round with insult, and during the active discussion, they did meet some weak objection. But the overwhelming effect of the Kerr flurry was to rally architects to a call for a recognition of their prerogatives. The president of the Royal Institute ratified the consensus when he thanked Kerr for at last giving architects the chance to have "had their say" on an urgent problem that the "moralists and philanthropists had got hold of" (74). Within the longer history of tense relations, Robert Kerr's nights at the institute stand out as the enactment of a recognition scene: the forcing into consciousness of an antiphilanthropic professionalism, which insisted on the boundaries of expertise and on an entirely autonomous mode of social practice: scientific, technical, detached.

9

This coda has a coda of its own. After the conclusion of the three meetings, one more contribution made its belated way to the rooms of the Royal Institute. It came in the form of a letter from Henry Roberts, who had once served as "honourary architect" of the Society Improving the Condition of the Labouring Classes, and who had made his reputation in the philanthropic housing movement under the patronage of Lord Shaftesbury and Prince Albert. As the one who designed Prince Albert's model houses for the Great Exhibition and who was responsible for some of the landmarks in domestic philanthropy—including buildings at Streatham Street and the Thanksgiving model buildings at Portpool Lane—Roberts recognized himself as a leading, if unnamed, target of Kerr's polemic.

The offended philanthropist, whose labors were "entirely free of pecuniary interest," responds angrily to the paper that had been sent to him in France. Its proposals are "unsound" and "tending to a retrograde course, instead of the progressive improvement which was the aim of those, with whom it has been my privilege to be associated, since 1844, in promoting the improvement of the dwellings of the Labouring Classes."[25] With pride Roberts recalls having introduced this subject to the institute in a paper of 1850 ("read in the presence of the late Earl de Grey" and "translated and widely circulated in France"). He also recalls that, when confronted with the same statistics on which Kerr relied, he had described the domestic condition of the poor as "a system of overcrowding that would not be tolerated in the farm-yard, the stable or even the dog kennel." There is indeed a bitter spatial irony not mentioned by Roberts: it lies in the fact that the single family room proposed by Kerr almost exactly matches the dimensions (20 by 17 feet as compared with 22 by 16) of the room in which Roberts had found forty to sixty human beings constantly lodging.

Yet what distinguishes Roberts' letter is that beneath its wounded tone lies such a palpable air of resignation. He admits that roughly 6 percent is the highest net return from these dwellings for the poor, conceding that the figure is too small to encourage builders to invest, but still hoping that other capitalists might be satisfied with the profit, especially if the investment were secured as are investments in railways and docks. Yet in his paper of 1850 he had hoped for a strong monetary return, quoting the earl of Carlisle on the need to bring "the impulses of generosity" in line with "the calculations of prudence."[26] In his least plausible suggestion, Roberts holds that even if Kerr is right and the model homes only attract the better paid workers, still, in leaving their old residences, they will make room for the more desperately poor. The growth of the population of London made a daily mockery of that prediction, vastly overwhelming the few hundreds of spaces made available on average each year.[27]

This long letter is stamped as received on January 30, 1867, weeks after the institute concluded its discussion. There is no reason to think that Kerr ever saw the document. But in this missed communication we have an evocative figure for the emerging situation. Even as the failure of domesticity is now seen as a national problem and an urban epidemic, a consensus on response is more distant than ever. The philanthropist continues to place hope in moral uplift through generous "model" provision on the small scale, whereas the professional architect develops a discourse of "realism" in which economic law is granted the same necessity as the laws of engineering. Neither party will disappear; they will simply continue to irritate one another, while the poor crowd into London.

PART FIVE

The Sensations of Respectability

Chapter Nine

THE EMPIRE OF DIVORCE: SINGLE WOMEN,
THE BILL OF 1857, AND REVOLT IN INDIA

1

At our outset, "to love" is the verb we are most prone to
conjugate; afterwards we discover, that though it is the first, it is
by no means the sole verb in the grammar of life.
—Dinah Mulock Craik[1]

"The common passion of woman generally . . .
is not love. . . . It is power."[2]

In 1851 the Queen had exulted in the prosperity of her nation, conspicuously displayed through her husband's cherished project, the Great Exhibition. Ten years later, the country anxiously witnessed another exhibition: the grief of a sovereign. First, in March 1861, Victoria's mother unexpectedly died, leaving her daughter to endure "the *blank* and the *loss* to me, in my isolated position." To her uncle Leopold, king of Belgium, Victoria explains the conditions of her solitude: "except Albert (who I very often don't see but very little in the day), I have *no human* being except our children, and that is not the same *Verhältniss*, to *open* myself to; and besides, a *woman* requires *woman's* society and sympathy sometimes, as men do men's."[3] Her experience of the blocked currents of private life was always sharp: she, who had been tutored so early in the ways of seclusion, was keenly alive to the depletions of intimacy and the dwindling of life to a sharp, still point.

The year could not have been more harsh to Victoria. In December, Albert, prince consort, also died after only a brief illness. The second abrupt blow confused the objects of sorrow: from her mother to Albert, and then quickly into mourning for herself. To Leopold, Victoria writes even more plaintively: "The poor Fatherless baby of eight months is now the utterly broken-hearted and crushed widow of forty-two!" Arthur's death signifies her own living demise: "to be cut off in the prime of life—to see our pure, happy, quiet, domestic life, which *alone* enabled me to bear my *much* disliked position, cut off fat forty-two . . . is too *awful*, too cruel!" (*Letters*, 3:603)

We have come recently from Robert Kerr's determined architecture of equilibrium, the gentleman's house as the physical embodiment of the dream of stability, "with a place for everything and everything in its place." Kerr's is the replete house. Its rooms await the full panoply of husband, wife, children, guests, and attendants; its design builds the image of the saturated household with every domestic possibility achieved. Victoria's shock in 1861, just as Kerr would have been conceiving *The Gentleman's House*, was a cold reminder of the limits of the daydream. Her widowhood was a sign of all those absences that jeopardize the replete house: the dead child, the emigrating young man or woman, and then, most immediately, the untimley death of husband or wife. Broken domesticity is what the queen both dreads and exemplifies. She understands the symbolic reach of her loss.

To Earl Canning, who had just lost his own wife in India, Victoria extends her sympathy but then insists on the difference between them. "To lose one's partner in life is, as Lord Canning knows, like losing *half* of one's *body* and *soul*. . . . But to the Queen—to a poor helpless woman—it is not that only. . . . To the Queen it is like *death* in life . . . and she feels *alone* in the wide world, with many helpless children . . . to look to her—and the whole nation to look to her—*now* when she can barely struggle with her wretched existence!" (*Letters*, 3:608) Immediately, she feels the double exposure, her presence before the eyes of her children and her nation; no matter how severe the debilities of grief, she knows that she will be a sovereign object on view.

Among those who watched her was the bishop of London, who placed the queen's loss within a rhetoric that others could share. "Indeed the great characteristic of this national mourning," said the bishop, "appears to be, that it has been felt with all the force of a domestic sorrow throughout the breadth of this land." Albert was a public icon, but he will be mourned for the life of privacy that made his public work possible. If he had never won the affection of the people through his enactment of family devotion, then he surely would have failed in those acts of symbolic persuasion on which his social initiatives relied. As the bishop puts it,

> Knowing that through the discharge of domestic duties political life gains its strength, and knowing also that he whom we this day mourn, if he had done nothing else, would have earned the love and admiration of Englishmen for the simple discharge of his duty in domestic life. We know there is nothing so dear to Englishmen as the due discharge of duty in domestic life. He first won our hearts in that simple manner, and then he was able to go forth into a more public sphere and perform great public duties . . . having begun by endearing himself to us in the discharge of all the duties of his home. . . . It is something to live in an age when our nation is united by that feeling of loyal love to the throne which binds us together as one family.[4]

The nation may be a family, but now the queen is alone. Even as Albert's death reanimated thoughts of exemplary royal domesticity, it built a difficult new picture of the single woman, queen or no queen, who could never live again within the ideal frame of family life. Margaret Oliphant recalled the shock of sympathetic recognition: "Understanding for the first time all that he had been to her, a flood of pity and terror burst forth, which was stronger than grief in the sensations of the moment. How was she to bear it?"[5]

Notoriously, she was not. The queen ran from the public gaze, keeping herself away from London, isolated for so long that a "For Let" sign appeared at Buckingham Palace.[6] Inconsolable, closed upon herself, intractable in her grief, averse to the thought of an emotional successor, Victoria became an emblematic portrait of woman alone. Even in the mantle of her royal privilege and within the embrace of public concern, she made her great refusal, and in her very withdrawal from visual spectacle, in the mix of her power and her need, she displayed the confused conditions of female singleness.

For all her singularity, the mourning queen, this young widow, belonged to a troop of women—single, divorced, or widowed, and of varying age, education, and status—who by the early 1860s had collected into a disruptive vortex. Whether she inspired ridicule or respect, a woman alone now forced the question of "self-dependence." Even in the agony of her loss, Victoria remained the queen; her sovereignty did not require her marriage: we might take this legal fact as a figure for the challenge of singleness. Dinah Mulock Craik includes this provoking utterance in her novel *Mistress and Maid*:

> Men will not believe what is nevertheless the truth, that we can "stand alone" much better than they can: that we can do without them far easier, and with less deterioration of character, than they can do without us; that we are better able to provide for ourselves interests, duties, and pleasures, in short, strange as it may appear, that we have more real self-sustaining independence than they.[7]

This strong view, of course, met strength on the opposing side. In an 1862 essay on "Our Single Women" published in the *North British Review*, Dora Greenwell turned a sorrowful conservative eye on her subject. Reaffirming an assumption of the inescapable natural subordination of women, she reminds her readers that

> It is not given to women to see, to grasp, things in their wholeness, to behold them in affinity, in relation. Not one of the keys which has unlocked the mighty synthesis of creation has been turned by her hand. In imaginative strength she has been proved deficient; she unfolds no new heaven, she breaks into no new worlds. She discovers, invents, creates nothing.[8]

Against the background of a root female insufficiency, Greenwell can only regret the attention now paid to the fate of the single women and especially to the problem of female vocation. "Single women," she writes, "must surely feel a little alarmed at discovering how much is expected from them—at finding themselves looked upon as a hitherto Unclaimed Dividend, which society is at length bent upon realizing" (62). Against the current of singleness, Greenwell combatively reasserts an axiom of normative domesticity, according to which

"No woman, we venture to say, is single from choice," "no woman, from the humblest to the highest, who has not had her dream of a heart that she might indeed call her own, of a home, of a husband" (64).

What gives edge to an otherwise familiar melody is the recognition that the normative arrangement faces inescapable historical challenge. Greenwell's essay, which wanders from the task of reviewing Anna Jameson's *Sisters of Charity and the Communion of Labour* (as well as *My Life, and What Shall I Do with It?* by "An Old Maid"), concedes that every passing year will reveal the need for woman's involvement in "housekeeping on a larger scale" (Jameson's phrase). Women will be needed for work in "charitable, penal, and reformatory institutions." Faced with the intractable conflict—on one side the unyielding ideal of the natural superiority of men and marriage, and on the other the growing social demand for working women—Greenwell retreats to a less exposed position. She ends by suggesting that if single women are required to work outside the home, then their efforts must be "provisional" and "exceptional," because "there is no such blight to the physical and moral well-being of a neighbourhood as that caused by such female labour" (71).

This concession can scarcely be enough. As contemporary commentators understood and as modern historical demographers have well established, the domestic dream of a world in pairs had become a statistical impossibility. During the European tour near the conclusion of Trollope's *Can You Forgive Her?*, Lady Glencora Palliser regrets that the "hundred and fifty thousand female operatives" working in Paris have no husbands—to which her mathematically minded husband responds that it "was impossible, because of the redundancy of the female population."[9] Contemporary historians have even better statistics than Plantagenet Palliser. Michael Anderson, for one, has calculated that there were just over a million unmarried women (aged twenty-five and above) and more than three quarters of a million widows, an imbalance that would become more marked, though only slightly, through the later part of the century. Partly this was due to "the better survival prospects of women" and partly to their "lower rates of emigration"; the results were predictable and often unhappy. Both widows and women who never married were victims of a weak position in the labor market, the latter finding it especially difficult "to break out into the less 'feminine,' less domestic sectors of the economy or into the self-employed sector."[10] As Trollope's narrator bluntly says of the unmarried Palliser sisters: "Being women they live a depressed life" (*Can You Forgive Her?*, 201). Anderson's work shows that other women, less favored than the Pallisers, could only look forward to declining prospects in their later years and were overrepresented in institutions, chiefly in workhouses but also in lunatic asylums.

This was not Queen Victoria's fate, though one might reasonably say that after the death of Albert, she too was more rigorously confined to an institution, namely the social apparatus of monarchy. Certainly, the tableau of her widowhood must be placed in the context of a large population of exposed women, who would have recognized in her grief a glowing image of their own deprivation, which would sometimes have been a comparable loss of love, sometimes the acute vulnerability to economic distress, and sometimes, of course, both.

In many respects, the condition of widows resembled that of women who had never married.[11] To the extent that marriage seemed an unchallenged norm—according to the Greenwellian axiom that no woman is single from choice—then the failure to marry would appear as a natural disaster, like the death of a husband. Within this interpretation the "spinster" and the "widow" were both objects of solicitude and targets of philanthropy.

Moreover, within the prevailing orthodoxy, unmarried women could resist the lure of outside work; they could remain associates in the great household enterprise, with no time for self-pity. One of the goals of Sarah Ellis's campaign had been to recruit all genteel women, of any age and condition, into the routines of home. By imagining an intricate array of responsibilities, Ellis was able to devise a task for each home-enclosed female. Death or disappointment were no excuse; anyone could find a place in the apparatus. With some pressing job always at hand, every woman of England should join in the ongoing, everlasting pursuit of comfort. In this vision of total assimilation to the domestic mission, no woman, married or not, widowed or not, was exempt.

But by the time Victorian domestic history reaches the 1860s the inherited terms of understanding receive a shock. Suppose "singleness" is not a biological or social cataclysm but an act of female assertion, like the assertion of the bloomer—or the Nightingale. Suppose it indicates doubt as to the necessity of marriage and even skepticism as to its felicities. Suppose work outside the home is desirable, as well as necessary. The sources for such a turn are many: they include the urgencies and opportunities of new vocations (like nursing), the (re)emergence of a feminist legal program, and, not least, changes within the dogma of domestic respectability itself.

2

Of these conditions at the end of the 1850s, none was more agitating than the specter of divorce. We say "specter," because the divorce legislation that ultimately passed was widely recognized as a far from radical act in its material legal consequences.[12] Indeed, the passage of legislation in 1857 exposed a discrepancy that had been reassuringly blurred through the domestic tracts and domestic novels. Those writings had often worked to adjust the balance of value, seeking to persuade the female reader that what a woman lost in the public world, she won back at the fireside. But once the famous bill was written into law as the Divorce and Matrimonial Causes Act, the resources of ambiguity could not conceal the invidious distinction. For a husband, the adultery of his wife was sufficient grounds for divorce. For a wife seeking divorce, her

husband's adultery was in itself not enough; it would have to be compounded
by additional harm: bigamy, incest, cruelty, or bestiality. At the same time the
effort to reform married woman's property law failed, and, together with the
provisions in the divorce law, this failure was a visible parliamentary sign of
the entrenchments of an inequality.[13]

In the "spectral" life of the culture, however—where this importantly includes the imaginative labors of politicians as well as poets, playwrights, and
novelists—the matter wasn't settled with the passage of the bill.[14] In this respect divorce stands within a line that also connects the Infant Custody Act of
1839 and the deceased wife's sister debates in the 1840s. Quite apart from
their different outcomes, the earlier legal conflicts had forced family trouble
to the surface. Even as the canons of domestic orthodoxy were becoming settled, the parliamentary and journalistic conflicts kept heterodoxy alive. We
suggested earlier that Victorian family norms at once feared the exceptions and
depended on them for justification. The norm needed the anomaly it dreaded.

The divorce debates grew out of this paradoxical disposition. But they represented a stage beyond infant custody and marriage with a dead wife's sister.
By the 1850s the idealization of home had developed further, making divorce
seem a devastating blow and also increasing the fascination of the horror.
Moreover, whereas the earlier controversies could be disarmed as strange and
unusual, the possibility of separation could be written into every marriage.
"Divorce" could thus become a figure for a wildly overdetermined set of anxieties and, even where marriages stayed intact, it remained intractably within
the repertoire of possibilities. Partly, this was because even with the unequal
outcome, women were at last given the right to sue for divorce. More significantly, because the difficult political struggle had made family breakdown so
conspicuous in the cultural reverie—in Parliament, in the press, and in prose
fiction—no legal act could relieve the turbulent fantasy. At a telling moment
in *Can You Forgive Her?*, when Burgo Fitzgerald allows himself to imagine a
successful elopement with Lady Glencora, he surmises that her husband would
"get a divorce, of course, and then we should be married" (257). Within
Burgo's "of course" resonates the full sound of a transformation. Divorce did
not suddenly become common after 1857, the number initially increasing only
to about 150 a year, but no count of legally terminated marriages can measure
the force of the disruption.

A small but illustrative trace of the effect occurs in Trollope's novel of the
year before, *The Small House at Allington*. When the pleasure-seeking
Adolphus Crosbie regrets that his (temporary) fiancée Lily Dale will bring no
fortune into the marriage, she nobly offers to break their engagement: "Though
I have given myself to you as your wife, I can bear to be divorced from you
now"—to which Crosbie will reply that they are bound "too firmly for any
such divorce as that."[15] In fact, he will within the week engage himself to

marry Lady Alexandrina of the noble DeCourcys, and though the breaking of his first engagement is not technically a divorce, it functions with all the violence (and all the scandal) of the emergent figure.

What these examples suggest is that even as a new age of divorce loomed, there were no conventions for representing its threat. Marriage had its elaborate tropology, but divorce erupted into imaginative life without coherent metaphors. It incited an anxious reflection that had no precedents for managing the worry, and here a particularly interesting sign of the trouble appears in the parliamentary debates leading up to the passage of the act. Gladstone, as part of his celebrated attack on the bill, mocked its makers for placing it within no tradition and for preparing a new legal system "which has been selected by a purely arbitrary choice."[16] This seems a fair characterization of the improvised character of the law making. But Gladstone's own attempt to fix firm biblical principles by which to understand the issue met with a scorn that rivaled his own. George Grey listened to the long speech with its soaring rhetoric, its religious indignation, its moral fury, and its colorful examples, and then tartly rejoined that, "I am afraid my right hon. Friend's memory is not quite so good as his imagination is vivid" (*Hansard*, July 31, 1865, col. 859). Grey observes that "the alarm which has been expressed as to the alteration of the law of marriage and divorce is entirely a fiction of the imagination" (col. 866).

"Fiction of the imagination," however, is what the divorce debates created in careless abundance.[17] Gladstone is hardly unique as an example of the parliamentary mind in full fictive flight. The prime minister, Lord Palmerston, had resolved to complete work on the bill through the heat of August, and with so many details yet to be settled, MPs grew agitated under the legislative pressure.[18] The need to settle large questions speedily, combined with the emotional charge inherent in the case, led parliamentarians into revelatory discussion of intimate questions. As proposed amendments circulated, the opponents of the bill brought forth salacious tales in order to dramatize the threats of the legislation. So Sir William Heathcote warns that "At the very moment in which they were carrying on this discussion the flame had burst forth, and the plague began to show itself. He was not speaking vaguely or without information. He knew that at this very time a body of dissolute and depraved men were already exulting over the license which they expected to receive at the hands of the Legislature" (*Hansard*, July 30, 1857, col. 742). The Honourable Mr. Bowyer adds another anecdote, remarking that "He knew a gentleman—one of the most amiable men in the world—whose wife, after one or two years of marriage, without any reason whatever, ceased to live with him. No doubt this was a form of insanity" (col. 766).

The well-tried procedure of hypothesis and thought experiment became the occasion for sordid fantasies of sexual misadventure. Mr. Clay, for instance, "would beg leave to suggest a case in which, under the influence of intoxication, or any other equally palliating circumstances, a man might once in his life be seduced into a house of ill-fame. Twenty years after, his wife, totally ignorant of the fact, might commit adultery; and on his seeking redress would, by the aid of spies and informers, who were always called into requisition in such proceedings, rake up the hitherto forgotten fact, and defeat his petition" (*Hansard*, August 17, 1857, col. 1723). Lord St. Leonards, imagines "the case of a wife who was anxious to get rid of her husband, and who might with that view place in his way an intriguing chambermaid, who might induce him to forget what he owed to himself and to society, and cause him to yield to temptation to which he had been designedly subjected" (*Hansard*, August 24, 1857, col. 2030). The Honourable Bowyer ruminates: "Suppose a woman preferred another man to her husband" (*Hansard*, July 30, 1857, col. 766), and the Honourable Henley meditates, "Supposing, then, a woman to present a petition alleging adultery combined with bigamy" (*Hansard*, August 17, 1857, col. 1717)

The attorney general had taken pains to calm the excitement that threatened to swamp the debates—"The Bill had excited great anxiety and even alarm in the country at large. . . . He was happy to say that alarm was groundless" (*Hansard*, July 30, 1857, col. 718)—but when the question turns to whether a single act of adultery can disqualify the husband from ever undertaking a suit for divorce, even he gives way to the lure of erotic supposition: "Supposing the case of a young man married twenty-five years ago, who then, without the knowledge of it ever reaching his wife until now, had committed a single act of adultery, it would surely be very hard at such a distance to dig up that remote circumstance" (*Hansard*, August 17, 1857, col. 1722).

The debates thus excited a sexual phantasmagoria, conducted in Parliament and reported in the daily press, and once the bill was passed, the question for the partisans of respectability was how to tame the demon that had got abroad. The fact that the new law retained such a clearly marked sexual double standard and that it had left married woman's property unreformed gave little relief. For those who had successfully opposed the Deceased Wife's Sister Bill, the success of the divorce legislation represented the long-dreaded fall into degraded modernity. In the earlier controversy, E. B. Pusey had asked, "Where, then, is this to end?" and had carried the day.[19] Now, faced with defeat, Gladstone worries that the passage of the divorce bill will be "the first of an interminable series" ("Bill," 283). Once the revolution has been legislated, why should it ever stop?[20]

3

In 1859 a novella was anonymously published under the simple title *Divorce*. Attributed only to "An Old Bachelor" and dedicated to "the matrons of England," the book stands as a rhetorically embossed emblem of the conservative reaction to the beginnings of a postdivorce society.[21] Refusing to make peace with the new legal order, the Old Bachelor spins a tale of marital catastrophe for two people finer than the legal regime that surrounds them. Colonel Elton, a worthy man of property—"no rent-exacter, but a feeling friend, a gentle governor" (6)—marries Amy Dashwood, with whom he enjoys a perfect domestic idyll in the antique confines of Elton Hall. ("If ever a man truly and fully appreciated the value of a domestic existence, it was my friend," 11). But the quiet peace is broken when little Harry Elton dies, leaving both parents bereft, the father inconsolable.

Only the crisis in India saves Colonel Elton from the melancholy of his mourning. He leaves to command a regiment to put down the uprising of 1857, and while his wife pleads to join him, emulating "the self-denial of Florence Nightingale" (20), he insists that the danger is too great. Left alone in Elton Hall, she only rouses herself when the colonel's friend, Captain Howard, returns from India on the sick list, thrilling her with tales of her husband's bravery.

But Howard is a villain. He is an atheistic rake, an erotic nihilist belonging to the same lineage as Trollope's George Vavasor: "malice was *imprinted* in every lineament, as *self* was written in every fibre of his worthless heart" (46). He casually seduces a farmer's daughter, then turns to the lady of the manor herself. Cloying, deferential, attentive, and smooth, he plays on the loneliness of "the high, the good, the lofty Amy Elton" (32), and by moonlight he tears her standard down. She sees through the cad almost immediately, but, alas, almost immediately is not soon enough. Although Howard dies in a fall from a horse, Mrs. Elton's mortification lives on. The colonel returns home, his spirits restored, triumphant, even raucous. But while he was in India, Parliament was passing the divorce bill. Elton is confounded by the new morality he finds at home, "the *easy morality* of modern society" (68), which has perfected a legal machinery for desecrating domestic life: "Why, with your convenient prescription, a man has only to tire of the marital yoke, invent a stratagem or enact a scene, and he has a bigwig at hand that unmakes him and remakes him—free. It is an ugly business" (53). Discovering that four of his friends have been "unwived" through the workings of the new court, he enacts a gesture of revulsion: he shows his wife a card with the names of four fallen women, insisting that, together with their lovers, they must be cast from the Elton social list. At which point, a stricken Amy Elton adds her name to the debased four. The colonel's frame shivers; his chest heaves; and then in his outrage he announces *their* divorce, not within the moral mockery of the new law, but within the absolute terms of divine justice. By her deed, his wife is "divorced from God—from virtue . . .—from the highest dignity that crowns your sex" (58).

Here is the stern lesson that the Old Bachelor sedulously teaches: divorce must not become an affair of courts and lawyers; it must remain a private prerogative of the strong and true. The good feudal Elton would never dream of stooping to the legal solution, "the filthy mire of a court of miscalled justice" (64). The only fit justice will come through the mutual moral recognition between the husband and the guilty wife. He suffers agony, while she feels a "sense of her own *entire* abasement" (59), so overwhelming that she collapses to the floor and into madness. Leering scandalmongers try to lay a trail of gossip, but Elton defeats their prurient curiosity by refusing to go to court. He tends to his mad wife, wasting away himself, until in the midst of his despair, he finds that he can forgive her. At this point she wakes from her madness, becomes a "conscious, penitent wife" (72) and then dies three months later. An unhappy end—but the Old Bachelor is uncompromising. It is far less unhappy, he insists, than what passes for the agreeable solutions of the divorce court.

Divorce is a tormented little work, made miserable by a social change that it refuses to accept. Its narrative is driven not only toward a contorted parable of how old virtues can resist the lure of modernity, but also toward a distinctive rhetoric that might fairly be called the rhetoric of baffled respectability, which one also finds in the conservative press and in the speeches of Tory MPs. It seeks a style that refuses any complicity with the modern; refuses to accept its terms, its tones, its rhythms; and yields passages such as this:

> Man never degrades what he loves. Oh, that I could write those words in indelible characters on every female heart; then, indeed, could I recall the time when the impregnable virtue of an English matron was the grandest quarter in our national escutcheon; then could I close the temple of our modern Janus, and consign the traders in domestic broils to the enjoyment of Arcadian peace. (33–34)

We have said that one feature of the eruption of divorce into domestic discourse was that it appeared as an epochal event but arrived with no conventions for its representation. One result is the windy rhetoric of such an emblematic piece as *Divorce*, which tries to reanimate old times through recourse to old tones. But there is a more focused motive to the stylistic project of the novella: the resistance to newspaper sensationalism, to what the story calls "the mass of impurity which is daily shovelled up in our Divorce Court" (4). For from the standpoint of the Old Bachelor, and he is hardly alone, the disaster of the new legislation is not so much that it permits married partners to separate, since this will happen one way or another in any human society. The far greater difficulty is that by establishing a public mechanism, the law invites a craving for detail, an endless appetite for "the exposé of domestic broils" (64). What can be tolerated as a private tragedy becomes morally intolerable and socially hazardous under the conditions of modern journalism. The becoming-known of personal scandal is seen as damaging to everyone, but of course most especially to women.

Woman is no longer surrounded by an atmosphere too pure for vice to breathe in; for vice meets her at every step—it lies on her breakfast-table in the columns of the *Times*—it flaunts in the park in a fashionable vehicle kept up at the cost of a broken-hearted wife—it speaks in the Senate in the form of some bloated *roué*, and it smiles in the drawing-room on the treacherous lip of a perjured matron, — all avenues are open to it. (2)

The law has tainted the "atmosphere"; this is its most poisonous effect. Much as in the growing controversies over the Deceased Wife's Sister Bill, the fear was that even to breathe a description of domestic failure was already to begin to create it. So in the last days of parliamentary debate Lord St. Leonards had advised the upper house to delete the references to bestial and unnatural acts, because "he thought it was desirable that no mention should be made of them in a Bill which would be in the hands of the purest women in England" (*Hansard*, August 24, 1857, col. 2029). A complex rhetoric of euphemism develops as the bill becomes more inevitable and finally passes into law. The wound of divorce seems so great that it must be addressed, but to address it is to risk contributing to its baneful effect. The difficult labor is to find a way to conduct a polemic against divorce, while suppressing the words that the law has put into circulation. The Old Bachelor must tell his tense story, even as he avoids any direct account of its central events: "It is not my intention to give a morbid interest to details which hurt by being dwelt upon, or to reproduce too minutely on paper events that even in retrospect bring pain: to sketch the facts of my story as delicately as possible, without damage to the moral is all I seek" (*Divorce*, 19). There could be no better indication that the challenge of divorce to the regime of respectability was as much a discursive as a moral provocation.

Yet we know that the Divorce and Matrimonial Causes Act of 1857 was an act of compromise, not revolution. By setting aside the demands for reform of the property laws, by continuing to make it difficult for those of modest means to pursue a divorce (by restricting the proceedings to a London court), and by refusing to grant women equal grounds to petition, the act stands as the cautious outcome to a long public brooding.[22] How, then, are we to understand the overwrought reaction to such a chastened legislative deed?

The answer must be that the deed was caught in circles of implication widening far beyond the command of any agent. To start to understand how far those circles reached, we turn to one last remark from *Divorce*. When Colonel Elton on his return from India first confronts the new divorce culture (and before he understands his place within it), he tartly remarks, "Why the deuce you have been turning morality upside down; and while I and other brave fellows have been quelling a revolution, at home you have been kindling a social one" (53). An entire cloud of suggestion condenses in this one poor witticism.

4

The uprising in India in 1857 came as such a shock and, what is more, from such a distance, that it took long weeks and months before those in the imperial capital could grasp what was occurring. When the first fragmentary reports made their way to London, the government reassured Parliament by remarking on the stable prices of the "funds" in India. But after another several weeks these wisps of reassurance scattered, as Britain began to understand the scale of the colonial revolt. General Hearsay was solemnly quoted in the Commons: "I fear we shall wake up some fine morning, and find that Her Majesty has lost India" (*Hansard*, August 11, 1857, col. 1417). As the uncertainty of June passed into the dread of July and August, Parliament held somber discussion on how to save the empire, and from our standpoint, the convergence of the Indian crisis and the divorce furor is one of the most arresting aspects of this historical moment. Colonel Elton was surely right to notice the uncanny coincidence of the parallel upheavals, imperial and domestic. All through July and August, MPs moved between these two great issues of the day, and the consuming questions—what to do about India? what to do with marriage?—became entangled in one another, to the point where in talking about one, members of Parliament could at the same time be talking about the other.

It would be misleading to suggest that the rebellion of 1857 brought India into the domestic debate for the first time. Our discussion of Sarah and William Ellis pointed to the prominence of suttee in the missionary literature surrounding the domestic polemic of the 1830s. In the following two decades the figure of the suttee persists, appearing in a strange double guise. First is the grotesque figure of the sacrificial woman, driven to self-destruction by a cruel pagan mythology—a rendering of the custom that astonishingly became a comic resource in popular journalism and fiction. An essay called "Husbands, Wives, Fathers, Mothers" in *Blackwood's* in 1852 acknowledged the decline of church weddings now that the Marriage Act permitted weddings at the registrar's office, but took the reassuring view that women would not so easily give up their spiritual devotion: "as long as we see widows in India throw themselves on the funeral-pile of their dead husbands, we trust in the pertinacity of the sex."[23] Trollope is another who smiles at the absurdity: in teasing Mrs. Greenow for her strategic acts of mourning, his narrator remarks that, "As regarded every item of the written law, her suttee worship was carried out to the letter" (*Can You Forgive Her?*, 351).

But in the second strain of figuration, no less unsettling, suttee appears as a sublime act of womanly devotion, horrific but inspiring. An essay in the *Quarterly Review*, nominally committed to an account of the end of "widow-burning," cannot resist describing the moral grandeur of the agent-victim. A selection quoted from Elphinstone's *History of India* lavishly praises "the more than human serenity of the victim," her "gentle demeanor," and goes on to note that

"The sight of a widow burning is a most painful one; but it is hard to say whether the spectator is most affected by pity or admiration." The reviewer includes this paean in his own voice:

> With very rare exceptions, the Suttee has been a voluntary victim. Resolute, undis-mayed, confident in her own inspiration, but betraying by the tone of her prophe-cies—which are almost always auspicious—and by the gracious acts with which she takes leave of her household, and by the gifts which she lavishes on the by-standers, that her tender woman's heart is the true source whence that inspiration flows, the child-widow has scarcely time to bewail her husband ere she makes ready to join him.[24]

The evident difficulty in keeping up the tone of disapproval might be fairly taken as nostalgia for the days of "tender" wifely subjugation, "serene" abjec-tion, "gracious" self-abuse. When the reviewer awkwardly quips that "Old maids, as our readers have probably heard, are sadly depreciated in the East" (264), one can almost hear the sound of the daydream. Suppose our superfluous women went the way of suttee, and suppose that no men ever needed to fear that his wife would love another.

In the crisis summer of 1857 suttee would assume a new and sharply defined role in the tense debates, but before its force can be gauged, we need to offer a closer reading of the immediate context. During the first serious debate on the Indian insurgency, Disraeli rose to make a long, closely argued, and verbally strenuous speech that stands as the counterpart to Gladstone's oration on di-vorce during this same summer. Setting the terms for the discussion to follow, Disraeli refused to accept that the events in India were a "mere" military insub-ordination that could be suppressed by a commanding show of force and ar-gued instead that a distressing question must now be posed: "Is it a military mutiny or is it a national revolt?" (*Hansard*, July 27, 1857, col. 442). His own answer is decisively the latter.

In the explanation that he offers in the House of Commons at that early date in the crisis, the eruption of violence is the nearly inevitable result of ill-considered policy and insensitive administration. During the preceding decade the government presided over a "new system," which broke with the long-standing tolerance of Hindu religion and national custom, and replaced it with a principle that "seems to be the reverse, and may be described as one which would destroy nationality": "Everything in India has been changed. Laws and manners, customs and usages, political organisations, the tenure of property, the religion of the people—everything in India has either been changed or attempted to be changed" (col. 448). Within the frame of this insight, Disraeli offers a reading of the colonial government that represents it as an aggressively insistent, modernizing agency, resolved to create an India that satisfies its own moral and religious norms, at whatever cost in native resentment. He is particu-larly incensed by what he calls the "revolution in property" (col. 459): under the new system millions of pounds in rental income have been seized by the government. Disraeli calls on the government to renounce the practice and to avow publicly that "the Queen of England is not a Sovereign who will disturb the settlement of property" (col. 479). Indeed, he insists, such disturbance is bound to fail, because the conquest of India has never taken place and can never take place. No tiny island can impose its will on a massive region and an ancient land: the destruction of Indian nationality is at once cruel and futile.

Can there be any doubt that the unhappy structure of the colonial relationship as described by Disraeli repeats, in close and extensive detail, the unsettled structure of married life as debated in those sessions that surround the quarrels on India? The picture of a hierarchical dyad, in which a strong figure subjugates a weaker one, in which dominance brings both the abstract privileges of power and the material advantages of property, but which is now riven by the revolt of the weak, who belatedly demand recognition and redress—this is at once an image of Britain and India, and a picture of the British husband and wife. How to preserve the empire? How to save marriage? These are very different questions, but their historical convergence and their structural similarity bring them confusingly close.

In the most general field of analogy, Britain and India are the married colonial pair, but one of the striking effects of the debate is the introduction of new characters into the imperial drama. The first of these is "the Sepoy," the once loyal native soldier who has broken the sacred bonds of loyalty and trust. The aging war hero, Sir De Lacy Evans, is dismayed by "the extreme ferocity and inhumanity which had been displayed by the Indian Sepoys. It might have been supposed from such conduct that they had been long suffering under some grievous oppression; but the fact was just the reverse. No troops in the world were treated with more consideration or enjoyed greater advantages than the Sepoys of the Bengal army" (*Hansard*, August 11, 1857, col. 1400). Whiteside will take up this theme that quickly becomes a commonplace: "The Sepoy was formerly respectful, docile, and obedient. Now he was insubordinate and mutinous" (col. 1418). In the view of Mangles, "The Bengal Sepoy was a simple-minded and almost childlike person"; no one "had ever been so indulgently and over-kindly treated"; he "believed that they had been spoilt" (*Hansard*, July 27, 1857, col. 531). Consistently, the metaphors place the Indian soldier in the position of a dependent wife (or child), who had until now always shown the angelic virtues of gentleness.

The second figure, emerging into angular visibility as the debates wear on, is the East India Company itself, which becomes personified as the failed authority. The complex imperial arrangement had entrusted a mercantile association with the administration of the subcontinent, from the exercise of legal power to the disposition of armies, and when the catastrophe occurred in 1857, it took no time for critics to name the company as the blameworthy agent.

From the first debates, the idea of taking authority back to the government is raised. As the events unfold over the next several months, the proposal gains force until in an act of 1858 the great change is made, and political power is taken out of private hands. For all the abuses one can lay at the feet of the East India Company, no one should doubt what a convenient target of abuse it made. In place of national failure, or the failure of one or several governments, now a single institution can be made to assume the burden of guilt.

Within the domestic metaphorics so freely released during the Indian revolt, the company takes on the aspect of the abusive husband, who has degraded the authority it was his to tend. Throughout the discussions over divorce, the figure of the bad man—careless, lascivious, amoral, even bestial—had threaded its way; the debates show clearly that women's right to divorce gained ground, largely thanks to the specter of the vile husband. As Poovey has shown, the polemical success of Caroline Norton's *English Laws for Women* on the eve of the divorce debates depended on its construction of the husband as the consummate example of the one who had sullied marriage, who had failed to protect his wife, and who had therefore made her revolt inevitable.[25] The East India Company fit easily into that role, with the result that the Indian catastrophe became a divorce in its own right. The woman who is India, or who was the gentle Sepoy, has been roused to fury; she must be punished; but the criminal weakness of her husband, John Company, gives grounds for imperial divorce. The new husband, the better man, will be the Nation itself through the agency of its government. The wild insurgence of the wife will be forgiven, now that a happy marriage has been arranged, one that firmly preserves the hierarchy of dominance and subjugation, but that promises to respect the reasonable wishes of its once-again-docile dependent.

Just at this point the question of suttee comes back into focus. For in the aftermath of the abolition of the practice, a law had been passed, permitting widows to marry again. The reasoning was brutally simple. If a wife was now to be saved from the horrifying death, then it was only humane to allow her to survive like any English widow, to survive, that is, in hopes of finding another husband. When the law was first proposed, Hindus on both sides of the question petitioned the government, but to no avail: despite the controversy the law came into force. Here, in other words, was a close transposition of the growing British anxiety over divorce, a point brought out clearly when Newdegate asks why the government had insisted "that Hindoo widows should marry again," when such a "second marriage" so clearly violated the terms of ancient custom (*Hansard*, August 11, 1857, col. 1414). Within the domain of its traditionalism, real and assigned, India played out the drama of remarriage, and if to the enlightened Liberal parliamentarian it seemed self-evident that widows should have the chance to marry again, Conservatives saw the law as another example of hostile modernization. Disraeli had concentrated on the issue in his keynote speech, arguing that one of the chief causes of Indian resentment had been the assertion of the rights of remarriage. Thus, within the imperial theater, politicians rehearse their parts in the drama of British domesticity.

Notably, when Vernon Smith rose to rebut Disraeli after that first debate-determining speech, he accused his opponent of wanting to allow a return to suttee. "No! No!" came the shouts from across the aisle, but Smith stubbornly soldiered on: "He certainly mentioned the abolition of Hindoo ceremonies as one of the causes of the present excitement" (*Hansard*, July 27, 1857, col. 484). Smith's certainty aside, the documentary record is clear: Disraeli had argued against allowing widows to remarry; he had never called for permitting suttee. Yet Smith gains a point when he willfully misunderstands his rival, because within the Disraelian perspective—the need to undo the modernization of the past decade and to leave India to its customs and traditions—it is difficult to find a principle forbidding a custom as central as suttee. The refusal of the Tories to accept the logic of their traditionalism, settling for a bifurcated policy—yes to the abolition of suttee, no to the permission for widows to remarry—exposes not only predictable party opportunism but the unsteady relations between modernity and tradition.

Certainly, one finds unembarrassed voices of reaction deploring the flaccid spirits of the present day. So the earl of Ellenborough mocks the timidity of the British military response: "My Lords, this is not the way in which war used to be carried on in India," and recalls how General Gillespie, when faced with sedition,

> burst open the gates with his gallopers, sabred all the mutineers, and there was an end of that mutiny. That was the way in which we carried on war in India when we were forming an empire—that is not the way we maintain one: those were the days of the red hand—these are the days of red tape. (*Hansard*, July 31, 1857, col. 786)

Such imperial anger parallels Gladstone's florid attack on the decadence of a divorce culture, his charge that we of the modern age have grown "feeble in our partial and narrow modes of handling emergencies, our inability to solve problems with which other times and men have not feared to grapple" ("Bill," 251). With "the general decay of the spirit of traditionary discipline" (253), we have forgotten that the key to marriage (like Ellenborough's key to imperial rule) lies in restraint: "restraint from the choice of more than a single wife; restraint from choosing her among near relatives by blood or affinity; restraint from the carnal use of woman in any relation inferior to marriage; restraint from forming any temporary or any other than a life-long contract" (285). Yet for all the rhetorical luster of the traditionalists, inconsistency—or, if one prefers, compromise—clearly became the controlling habit. In both crises, in that of empire and of domesticity, there emerged a consensus, though nothing like a unanimity, that history had worked its inevitabilities and there was no more going back to Ellenborough's "red hand" than to Gladstone's biblical literalism.

5

As members of Parliament tried to make their way through the cunning corridors of divorce, India appeared as an immense screen on which the fantasy structures of a threatened domesticity could be projected. Would India be allowed to divorce Britain? Never. But would she be permitted to divorce the East India Company, which had seized her property and abused her integrity? Yes, in the interests of a better and stronger bond, she would.

It is impossible to know how the terrors excited by the India revolt affected the sharper details of the divorce debates: the last amendments, the improvised adjustments, the votes. But the recurring figures of the self-destroying widow and the mutinous Sepoy gave urgency to the question of the moment: how to manage dependency in a time of historical transition? "Divorce" was no longer just the description of a failed domesticity; now it could describe failed relations in the grandest domain. The put-together compromise of the Divorce and Matrimonial Causes Act was no more elegant than the patched-over connection with India in the following year. There is good reason to believe that the two "solutions" confirmed and reassured one another, encouraging the complacent view that small concessions could preserve large entrenchments.

But while compromise was trying to achieve its anodyne work, another exemplary character loomed out of the Indian emergency, this one not a figure for the British wife but the literal woman herself. In the first narratives coming back to the capital it was the scene of victimage that transfixed the national mind: the horrors of Cawnpore, the slaughter, the (unnamed) rape of women. A well-known painting by Paton was originally drawn not with the Scottish Highlanders appearing just in time to save threatened womanhood, but with Sepoys bursting through the door, bringing bloodlust and the final indignity.[26] That image proved so horrifying that it was painted over in favor of the image of salvation, but in either version the painting crystallizes the pervasive dread: the fear for an ethereal feminine innocence threatened by the racial other.

Such images, and the stories accompanying them, never disappeared from the body of legend excited by the uprising, but they were soon overlaid with another strain of imagery and anecdote. This emphasized not the passive victimage of the British but their heroic resistance against impossible odds. Here it was the resistance of women that proved most captivating. Miss Wheeler (Figure 9) is upright, armed, and resolute: not content to wait for the horror,

Figure 9. "Miss Wheeler Defending Herself against the Sepoys at Cawnpore."
Courtesy of the Director, National Army Museum, London.

she performs another influential "mutiny" topos: the British woman roused to righteous violence.

Dickens was another whose imperial rage discharged itself in images of Women Militant. In the face of the great Indian "betrayal," he acknowledges that he has "become Demoniacal," and that if he were "Commander in Chief in India," he would "do my utmost to exterminate the Race upon whom the stain of the late cruelties rested."[27] Central to his fantasy of retaliation is the ardent British woman, who, having once inspired men with her grace and innocence, will now fight alongside them. He projects a story of the mutiny that will change the scene to South America, noting to Henry Morley that, "I wish to avoid India itself; but I want to shadow out, in what I do, the bravery of our ladies in India" (*Letters*, 469).

The result is "The Perils of Certain English Prisoners," written with Wilkie Collins and published in the 1857 Christmas number of *Household Words*, in which the heroism of the colonial British shows itself in the valor, pluck, and mettle of the beautiful young women who put down domestic implements and pick up instruments of war. In the last moments of preparation before attack, the ever doting narrator Gill Davis stares in astonishment, as the adorable Miss Maryon and Mrs. Fisher (she whom he had "taken for a doll and a baby") enter the military line: "Steady and busy behind where I stood, those two beautiful and delicate young women fell to handling the guns, hammering the flints, looking to the locks, and quietly directing others to pass up powder and bullets from hand to hand, as unflinching as the best of tried soldiers."[28] Then, as the pirates overwhelm the defenses, there they are again, "their hands and dresses blackened with the spoilt gunpowder," as they "worked on their knees, tying such things as knives, old bayonets, and spear-heads, to the muzzles of the useless muskets" (12).

In a story in which Dickens seems to have almost no distance from the animating fantasies, the retaliation against revolt is sealed through the erotics of women in arms. One needn't credit his readers with the same violent-erotic reverie in order to see how the events in India created a drama in which new roles were granted to (or seized by) women who lived through the trauma. Dickens strives for continuity between the domestic personality of his hero-ines—so neat, so pert, so active—and their new guise as gun handlers and bayonet fixers. Ultimately, "The Perils of Certain English Prisoners" returns these women to married life and the household circle, Dickens having com-pleted his act of acknowledgment toward "the bravery of our ladies." The guns will again be replaced by housekeeping keys, and the heroism of men will remain unchallenged by these heroic women.

Elsewhere, however, the transformed woman was not so easily returned to the parlor. In 1859 R. M. Coopland published a memoir of the revolt, under the title *A Lady's Escape from Gwalior: During the Mutinies of 1857*. As the wife of George Coopland, chaplain to the East India Company, she had gone out to India only shortly before the rebellion. Her narrative records the brief idyll of her early stay, the elephant rides and the sketching of picturesque scenery. It then moves into an account of weeks of uneasiness followed by the Sepoy violence, which led to her husband's death and to her difficult flight from Gwalior to Agra (where she delivered a child). Mrs. Coopland is unspar-ing in her representation of the horrors of India; not for her to expend any time on the social and political causes of imperial resentment. But what distin-guishes the work for our purposes is the emphasis on women's strength, her own and the others with whom she fled. The epigraph of the memoir is from Goethe:

> I saw the youth become at once a man, the greybeard
> Turn young again, the child grow to a lusty youth—
> Yes, and that sex, the weak, as men most call it,
> Show itself brave and strong, and of a ready mind.[29]

Coopland offers herself as one compelled to bravery, driven to heroism, but what gives edge to the rendition is that it accompanies such a skeptical view of male strength. Embedded in the memoir is the uneasy suggestion that at moments of stress, women are at least as commanding as those who would protect them. Early in their flight, the women enter the house of a European telegraph employee disguised as a native; from Coopland's point of view, he is contemptible in his fear: "The weak childish conduct of this man was sickening; he almost cried, and kept saying, 'O we shall all be killed': instead of trying to help, he only proved a burden to us" (131). In the same spirit, she offers a reticent but critical account of one Captain Campbell who won't dare to venture into the countryside to rescue his wife, but waits until she makes her way near to him. This strain of subtle but pronounced critique culminates in a defense of the powers of womanhood.

> Some may think that women are weak and only fitted to do trivial things, and endure petty troubles; and there are women who deserve no higher opinion: such as faint at the sight of blood, and are terrified at a harmless cow, or make themselves miserable by imagining terrors, and unreal sorrows; but there are many who can endure with fortitude and patience what even soldiers shrink from. Men are fitted by education and constitution to dare and to do; yet they have been surpassed, in presence of mind and in the power of endurance of weak women. (116)

Of all the tones struck in this elusive narrative, the most arresting is the note of disappointment in those men (including, one can only assume, her husband) who have always laid claim to physical prowess and moral authority but who, in the time of crisis, may reveal that the male shelter has been a fiction. Then women, left on their own, have no choice but to discover their strength. Coopland's difficult career falls within a lineage of midcentury women forced back upon themselves—separated from domestic comfort by widowhood (like the queen) or vocation (like Nightingale) or economic need (like unremembered thousands) or the divorce court or the crisis in India. For all the burdens in these accumulating separate lives, every emergency was an opportunity.

Chapter Ten

BIGAMY AND MODERNITY: THE CASE OF
MARY ELIZABETH BRADDON

1

Through the length of the 1850s, a series of episodes brought an accumulation of exemplary new roles for women. From the bloomer to the pistol-wielding Mrs. Wheeler, from Caroline Norton to Florence Nightingale, from an emergent feminism to an eager philanthropy, these highly visible instances spread themselves across the cultural expanse. It's true that their diversity resolved into nothing like a coherent new womanhood, and also true that, with some rhetorical effort, several of these challenging figures—the nurse, the philanthropist, the militant imperial wife—could be absorbed within existing conventions. Nevertheless, the force of such examples of resistance, anger, courage, and professionalism had a determining effect on the course of imaginative life in the following decade, most immediately in that region of imaginative life that fed itself on the new "sensation fiction."

Within our larger account, it is of great importance that "stormy" female nature showed itself not just under the aspect of sensationalism but also within the specific narrative paradigm that suddenly flourished in the early 1860s: the novel of bigamy. Several years ago Jeanne Fahnestock trawled through the records of publishers and the pages of contemporary reviews in order to gauge the full extent of the narrative formula. In estimates termed conservative, she counts twelve bigamy novels in 1862 and 1863, thirteen in 1864, and sixteen in 1865.[1] Fahnestock uncovered a telling remark from a review by Geraldine Jewsbury, which is worth quoting at some length:

> If in after-times the manners and customs of English life in 1864 were to be judged from the novels of the day, it would naturally be believed that people, in the best regulated families, were in the habit of marrying two wives, or two husbands, as the case might be; and of suppressing the one that proved inconvenient, either by "painless extinction" or by more forcible methods, regardless of the cost of suffering to the victim. Heroes and heroines of the present generation of novels rarely dispense with the marriage ceremony altogether, —it would be a want of propriety which would shock both author and reader; but illegal marriages and supernumerary ceremonies are the order of the day. Novels have always some basis of probability; they seldom paint an entirely false picture of manners: and as bigamy and the conditions to which bigamy is allied form the basis of every second novel that

has been published for some time past, we must conclude that there is a great deal
of latent sympathy with this state of things, which an author can appeal to with
the certainty of exciting the reader's lively interest.[2]

The explanation offered by Fahnestock is that the bigamy convention is a
product of the confused marriage laws, the legal disarray permitting the well-
known and mortifying possibility "that a man could simultaneously have legal
wives in England, Scotland, and Ireland" ("Bigamy," 60). No doubt the confusion was a narrative incitement, but there is another pressure tending toward
the formation of the subgenre, which can be approached through a remark
from a novel that stands as a defining instance of the new convention. The
remark is made by the eponymous protagonist of Mary Elizabeth Braddon's
Lady Audley's Secret, after Robert Audley has described the suicidal grief of
the man whom we will come to know as her first husband. George Talboys,
asserts his friend, has never got over the (apparent) death of his wife—to which
Lady Audley coolly responds.

> "Dear me!" she said, "This is very strange. I did not think men were capable of
> these deep and lasting affections. I thought that one pretty face was as good as
> another pretty face to them, and that when number one with blue eyes and fair
> hair died, they had only to look out for number two with black eyes and hair, by
> way of variety."[3]

What gives biting force to the speech, of course, is that Lady Audley challenges
male promiscuity not only through verbal ridicule but by conducting her own
experiment with a "number two." She begins wedded life with Sir Michael
Audley even as her first husband is returning to England, an audacious act that
captures a salient feature of the bigamy formula: it is indifferent to gender. In
the unresolved flutter over the Deceased Wife's Sister Bill we saw a vivid
example of a male fantasy of mobile affection: the transfer of love from one
sister to the next. As Braddon shows in both *Lady Audley's Secret* and *Aurora
Floyd*, definitively and spectacularly, bigamy extends the reach of fantasy to
women.

Certainly the bigamy novel was a precipitate of the buzzing divorce conversation conducted through the length and breadth of every genteel breakfast
table in Britain.[4] But the question can fairly be asked: why did divorce yield
bigamy novels and not divorce novels? A bit of tortured explanation in Braddon's next novel, *Aurora Floyd*, may point toward an answer. Aurora, who has
shown herself to be fully conversant with the Divorce and Matrimonial Causes
Act, knows that the "brutality" and "infidelity" of her first husband, James
Conyers, entitles her to sue for divorce: "The law would have set me free from
him."[5] But to pursue the legal remedy would have been to raise scandal, to
humiliate her father, in short to fall into the realm of the *Times*. Aurora, that
is, accepts the viewpoint of the Old Bachelor, who warns that the poison of

divorce is its publicity, and the result is that she leads the tormented, breathless, subterranean life of the bigamous woman, vulnerable to scheming cads on every side.

Partly, then, bigamy is the imaginative manifestation of postdivorce culture because it is the preferred "quiet" alternative to the divorce pandemonium. And yet, Mrs. Henry Wood's *East Lynne*, one of the few novels of the sixties to represent a legal divorce, suggests that what makes bigamy a compelling alternative is that it is so close to the divorce it replaces. The woodenly decent Archibald Carlyle divorced his wife after her rash elopement with Francis Levison—a divorce, he believed, that was consummated with her death. But in the last overwrought pages of the novel Carlyle realizes that his veiled governess is his first wife; she is Isabel Vane, not dead after all, but living by his side, tending their children and watching the course of his second marriage. In the cataclysm of Carlyle's recognition, "The first clear thought that came thumping through his brain, was, that he must be a man of two wives."[6] This is the tremulous insight that leaves the reader panting: that divorce has failed to work its effect, that the legal mechanism has been unable to change the course of affective life. Within this novel, as within a culture still struggling to represent the change, marriage after divorce remains a form of bigamy. In the uncertain new world of the Matrimonial Causes Act, love for a second spouse, while the first spouse lived, was bound to seem an infidelity. In this respect, the bigamy novels of the sixties are all divorce novels, which is to say, novels about the failure of divorce to achieve a true separation.

2

It is one thing for men to participate in the divorce-bigamy culture; for this there are precedents and conventions. The startling case, we have suggested, is the woman who dares to take up the newly circulating possibility. Braddon's twin bigamy novels of the early 1860s differ in some significant respects, but they share a vision of the bigamous wife as the woman of scarcely conceivable will. It's not only that Lady Audley is capable of such sensational gestures as throwing her husband down a well and setting fire to the Castle Inn; it's also that she dares to perform smaller acts, such as taking a train alone to London or sending a telegram. In ordinary as well as extraordinary ways she emancipates herself from the embrace of male "protection," that gaudy concept hovering over domestic life. To be a murderess is to take on an awful aspect; but to be a mobile female agent, moving with self-possession around England, is scarcely less dreadful. The ability to maneuver through mass society by herself, to be a self-promoting entrepreneur, to calculate close odds, and to arrange complex plans—these arc signs of mastery as definitive as murder.

The critics of sensation fiction complained of its quaking and trembling, but the plots of Braddon, Collins, and others need to be set within the agitating

social circumstances that changed the texture of everyday life.[7] The wars of
the fifties, the expanding network of railways, the extension of the telegraph,
the urban building boom, and the emergence of conspicuous consumerism
helped to breed an enervated subjectivity, too narrowly sorted under the heading of "sensation fiction." Lady Audley is capable of sensational aberration,
but her restlessness and distraction link her to the lives of readers.[8] All those
who are told to be still and yet find their minds wandering can recognize her
as a monstrous counterpart, an infernal double of their doubleness.

Readers quickly understand that what makes the command of Helen Maldon / Lucy Graham / Lady Audley so sinister is that it is concealed beneath
an exquisite mask of flaxen hair and blue-eyed delicacy.[9] Because she has
successfully appeared within the conventions of the "amiable," the "gentle,"
the "light-hearted, happy and contented" (*Lady Audley*, 5), her turn to murder
tickles the spine more thrillingly. What Robert Audley calls "the hellish power
of dissimulation" is scarcely something new in the representation of women:
what indeed could be older?[10] But what gives the aura of contemporaneity to
Lady Audley's Secret is the timeliness of its contrast between the banal surface
of mid-Victorian respectability—she visits the old and the poor—and the
thrashing violence of the female demon.[11] The transformation of Lady Audley
has been prepared, after all, in those recent changes of the fifties. The daughter
who one morning appears in bloomers, the imperial wife who learns to shoot
a gun, the unmarried sister who trains to be a nurse—these changes, too, were
often treated as cases of demonic possession: yesterday, she sat in my drawing
room; today she carries a petition for Girton College. Within this complex of
examples we must also recall the disruptive case of the Indian Sepoy, that
other figure seen as converting obedience into homicide. (At a tense moment
in *Aurora Floyd* a husband who served in the India campaign will stare
"in blank amazement at his *mutinous* wife" [293, emphasis added].) Lady Audley is herself painted as a kind of domestic Sepoy, capable of obedient district-
vising in the morning and arson at night, at one moment demure in the drawing
room and in the next hoarse with murderous design. In all these respects, the
melodrama of the sensation narrative belongs to a broadly sensational cultural
moment.[12]

Braddon understands that moment in complex terms. On the one hand, it is
the moment of a mature modernity that has outgrown the moral infancy of the
first decades of the century. An early passage in *Aurora Floyd*, almost certainly
written during the composition of *Lady Audley's Secret*, emphasizes the contrast, frequently met in the early 1860s, between an early nineteenth-century
"then" and a mid-nineteenth-century "now." The passage evokes the recent
death of Prince Albert, "when a whole nation mourned with one voice for the
untimely end of a blameless life," and when "the words that rose simultaneously to every lip dwelt most upon the spotless character of him who was lost;

the tender husband, the watchful father, the kindly master, the liberal patron." From this summit of national grandeur, Braddon looks back to the death of George IV, still available to living memory, and describes the contrast between the two moral conditions.

> It is many years since England mourned for another royal personage who was called a "gentleman." A gentleman who played practical jokes, and held infamous orgies, and persecuted a wretched foreign woman, whose chief sin and misfortune it was to be his wife; a gentleman who cut out his own nether garments, and left the companion of his gayest revels, the genius whose brightness had flung a spurious lustre upon the dreary saturnalia of vice, to die destitute and despairing. Surely there is some hope that we have changed for the better within the last thirty years, inasmuch as we attach a new meaning to-day to this simple title of "gentleman."
> (*Aurora Floyd*, 51)

Braddon's two novels meditate on the cultural settlements that have grown rooted in Britain and that measure a distance between the 1860s and "thirty years since." In the earlier of the two books, where Lady Audley makes her challenge to the reign of the new gentlemen, what gives attraction to her revolt is that the gentlemanly rule appears weak, ineffectual, and, most of all, tedious. When Sir Michael Audley first quickens with desire for the governess Lucy Graham, he recalls his earlier marriage, recognizing it as "a dull, jog-trot bargain, made to keep some estate in the family that would have been just as well out of it." He now sees his love for his first wife as "a poor, pitiful smouldering spark, too dull to be extinguished, too feeble to burn" (*Lady Audley*, 6–7).[13] The novel maintains a running commentary on dullness, on the feebleness of respectable life. If Sir Michael's marriage is dull, so has his nephew, Robert, tricked out a lifeless career as a lazy barrister. Audley Court itself, the great house, often appears as an overwhelmingly tedious place. Throughout, Braddon satirizes the heavy weight of polite society, even as she suggests that the placid surface is yet another mask. Early in the novel Lady Audley's maid Phoebe wanders through the house with her beau, the aspiring publican Luke.

> "It's a mortal dull place, Phoebe," he said, as they emerged from a passage into the principal hall, which was not yet lighted; "I've heard tell of a murder that was done here in old times."
> "There are murders enough in these times, as to that, Luke," answered the girl.
> (*Lady Audley*, 28)

The Newgate crime novels had been the targets of harsh critique in the late 1830s, leading Dickens and others to retreat from the scarifying plots of a roguish underworld (the world of *Oliver Twist* or *Jack Sheppard*). While there were, of course, exceptions (as, for instance, in the fiction of Reynolds), the midcentury force of the domestic ideal had clearly softened the edge of narra-

tive violence. The historical project of *Lady Audley's Secret* is to insist that
sensation is not a thing of the past, that it lives on, flourishing secretly in the
dark corridors of modernity.[14] Indeed, what many sensation novels suggest—
in the display of heightened emotions, and the absorption in motifs of sexual
ambition and physical brutality—is a historical recursus, sensationalism not as
something new but as something recalled from the first third of the century,
before the entrenchment of the home ideal. In this aspect, the 1860s are seen
not as a surpassing of the bad old days of George IV, rather as a return to
depravity, corruption, coarseness, and violence.

A return, though, with a difference. Now the thrills and tickles are no longer
the privilege of the high-born and the fantastically wealthy. The narrator of
Aurora Floyd implicates her readers in the frantic, urban-centered, overwrought life of modernity: "Have you ever visited some still country town
after a lapse of years, and wondered, O fast-living reader!, to find the people
you knew in your last visit still alive and thriving, with hair unbleached as yet,
although you have lived and suffered whole centuries since then?" (95). What
had been the privileged decadence of the elite in the 1820s and 1830s becomes,
in effect, more fully democratized in the 1860s, extending downward into the
lower reaches of the middle class, to all those who read newspapers, ride trains,
send telegrams—or read novels.

Which is it then? Are the early sixties a modernity of mature moral self-
possession, measured by the distance between "the tender husband" and
"watchful father" who was Albert and the dissolute hedonist who was the last
of the Georges? Or are those sixties a revival (with a difference) of the "fast-
living" social vortex that makes the pulse strong and the morals weak? The
answer, of course, is both: sensation fiction trades heavily on the portrait of a
ponderously insistent respectability finding itself appalled (but also thrilled)
by the hectic pleasures that its own dullness secretly enjoys.[15] The novels keep
affirming that things are not as dull as they seem, here, now, in the 1860s, that
we may be promised suburban peace only to encounter murder in the night.

Or at least to encounter it in the newspapers. The central recognition of the
genre is that an enclosed daily life may enshrine the norms of respectable
routine, but in a mass society described by avid journalists, even the most
protected are made aware of violence, brutality, and sexual aberration. Drawing on the work of Raymond Williams and Richard Altick, William Cohen has
argued that the period of 1855–60 created the material conditions for a new
age of scandal, noting in particular how the repeal of the stamp tax in 1855
and the paper duty in 1860 dramatically expanded the power of the newspaper:
"This burgeoning medium generated stories for popular consumption on a
scale that had not been possible before, and the character of both newspapers
and the news changed significantly."[16] The spectacular events may be rare, but
they are part of the texture of consciousness, because consciousness is now

steeped in the newspaper medium.[17] And so you will fear what you have never seen, you will be thrilled by what you have never met, because it will exist in the newspaper consciousness, the mediated consciousness, that has become your own.

Stimulated by this "fast-living" newspaper culture, *Lady Audley's Secret* releases a series of extraordinary wish fulfillments for its protagonist—to choose the love object (George), to replace him, to invent a new identity, to become wealthy, pampered, indolent, and dominant—that make a mockery of the stable household. The narrative, like its protagonist, remains conscious that it is hemmed in by the world of earnest obligation, the realm outside fantasy that must finally reassert its dominance. Yet that earnest world is unsettled and divided. The novel sees that the forces of respectability occupy two distinct social sites: the world of the country house with its aura of landed tradition, and the emerging world of the new professional classes, the lawyers and doctors identified with the metropolis, rather than the rural seat. The troubled relation between Sir Michael Audley, anticipating married pleasure at Audley Court, and his nephew Robert, struggling in London as a barrister, captures the distinction between a respectability of aristocratic nostalgia and a respectability of modernizing professional experts. Lady Audley's success in reinventing herself depends on exploiting the gap between nostalgia and modernity, the land and an urban professionalism. She is able to hide in the interstices of a mass society incapable of controlling its anomalies. When she first appears, we read that, "She had come into the neighbourhood as a governess in the family of a surgeon in the village near Audley Court. No one knew anything of her except that she came in answer to an advertisement which Mr Dawson, the surgeon, had inserted in the *Times*. She came from London" (5). As she emerges out of the social welter of London and travels across England, as she sends telegrams at short notice, as she changes her name and her story, Lady Audley thrives in the space between an aged tradition and a still uncertain contemporaneity.

The still chilling force of the novel is that it carries the domestic nightmare so close to catastrophe. The bewitching wife has overwhelmed the doting husband: "I can twist him which way I like, I can put black before him, and if I say it is white, he will believe me" (282). As Robert Audley closes upon her, she prepares Sir Michael to believe in his nephew's lunacy; and beyond that, she burns down an inn, hoping to turn her antagonist to ash. In the extremity of these gestures, the novel allows its antidomestic reverie to discharge itself, and Braddon finally rouses her narrative to incarcerate the fantasy.[18] Notably, she does this by bringing together the separate respectabilities. When Robert Audley returns from the charred Castle Inn, confronts Lady Audley, and forces her to confess, he then immediately sends off telegrams to London, summoning the eminent physician Dr. Alwyn Mosgrave. In this last phase, when Robert, the no longer listless barrister, and Mosgrave, the consummate medical professional, meet at Audley Court, they work to seal the breach between modernity and tradition.[19] The great terror of aristocratic family virtue, the loss of a good name, is averted through the close compact of a doctor and a lawyer.

Notoriously, Lady Audley, the unbridled female agent, is condemned to madness. It has been fairly said that the diagnosis of "latent insanity" is the punishment for her "unfeminine assertiveness,"[20] and to that judgment we might add that it is just to the extent that the culture lacks conventions to describe her agency, madness comes forward as the strategic improvisation of a professional class.[21] Where her brazen refusal of passive dependence might have invited female readers to see her as exemplary—and this in spite of her crimes—the name "madness" marks her revolt as an anomaly; no longer an intelligible response to suffocating constraint, it is a "hereditary taint," a diagnosis that safely particularizes her wild abandonment of wifely duty.

There is a further point. We know that much of the dread of divorce, like the dread of the deceased wife's sister reform, turned not on the likelihood of more failing marriages but on the prospect of a new public consciousness, the visibility of a shameful epidemic. The bigamy plot, as we have seen, is the improbably discreet alternative to the noise of a public divorce.[22] Similarly, in *Lady Audley's Secret* the terror that grips Robert Audley is that his uncle's life will be ravaged by the exposure that would come from the criminal trial of his wife. What is so narratively convenient and historically apt in the expedient of Lady Audley's madness is that it permits the eerily *silent* arrangement of the lunatic asylum. In this respect, madness is to criminality, as bigamy is to divorce: the sensational extralegal plot device that allows fiction to imagine a private solution in place of a public cataclysm.

3

But Aurora Floyd is not mad. The companion novel, begun while the writing of *Lady Audley's Secret* was still in motion, has been largely cast into the shadows for our century's readers. Yet at the cultural moment we are seeking to resuscitate, it had its own strong success, and must stand alongside its more glamorous twin as a second genre-defining work of the early 1860s. To place the two novels together is to adjust the valence too quickly assigned to Lady Audley, Braddon, and sensation fiction. One strong tendency has been to identify the subversions of sensationalism, and certainly no one can doubt the disruptions created by the portrait of the untamed, amoral, murderous, and bigamous wife, refusing to cower in dependence and penury. It is a short interpretive step to conclude that such a figure makes a challenge to the minions of respectability. *Aurora Floyd*, however, forces us to turn that straightforward step into a little dance.

Where the will is concerned, Aurora yields nothing to Lady Audley. With her "proud defiance" and her "haughty insouciance" (*Aurora Floyd*, 63), with her "unfeminine tastes and mysterious propensities" (42), she is an "Eastern empress" (35), a Cleopatra, if not a Lola Montes, a Nell Gwynne, or Charlotte Corday (40). Like her counterpart in Audley Court, Aurora Floyd has mastered the modernity of trains and telegrams. The men in her life pay homage to her imperious domestic force. Dominating her father's household and then her husband's, she is capable of leaping (like a "beautiful tigress," 116) upon the brutal stablehand, Steeve "Softy" Hargreaves, "after he has kicked her favorite dog (Bow-wow). At the great moment of crisis, when Aurora faces exposure at the hands of her blackmailing first husband, once a jockey but now a groom on her estate, she quiets her outraged second husband, saying with supreme confidence, "Leave all to me" (228). Like *Lady Audley's Secret*, in short, *Aurora Floyd* provides a timely portrait of unembarrassed female agency, a striking imaginative consolidation of many social pressures of the previous decade. In a mood of despondency Robert Audley had concluded that "To call [women] the weaker sex is to utter a hideous mockery. They are the stronger sex, the noisier, the more persevering, the most self-assertive sex" (207). Although Robert will rouse himself for the final combat, his views continue to echo.

No less than Lady Audley, Aurora is a conscious bigamist, who understands the scandal of her transgression and actively hides it. When the blackmail becomes too pressing, she meets her groom-husband in the woods, delivering two thousand pounds in return for his promise to emigrate to Australia. She screams out her hatred to the vulgar seductive Adonis, and moments later the man Conyers is murdered. No reader has any reason to doubt that the superb Aurora Floyd is capable of the act. Even her husband believes she is guilty. In this way the novel carefully repeats the structural disposition of *Lady Audley's Secret*: an unrepentant woman dares to commit bigamy, schemes to suppress the truth, and finally confronts the living first husband, whose return threatens to destroy her new life of ease and privilege.

At this node in the earlier novel, Lady Audley steps beyond the pale and commits the violence that brands her as a madwoman. But in the second novel a telling "correction" is made. Others were walking in the wood that evening, and though Aurora uttered her contempt, she was never close to the act of murder. It was all a mistake; she never took that pistol she was polishing; she never forgot herself or her position. The villain was indeed mad, but the free female agent was not the villain. It was all along the brute, the half-wit, dog-beating "Softy," who shambled and leered, and finally murdered, who "was more awkward, and perhaps more repulsive, than the ugliest of the lower animals." (The former soldier, who finally subdues him and uncovers the incriminating garment, shouts out a tangle of compressed epithets: "I've been accus-

tomed to deal with refractory Sepoys in India, and I've had a struggle with a
tiger before now. Show me that waistcoat!" *Aurora Floyd*, 380.)

In this unpleasant downward displacement of guilt, the novel recuperates
the bigamous wife, whose fault, we finally learn, was real but forgivable. She
was young when the groom lured her from her father's influence; she took a
"sentimental fancy for his dashing manner"; it was "only a school-girl's frivolous admiration"; he pretended to be "a prince in disguise," "a gentleman's
son"; the governess encouraged the wild fancy. Aurora is guilty, in short, not
of murderous *folie* but only of adolescent folly. Yet even in this catastrophic
marriage, she shows her defiant strength. As a witness of her secret life recalls,
"I've seen her look at [Conyers], as if she'd wither him up from off the ground
he trod upon, with that contempt she felt for him"—adding that "she was a
tartar . . . but she was the right sort, too" (323).

This last remark condenses the daydream that hovers over the entire novel:
the image of the sublime imperial woman, the ferocious tartar, who nevertheless belongs to the right sort, the polite sort, the gracious, comfortable, and
privileged sort. Against her are arrayed the small evil people, the ones responsible for the sensational disruption to the good life: the groom who seduced
her, the softheaded stable-hand, and finally the companion, Mrs. Powell, who
keeps up the face of loyal service, while writing secret letters of accusation.
Aroused by this last figure in the triad, the treacherous domestic companion,
Braddon's narrator assails the unreliability of the servant class:

> Remember this, husbands, and wives, fathers and sons, mothers and daughters,
> brothers and sisters. . . . *Your servants enjoy the fun.* . . . Nothing that is done in
> the parlour is lost upon these quiet, well-behaved watchers from the kitchen. They
> laugh at you; nay, worse, they pity you. They discuss your affairs, and make
> out your income, and settle what you can afford to do and what you can't afford
> to do; they prearrange the disposal of your wife's fortune, and look prophetically
> forward to the day when you will avail yourself of the advantages of the Bank-
> ruptcy Act. (149)

The unholy triangle of companion, groom, and stablehand join to destroy the
splendid Aurora, and if they fail, it is because respectable and monied society
arrays its inborn strength against them. The envious upstarts have invaded the
noble precincts of Mellish Park, but merely to set the high-born beside the
low-spawned is to see that gentility will triumph. In one resonant tableau,
Aurora's two husbands, the good Mellish and the vile Conyers, stand alongside
one another, while the bigamous wife gazes on the difference. Conyers is as
handsome "as it is possible for this human clay to be," and yet "every inch of
him" reveals "a boor," coarse, slouching, unkempt. Mellish, on the other hand,
has no Grecian beauty, but, better than such a dubious gift is his "broad-shouldered and stalwart" posture, "everything about him made beautiful by the easy

grace which is the peculiar property of the man who has been born a gentle-man" (223). The contrast—graceful gentility versus boorish (though beautiful) animality—is conventional, but it plays a striking role within the workings of the new sensationalism, where it will persist within the unfoldings of the genre.

Free of her schoolgirl infatuations, Aurora seeks a return to the world of settled value, anchored by birth and wealth. She glows with health and high spirits, a physical vigor and psychic strength that might have yielded the trans-gressions of her predecessor from Audley Court. But the labor of the novel is to channel the heroine's will into a defense of the union between old family and new money. The daughter of an amiable actress and a rich banker, she has married into the genteel Yorkshire lineage of John Mellish, where she rules her grand household with benevolent heartiness, the "pretty tyrant," who domi-nates her husband, the "big, blustering" man, who "laid himself down to be trampled upon by her gracious feet" (120). She never abuses the respectable privileges of her power. Although she keeps her secret, she wears no mask. She is the good-natured beauty: "it was impossible for honest people to know Aurora without loving her" (230).

What stain is then left to bigamy? Despite all the narrative tangles—Who was the man in the park wearing the waistcoat with the missing brass button?—the central bigamy plot barely ruffles the reader's sympathy. In her legal embar-rassment Aurora is the guiltless agent, more victim than perpetrator, who con-fesses her faults so frankly that we are invited to forgive her heartily.

More difficult than the legal bigamy is the romantic knot that the novel struggles to untie in its first chapters. When Aurora still believes that Conyers is dead and that her only shame lies in having run off to marry such a coarse man, she is courted by both Mellish and his friend Talbot Bulstrode, of the Cornwall Bulstrodes, the proud heir to an old baronetcy. Although embarrassed by her past, Aurora lets herself love Bulstrode; their engagement is approved by all the world; but when the dour fiancé learns the most mild version of her secret—that she left her French school and passed a year of her life that she refuses to explain—he breaks off the engagement. It's during Aurora's collapse after this episode that the agreeable John Mellish tends and courts and marries her, secrets and all. But the novel then faces an awkwardness greater than the turn from the handsome groom to the broad-shouldered landowner. How can it be that the affectionate girl loves the future baronet, and then so quickly turns to the second suitor? The narrator, who knows that this will be a question for the reader, asks it first.

> Have I any need to be ashamed of my heroine in that she had forgotten her straight-
> nosed, grey-eyed Cornish lover, who had set his pride and his pedigree between
> himself and his affection, and had loved her at best with a reservation, dearly
> though he had loved her? Have I any cause to blush for this poor impetuous girl, if,

turning in the sickness of her sorrowful heart, with a sense of relief and gratitude, to
the honest shelter of John's love, she had quickly learnt to feel for him an affection
which repaid him a thousandfold for his long-suffering devotion? (119)

The answer, of course, is no: no shame, no blush. This is where the reflections
on "fast-living" modernity occur, and the unsentimental conclusion is that in
these modern times we need to expect that we will convalesce from the pain
of old love, shake ourselves, and love again: "The sharper the disease, the
shorter its continuance." Talbot Bulstrode, pained by his breaking of the engagement, "will be better by-and-by, and will look back at his old self, and
laugh at his old agonies" (95). On Aurora's side the healing is equally complete: "With these impetuous and impressionable people, who live quickly, a
year is sometimes as twenty years; so Aurora looked back at Talbot Bulstrode
across a gulf which stretched for weary miles between them, and wondered if
they had really ever stood side by side, allied by Hope and Love, in the days
that were gone" (125).

Here, one might say, is the real bigamy, the capacity to move abruptly from
one heartfelt love to the next. The excuse offered for both impetuous Aurora
and proud Bulstrode—for good or ill, they lead the fast lives of the new era,
within which "we cast off our former selves with no more compunction than
we feel in flinging away a worn-out garment"—amounts to nothing less than
a rehabilitation of bigamous love, and by extension an acceptance of divorce,
for which bigamy serves as the figure. Circumstances will supervene; old love
will fade; new love will descend. It's not easy to learn the lessons of modern
discontinuity—"Shall I feel the same contempt ten years hence for myself as
I am to-day, as I feel to-day for myself as I was ten years ago?" (95)—but they
must be learned nonetheless. The burden of Braddon's early, influential, and
convention-establishing sensation novels is that the best circles cannot rest on
ancient stability; they must rouse themselves and grow vigorous enough to
accept the faster movements of both social life and private affection.

Yet the other side of the canny perception in these two novels is that the
forces of respectability (measured by those thirty years that separate the pleasure-seeking George IV from that of the blameless Albert) are gathering to the
point where they can absorb, and even enjoy, the challenges of sensation. As
Braddon was working on her two books, Margaret Oliphant was remarking (in
Salem Chapel, 1862–63) on the change of tone in "late days": "The 'Times'
and the Magazines take it for granted that all their readers dine out at splendid
tables, and are used to a solemn attendant behind their chair."[23] In the course
of her two novels Braddon moves to just this assertion of brazen respectability.
She plays out her own bigamy with the two eponymous heroines, giving herself
to the lawless Lady Audley and then giving herself again to merely "impul-
sive" Aurora. Lady Audley defiantly affirmed that women have the same rights
and powers as men to choose new objects of affection and to marry second

spouses. Aurora Floyd, without surrendering those rights, assimilates them to the world identified with Prince Albert: the world of the mature, the decent, the fine, and the high.

Aurora Floyd puts sensation in the service of respectability. Partly, it does so by identifying villainy with the class of menials, and partly by confirming Aurora's search for vindication. Unlike Lady Audley's curled-lip contempt for domestic propriety, Aurora wants only to coincide with social privilege. In the late crisis of the novel she returns to Talbot Bulstrode, now a distinguished member of Parliament, married to Aurora's quiet cousin Lucy. In his lofty integrity, he will serve Aurora "as a wise judge, to whose sentence she would be willing to submit" (302). When Bulstrode meets her in London, his first reflex is to exclude her from his stainless home: she "was a guilty creature, whom it would be his painful duty to cast out of that pure household. She was a poor, lost, polluted wretch, who must not be admitted into the holy atmosphere of a Christian gentleman's home" (294). But when she rehearses the entire sensational narrative, telling him for the first time of the marriage to Conyers, the bigamy, and the blackmail, the staid MP relents. He decides not only to heal her threatened second marriage but also to catch the real murderer.

The reconciliation between the bigamous wife and the parliamentary judge serves as an emblem for the movement from *Lady Audley's Secret* to *Aurora Floyd*. Sensation will make its peace with polite society, on the understanding that society heed the lessons of sensation. The teaching of *Aurora Floyd* is that this will be the age of both Prince Albert and fast living, the tender husband and the bigamous wife. Divorce will continue to provoke howls of outrage, and the bigamy novels will create outrage of their own. But Braddon's wildly successful books suggest the appetite for domestic doubleness, for the safety of a Christian gentleman's home and the transgressions of household mystery. After 1857 the disruptions of a divorce culture could not be locked back in the cabinet, but they could be wrapped within extravagant forms of story, allowing fantasies to be released and then orthodoxies to be resumed.

BETWEEN MANUAL AND SPECTACLE

THERE ARE TIMES when the imaginative investments of a culture become so conspicuous, so overheated, that a second order of discourse emerges. Where there had been the affirmation of a value, now affirmation affirms itself. What had appeared as a reflex begins to conduct itself as a program. Exactly when this happened to the Victorian investment in domestic life is impossible to say, but by the opening of the 1860s the terms of the conversation had clearly changed. The fireside reverie lost its simplicity when it took itself as a subject: to enjoy home was one thing, but to watch oneself chant out enjoyment was another. By the end of the 1850s the fascination with family life watched itself in a mirror.

A central cause for the change lies in what we have been calling the spectacle of intimacy, the wild efflorescence in the public signs, traces, slogans, and figures of domesticity, until it was scarcely possible to see the home beneath the mottoes enshrining it. The fifties were the great age of a widely popular domestic journalism, which followed Dickens's *Household Words* with a parade of more narrowly focused periodicals such as *The Home Circle*, *The Home Friend*, *Home Companion*, *The Home*, *The Family Friend*, *Family Herald*, *Family Economist*, and *The Englishwoman's Domestic Magazine*. Nor was it only a matter of a dense fog of domestic symbols. The construction boom in the middle decades of the century transformed the built environment, laying out material traces of the vast extension of middle-class domesticity. Everywhere one looked there were more homes shrouded in more utterances about home.

In a biting essay in the *Cornhill* at the very beginning of the 1860s, James Fitzjames Stephen described the triumph of domesticity as a cultural catastrophe: "it is in the highest degree dangerous . . . to allow any one side of life to become the object of idolatry; and there are many reasons for thinking that domestic happiness is rapidly assuming that position in the minds of the more comfortable classes of Englishmen."[1] Partly, he suggests, the English fetish is a reaction to Continental revolution, and partly a revulsion against the vice of the previous century, but, in whatever historical frame it is placed, the "worship of domestic comfort" (351) has had poisonous effects. It has led to a low, creeping practicality that cancels high ambition. Nowadays, the husband

> thinks himself bound to earn what will keep himself, his wife, and his six or seven
> children, up to the established standard of comfort. What was at first a necessity,
> perhaps an unwelcome one, becomes by degrees a habit and a pleasure, and men
> who might have done memorable and noble things . . . lose the power and the wish
> to live for other than fireside purposes.

What alarms the fretful Stephen is that his countrymen will lower themselves further into the warm bath of prudence; they will choose the pleasures of "cheerful families and happy homes" (351) over the strenuous demands of distinguished achievement; they will smile at the recession of excellence. For these reasons, "it would be an unspeakable misfortune if the procuring of domestic comfort came to be recognized as the ideal of human life" (350). In prophetic phrase, "a paradise of comfort would be a hell, ignorant of its own misery" (351).

Stephen's vexation is one sign of the embedding of the normative domestic order, and it is also a sign of the aging of the norm. The career of fireside comfort has assumed the rounded shape of an old familiarity: if this is what makes it an object of disdain for Stephen, it is also what lends it power for its defenders. The recognition that a consensus has gathered around the sanctity of the hearth allows the partisans of domestic respectability to brandish their daydream ruthlessly.

Dickens's Podsnap is the grotesque example, the militantly contented man who "never could make out why everybody was not quite satisfied."[2] With his heavy furniture and his weighty plate, Podsnap wields his complacency against his helpless dinner guests and bullies them into agreement over the mutton and the sweets. The "meek man" at his table, who mentions starvation in the streets of London and futilely asks Podsnap merely to acknowledge the existence of poverty, epitomizes the weak opposition to the belligerent powers. Dickens's career spans a long arc in the history of domestic imagination; at every stage he is an architect of the curving; but here at the end he sees more clearly than ever that the defense of home life can become an instrument of cruelty.

Even when it is solicitous rather than cruel, the home mission begins to seem mature, even overripe. When Lucilla Marjoribanks arrives home after the death of her mother, she mourns briefly and then ponders the vocation before her. She is to be a "comfort to papa," a phrase that she self-consciously makes her tag, abetted by the narrator of *Miss Marjoribanks*, who never fails to put the motto within winking quotation marks. These marks are the typographical signs of a dated domestic rhetoric: what had seemed vigorous in the young Sarah Ellis or in *A Christmas Carol* now seems quaint. Oliphant shares the perception that domestic values have grown aged and seasoned; it won't do any longer, certainly not if one has any ear for cliché, to speak out the old convictions in the same tones. Part of the virtuosity of *Miss Marjoribanks*, and also *Our Mutual Friend*, lies in the ability to reaffirm conventions while keeping a distance from cliché. Miss Marjoribanks indeed wants to be a "comfort to papa," and if she can wink as she recites her creed, it's because winking is to the sixties what dewy eyes were to the thirties and forties.

"I have until now suppressed my domestic destiny" (bk. 1, ch. 12) announces Eugene Wrayburn in wry mockery, a mockery that will grow when he leads Mortimer Lightwood through a tour of their new chambers in the Temple.

> "See!" said Eugene, "miniature flour-barrel, rolling-pin, spice-box, shelf of brown jars, chopping-board, coffee-mill, dresser elegantly furnished with crockery, saucepans and pans, roasting-jack, a charming kettle, an armoury of dish-covers. The moral influence of these objects, in forming the domestic virtues, may have an immense influence upon me; not upon you, for you are a hopeless case, but upon me. In fact, I have an idea that I feel the domestic virtues already forming." (bk. 2, ch. 6)

Had there been anyone more convinced than Dickens of the morally regenerative power of the flour barrel, the rolling pin, and the kettle, of "every little household favourite which old associations made a dear and precious thing"?[3] Wasn't it precisely the burden of so many Christmas tales and early novels that the routines of home life gave the path to virtue? Indeed, won't it become Eugene's own destiny in *Our Mutual Friend* to accept the moral influence of a cherished wife? The ironies in this rendition of "domestic virtue" are nothing like a repudiation of an earlier Dickensian axiom, but they too indicate the changing circumstances of affirmation. One might say that Dickens can offer a pastiche of his old earnestness, exactly because he must. He must now flee from his own rhetoric that had once found easy comfort in sentimental conventions. Wrayburn's mockery registers the strain on earnest utterance; through Wrayburn the novel invokes the old home discourse only to place it in brackets, as much to acknowledge that the earlier images have been so thoroughly coded, so much a part of the symbolic furniture of the age, that it is now a strain, even an indelicacy, to speak them in tones of simple conviction. Every earnest Lizzie Hexam now needs an ironizing Wrayburn.

When Bella Wilfer marries the man she does not yet know as John Harmon and takes up with her Rokesmith a modest life in Blackheath, she develops a "perfect genius for home. All the loves and graces seemed (her husband thought) to have taken domestic service with her, and to help her to make home engaging." Bella twitters and hums "in the charm-ingest of dolls' houses"; she bustles and coos; and in the glow of love she makes "amazing progress in her domestic efficiency." We have heard this story before. With tuneful eagerness the young wife spends her days alone with her responsibilities, fully dedicated to the participles of home. "Such weighing and mixing and chopping and grating, such dusting and washing and polishing, such snipping and weeding and trowelling and other small gardening, such making and mending and folding and airing, such diverse arrangements, and above all such severe study!" (bk. 4, ch. 5). But the final phrase marks new conditions in the career of the good Dickensian wife, and it also suggests the changing terms of intimate domesticity. What Bella studies is the advice manual, *The Complete British Family Housewife*, with its empty promises of household harmony. Through some perfunctory satire, the manual is jeered at for its bad prose and its unexecutable commands ("Take a salamander"), but the formulaic comedy doesn't disguise the challenge it presents. The rising arc of Dickens's novelistic triumph was mirrored by that other successful publishing episode, the production of manuals of domestic advice. The female characters in the earlier fiction could disregard these authorities and could adorn the home by reflex and instinct. By the time of *Our Mutual Friend* Dickens cannot ignore the pervasive chatter that shadows his fictions, the tireless rehearsal of norms and tactics directed at the wide audience of middle-class women aspiring to the satisfactions of gentility.

Our introduction mentioned the case of young Rosina, the newlywed in the sketch "A Home Picture," who sweetly asks her husband to point out all her faults and in this way to guide her improvement. Often through the 1860s a task of the novel will be just such stern instruction of the young, especially the heedless young woman, to give up thoughtlessness, selfishness, and frivolity, on the path to moral marriage. And yet a leading assertion of these narratives is that change cannot follow the course of a primer, that it can be neither routine nor rule-governed. Bella Wilfer's brief tussle with the *Complete British Family Housewife* stands as a sign of the quarrel between novelists and manualists. From the standpoint of the novel, the manual is the crystallization of Podsnappery, of all those forces of respectability that have brought the overripening of domestic values, converting them into copybook slogans. The book of rules is the physical emblem of a hectoring conventionality. It is be resisted both because it is cruel and because it is a lie: its simplicity overlooks the catastrophes before its very eyes.

The icons and episodes that have attracted our attention—from the bloomer to the queen, from the deceased wife's sister to the divorced husband, from the sprawling bodies in the lodging houses to the fantasies of bigamy in country mansions—all interrupted the code of splendid intimacy at home. One of the vocations of the midcentury novel was to register the disruptions within the aging norm. Too often the rubric of the sensation novel has been confined to a subgenre on the literary margins. In fact, sensational domesticity was pervasive in the fiction of the sixties. *East Lynne* and *Lady Audley's Secret* made the pulse race and the flesh creep, but though the tones of the "liberal" novel were not as frantic, the works were just as preoccupied with the imminence of domestic catastrophe. *Romola, Can You Forgive Her?, Our Mutual Friend, Miss Marjoribanks*, each displayed scenes of horror within their own terms and tones.

We take "sensationalism" and "manualism" as twin cultural pressures rising through the middle decades of the century. More public exposure, more conventionalized social practice—together they create the agitated confidence of the 1860s. Part of the task of liberal fiction of the sixties was to devise plots that would resist both opposing forces: both the coded routines of the manuals and the moral bafflement of scandal.

In the midst of Trollope's *Can You Forgive Her?* John Grey receives a letter from his sometime fiancée Alice Vavasor, announcing that she has become engaged (for a second time) to her cousin George. Shaken by the news but not prepared to give up Alice, Grey confides to his friend Seward that a new trouble has come into his life. But when Seward delicately asks if he can help, Grey feels unable to say more: "I do not know that I can tell it you all. I would if I could, but the whole story is one not to be told in a hurry. I should leave false impressions" (319), and then he immediately goes on, "I wish with all my heart that you knew it all as I know it; but that is impossible. There are things which happen in a day which it would take a lifetime to explain" (320).

Among other things, Grey's sentiments represent the strategic confession of a novelist who has come to realize how long his book is likely to be. Just a few pages later, after discharging a stern critique of Alice's return to her cousin, the narrator turns to us, "But can you forgive her, delicate reader? Or am I asking the question too early?" and when this narrator goes on to confess that "the story of the struggle has been present to my mind for many years" (326), the motif receives its clinching emphasis. The novel, still less than halfway to its close, defends the length to come, on the grounds that it cannot but be long. Trollope is arguing, in effect, that the story of romantic sin and domestic forgiveness, of the turn from self-will to reverence, is so deep and disturbing that it cannot be told as a sketch, anecdote, or a homely exemplum (as in a manual), but that it requires great narrative patience. It is a story on which one must brood "for many years," and then it may take a "lifetime" to tell.

This obligation to be deliberate and painstaking appears in many guises within the narrative tradition. But in the novels of the 1860s the emphatic self-consciousness of duration (and endurance) is a chief instrument in the moral campaign of the fiction. It frequently takes the form of an effort to vindicate a domestic career under assault, as it were, from beneath and below, from a frankly sexualized passion and from an overstrict code of respectability. What is in Trollope the willfully slow movement to forgiveness and marriage is in Dickens the gradual transformation of Eugene Wrayburn from a man who mocks to a man who marries and, even more strikingly, the long deception of Bella Wilfer that brings her from a search for money to an acceptance of love. Miss Marjoribanks has to traverse every small step of the passage from youth to maturity, anticipation to retrospection; and Romola must endure an arduous course of trials, including a bigamous husband and shattered faith, before she invents an improbable household.

The prevailing assumption is that the achievement of the domestic virtues cannot be ready-to-hand and universally available. The "instruction" of a manual, whether it take the form of a weighty handbook or the ritualized advice of a meddling relative, can never be enough: by itself it can only bring the veneer of improvement. What is needed is an unhurried change in the dispositions of character. The novel develops a form for this patience. Refined through decades of Victorian fiction making, its narrative rhythms can adjust to the twin tableaus that we identified in Braddon's designs: the compacting of solid respectability and the quickening of newspaper consciousness. The liberal novel offers an ongoing process, an unending conversation between routine and anomaly; its plots depend on a training of the emotions that must be experienced, both by characters and readers, not as a quick lesson, but as a long, strenuous *durée*.

By the 1860s, manual and spectacle, respectability and sensation, had entrenched themselves as separate powers: the history of family life will henceforth divide between them. The everyday routines of life were now no more deeply lodged than the spectacular interruptions; the code of the happy home could never again ignore the presence of intimacy on display. From this moment onward, domestic culture found it impossible to know whether it had reached the dullness of perfect safety or the last pitch of terror. Were we going to die of boredom in the drawing room, or were we all going to be murdered in our beds? The press of novels and novelty in the press created the picture of a world both astonished by its security and never certain that it was immune from disaster. Who could say, even in the midst of domestic ease, that a family would withstand the release of an old secret shattering its privacy, exposing it to the public eye, and leaving it as another casualty of the divorce court and the machinery of narrative?

NOTES

Introduction
The Trouble with Families

1. Dr. C. G. Carus, *The King of Saxony's Journey through England and Scotland, in the Year 1844* trans. S. A. Davison (London: Chapman and Hall, 1846), 32.

2. *Census of Great Britain, 1851* (London: Longman, Brown, 1854), xxxvi. "Own voice" may well be disingenuous. Edward Higgs reports the contemporary assumption that William Farr, the superintendent of statistics at the General Register Office and a commissioner for the census from 1851 to 1871, was the author of the census reports during those years. *A Clearer Sense of the Census* (London: HMSO, 1996), 17.

3. Higgs, *A Clearer Sense of the Census*, 8.

4. John Burnett, *A Social History of Housing, 1815–1985*, 2nd ed. (London: Methuen, 1986), 98.

5. Jürgen Habermas, "The Public Sphere," *New German Critique* 1, no. 3 (Fall 1974): 50, and *The Structural Transformation of the Public Sphere: An Inquiry into a Category of Bourgeois Society*, trans. Thomas Burger, with the assistance of Frederick Lawrence (Cambridge, Mass.: MIT Press, 1991); Richard Sennett, *The Fall of Public Man* (Cambridge: Cambridge University Press, 1977).

6. Habermas, "The Public Sphere," 50. Sennett writes that this "was the era in which coffeehouses, then cafés and coaching inns, became social centers; in which the theater and opera houses became open to a wide public through the open sale of tickets rather than the older practice whereby aristocratic patrons distributed places." *The Fall of Public Man*, 17.

7. Habermas, "The Public Sphere," 51, and Sennett, *The Fall of Public Man*, 19.

8. Thaïs E. Morgan has usefully asked to what extent our own methodological categories of public and private retain Victorian investments. "Afterword: Victorian Scandals, Victorian Strategies," in *Victorian Scandals: Representations of Gender and Class*, ed. Kristine Ottesen Garrigan (Athens: Ohio University Press, 1992), 311.

9. William Cohen notices "how the privacy constitutive of the Victorian subject is structured in and through the public sphere against which it positions itself." *Sex Scandal: The Private Parts of Victorian Fiction* (Durham: Duke University Press, 1996), 110.

10. Alexander Welsh, *George Eliot and Blackmail* (Cambridge, Mass.: Harvard University Press, 1985), 73, 71.

11. *Home Is Home: A Domestic Tale* (London: William Pickering, 1851), 2.

12. Charles Dickens, *David Copperfield,* Oxford Illustrated Dickens (Oxford: Oxford University Press, 1989), ch. 3.

13. M.B.H., *Home Truths for Home Peace, or "Muddle" Defeated, a Practical Inquiry into What Chiefly Mars or Makes the Comfort of Domestic Life* (London: Effingham Wilson, 1851), 159.

14. Charles Dickens, *A Tale of Two Cities,* Oxford Illustrated Dickens (Oxford: Oxford University Press, 1991), ch. 3.

15. "A Home Picture," *Home Companion* 3 (November 1855): 77–78.

16. "Family Troubles," *Saturday Review* 18 (September 10, 1864): 329.

17. Sarah Ellis, *The Daughters of England, Their Position in Society, Character and Responsibilities* (London: Peter Jackson, 1842), 273.

18. Caroline Norton, "Curious Customs in the County of Middlesex," in *The Coquette* and Other Tales and Sketches, in Prose and Verse (London: E. Churton, 1835), 1:203.

19. Catherine Gallagher, *The Industrial Reformation of English Fiction, 1832–1867* (Chicago: University of Chicago Press, 1985); Mary Poovey, *Uneven Developments: The Ideological Work of Gender in Mid-Victorian England* (Chicago: University of Chicago Press, 1988); Catherine Hall, "The Early Formation of Victorian Domestic Ideology," in *White, Male and Middle Class: Explorations in Feminism and History* (New York: Routledge, 1992), 75–93; Leonore Davidoff and Catherine Hall, *Family Fortunes: Men and Women of the English Middle Class, 1780–1850* (Chicago: University of Chicago Press, 1987); Elizabeth Langland, *Nobody's Angels: Middle-Class Women and Domestic Ideology in Victorian Culture* (Ithaca: Cornell University Press, 1995); Mark Girouard, *The* Victorian Country House (New Haven: Yale University Press, 1979); F.M.L. Thompson, *The Rise of Respectable Society: A Social History of Britain, 1830–1900* (London: Fontana, 1988); Adrienne Munich, *Queen Victoria's Secrets* (New York: Columbia University Press, 1996); Margaret Homans, *Royal Representations: Queen* Victoria and British Culture, 1837–1876 (Chicago: University of Chicago Press, 1998); Michael Anderson, "The Social Implications of Demographic Change," *Cambridge Social History of Britain*, ed. F.M.L. Thompson (Cambridge: Cambridge University Press, 1990), 2:1–70; Mary Lyndon Shanley, *Feminism, Marriage, and the* Law in Victorian England, 1850–1895 (Princeton: Princeton University Press, 1989); Cohen, *Sex Scandal.*

20. Compare Joseph Litvak's interpretation in *Caught in the Act: Theatricality in the Nineteenth-Century English Novel* (Berkeley: University of California Press, 1992) of the the relationship between the nontheatrical dispositions of many Victorian novels and their telling moments of eruptive theatricality.

21. As will be clear in the exposition that follows, moments of public display in the nineteenth century do not fit Debord's account of late modernity as a period of total spectacular absorption: "The whole life of those societies in which modern conditions of production prevail presents itself as an immense accumulation of *spectacles.* All that once was directly lived has become mere representation." What rather characterizes the Victorian public condition is the intermittence of the spectacle, and the confidence that once the theatrics end, it will be possible to leave the arena and return to the quiet of home. Guy Debord, *The Society of the Spectacle* (New York: Zone Books, 1994), 12.

Chapter One

The Trials of Caroline Norton: Poetry, Publicity, and the Prime Minister

1. Caroline Norton, *Letters, etc. dated from June 1836 to July 1841* (London: privately printed), Third Correspondence, 4.

2. In his diary entry for May 17, 1826, Tom Moore records his glimpse of Caroline Norton on display: "I had heard that the Fancy Quadrille of the Twelve Months that

was danced at the Spitalfields ball last week was to be repeated to-night at Almack's; but the sister of one of the Months has died since then, and it is given up. The Quadrille of the Paysannes Provençale, however, was danced; some pretty girls—among them a daughter of Lord Talbot—the Miss Duncombes, Mrs. Sheridan's second daughter, strikingly like old Brinsley, yet very pretty." Quoted in Jane Gray Perkins, *The Life of Mrs. Norton* (London: John Murray, 1909), 12.

3. Caroline Norton *The Undying One; Sorrows of Rosalie; and Other Poems* (New York: C. S. Francis, 1854), 12.

4. Although she writes of episodes later in the century, Judith Walkowitz offers exemplary accounts of the eruptions of sensational celebrity. *City of Dreadful Delight: Narratives of Sexual Danger in Late-Victorian London* (Chicago: University of Chicago Press, 1992).

5. Caroline Norton, "The Favourite Flower," in *The Keepsake for MDCCCXXXVI* (London: Longman, Rees, 1836), 75–76.

6. Hartley Coleridge, "Modern English Poetesses," *Quarterly Review* 66 (1840): 376.

7. Caroline Norton, *English Laws for Women in the Nineteenth Century* (London: printed for private circulation, 1854), 26.

8. As Mary Poovey puts it, "To the extent that she insisted on articulating her own desires independent of her husband's will, and to the extent that her history exposed the nexus of economic, social and ideological factors concerning married women, Caroline Norton . . . threatened to subvert the conceptual oppositions crucial to the middle-class ideology of separate spheres." *Uneven Developments: The Ideological Work of Gender in Mid-Victorian England*: (Chicago: University of Chicago Press, 1988), 81.

9. Caroline Norton, "Fashion's Idol," in *The Keepsake for MDCCCXXXVI*, 254.

10. Caroline Norton, "The Broken Vow," in *The Coquette and Other Tales and Sketches, in Prose and Verse* (London: Edward Churton, 1835), 1:144.

11. Norton, "The Coquette," in ibid., 1:15.

12. Caroline Norton, "Count Rodolphe's Heir," in *Keepsake MDCCCXXXVI*, 98.

13. Caroline Norton, "Kate Bouverie," in *The Coquette and Other Tales*, 2:221.

14. Caroline Norton, *The Wife and Woman's Reward* (New York: Harper and Brothers, 1835): 1:12, 184; 2:15.

15. *The Letters of Caroline Norton to Lord Melbourne*, ed. James O. Hoge and Clarke Olney (Athens: Ohio State University Press, 1974), 70.

16. *Morning Chronicle*, June 25, 1836, 1.

17. *Extraordinary Trial! Norton v. Viscount Melbourne for CRIM. CON.* (London: William Marshall, 1836), 12.

18. Caroline Norton, writing under the name Pearce Stevenson, *A Plain Letter to the Lord Chancellor on the Infant Custody Bill* (London: J. Ridgway, 1839), 9–10.

19. Mary Lyndon Shanley explains the legal intricacies of Norton's predicament in close detail. *Feminism, Marriage, and the Law in Victorian England, 1850–1895* (Princeton: Princeton University Press, 1989): 22–29.

20. *Morning Chronicle*, June 25, 1836, 1.

21. Jonathan Parry, *The Rise and Fall of Liberal Government in Victorian Britain* (New Haven: Yale University Press, 1993), 27.

22. It's altogether fitting that the best that the tainted witnesses could provide were recollections of "rouging" and Fluke's memory of a vision of Norton's thigh, because

the telling event was not the exposure of carnal desire, so much as the exciting revelation of the apparatus of intimacy.

23. *Letters, etc.*, Third Correspondence, 44.

24. "Scandal," notes William Cohen, "in fact always hangs upon a name, since reputation itself about maintaining a good name, and keeping one's name out of the mouths of others is the principal goal of avoiding scandal." *Sex Scandal: The Private Parts of Victorian Fiction* (Durham: Duke University Press, 1996), 22.

25. In this respect Norton exemplifies Cohen's recognition that "while scandal teaches punitive lessons, often deliberately intended to induce conformity in its audience, its thrilling terrors always pose the danger of inciting disobedience to the norms they advertise." Ibid., 5.

26. *Letters, etc.*, Second Correspondence, 29, 35, 48.

27. Ibid., Third Correspondence, 44.

28. Ibid., 24, 36.

29. See Shanley's important analysis of Norton's struggles to reform the law. *Feminism, Marriage, and the Law*, 26–29.

30. Mixing his admiration with his male pride, Charles Sumner wrote of Norton's pamphlet that "it is one of the most remarkable things from the pen of a woman. The world here does not suspect her, but supposes that the tract is the production of some grave barrister. It is one of the best discussions on a legislative matter I have ever read." Perkins, *The Life of Mrs. Norton*, 155.

31. Dorothy E. Zaborsky has offered a narrative account and a strong coherent interpretation of the texts that accumulated around the infant custody campaign. See " 'Domestic Anarchy and the Destruction of the Family': Caroline Norton and the Custody of Infants Bill," *International Journal of Women's Studies* 7, no. 5 (November–December 1984): 397–411.

32. In her subtle chapter on the 1857 Matrimonial Causes Act, Mary Poovey narrates the events of Norton's second great reform campaign, her ardent agitation for reform in the law of divorce. See *Uneven Developments*, 62–88.

33. Caroline Norton, *Separation of Mother and Child by the Law of Custody of Infants Considered* (London: Roake and Varty, 1838), 3.

34. See Shanley, *Feminism, Marriage and the Law*, 136, 137.

35. See useful accounts of the polemic in Zaborsky, " 'Domestic Anarchy,' " and in John Killham, *Tennyson and* The Princess (London: Athlone Press, 1958). In close-grained detail Killham sketches the curving line that connects Norton's agony, the essay in the *British and Foreign Review*, and Tennyson's meditation on female education.

36. "Custody of Infants' Bill," *British and Foreign Review* 7 (July 1838): 384. Although the author of the essay was unknown, Caroline Norton naturally held the editor Kemble responsible. Surviving documents make clear that he took great pride in the verbal assault and suggest that he was actively engaged in the composition. Killham writes that "Whether he was the sole *author* is difficult to say, but it is not to be overlooked that Kemble was well known for the virulence of his expression when dealing with subjects near his heart." *Tennyson and* The Princess, 167.

37. Caroline Norton, *The Dream and Other Poems* (New York: C. S. Francis, 1845), 45.

38. Caroline Norton, *The Child of the Islands*, 2nd ed. (London: Chapman and Hall, 1846), 112.

CHAPTER TWO
THE YOUNG QUEEN AND THE PARLIAMENTARY BEDCHAMBER:
"I NEVER SAW A MAN SO FRIGHTENED"

1. *Speeches of Brougham* (Philadelphia: Lea and Blanchard, 1841), 418.

2. For several years Brougham had been an eloquent tangle in the hair of the Whigs. He and Melbourne had clashed sharply in 1837, and over the next several years, even when the conflict was not so direct or open, Brougham's insinuations were a chronic irritant. See, for instance, Lord Holland's account in *The Holland House Diaries*, ed. Abraham D. Kriegel (London: Routledge and Kegan Paul, 1977), 376.

3. Of the 445 members of the queen's household, at issue were the mistress of the robes, the duchess of Sutherland, and the eight ladies of the bedchamber, including the Marchioness Tavistock, the Marchioness Lansdowne, the countess of Charlemont, the countess of Mulgrave, Baroness Portman, Baroness Lyttleton, Lady Barham, and the countess of Durham. For an account of the structure of the queen's household, see Monica Charlot, *Victoria: The Young Queen* (Oxford: Blackwell, 1991), 111.

4. Adrienne Munich's fine study of Queen Victoria reveals the tensions between the public constructions and the self-representations of the queen, and demonstrates how Victoria consistently "blended into her age while standing apart from it." *Queen Victoria's Secrets* (New York: Columbia University Press, 1996), 13.

5. Margaret Homans astutely captures the "paradox of [the Queen's] agency" with reference to the fissure between her public function and private life in *Royal Representations: Queen Victoria and British Culture, 1837–1876* (Chicago: University of Chicago Press, 1998), xix–xxxvii.

6. For concise narratives of the political and personal events, see Elizabeth Longford, *Queen Victoria: Born to Succeed* (New York: Harper and Row, 1964), 108–14, and Charlot, *Victoria: The Young Queen*, 140–46.

7. *The Letters of Queen Victoria*, ed. Arthur Christopher Benson and Viscount Esher, 3 vols. (New York: Longmans, Green, 1907), 1:194–95.

8. Later, within the difficult terms of her marriage, Victoria will have to negotiate again the difficult pass between private and public realms. The queen anxiously appealed to her ministers and to Parliament to grant formal titles and dignities to Albert on the grounds that it was unseemly for the husband to be absorbed by his wife. As Gail Turley Houston has argued, Victoria's dilemma was to adjudicate between the conduct-book standards of married life, which were sanctified by legal dispensation, and the exceptional strains her public position imposed upon her marriage. See "Reading and Writing Victoria: The Conduct Book and the Legal Constitution of Female Sovereignty," in *Remaking Queen Victoria*, ed. Margaret Homans and Adrienne Munich (Cambridge: Cambridge University Press, 1977), 159–81, esp. 172–76.

9. *Sir Robert Peel from His Private Papers*, ed. Charles Stuart Parker (London: John Murray, 1899), 1:389.

10. Edward Bulwer Lytton, "The Late Political Events," *Blackwood's* 70 (June 1839): 135.

11. Charles C. F. Greville, *The Greville Memoirs*, vol. 1, pt. 2, ed. Henry Reeve (New York: D. Appleton, 1885), 113.

12. A seething J. W. Croker summarizes the tableau: "The *wife* of the *Lord President of the Council* was *First Lady of the Bedchamber*; one *sister* of the *Secretary for Ireland* is *Mistress* of the Robes, and another, *Lady of the Bedchamber*—as was also the *wife* of the *Lord Lieutenant of Ireland*: the *sister* of the *Secretary* at War is *Bedchamber Woman*; the *sister-in-law* of the *Home Secretary* and the *daughter* of the *Chancellor of the Exchequer* are *Maids of Honour*—not to mention the *wife, sister,* and *daughter* of Lords Durham, Spencer, and Grey, who though not now in the Cabinet, are even more prominent in the Whig party than any of the Ministers." J. W. Croker, "The Household and the Ministry," *Quarterly Review* 64 (1839): 236.

13. On the other hand, Lord Liverpool, in his own letter to Peel, resists the prevailing overstatement. Drawing on his personal connection to the queen (through his daughter), Liverpool writes that "it is but fair and just for me to say that no objection was made by Lord Melbourne in several instances to appointments, or offers of appointments, to persons of adverse politics to himself." Liverpool goes on to note that "Lady Manvers was offered a ladyship of the Bedchamber, Lady Harriet Clive was made Bedchamber Woman, and Miss Pitt and Miss Cox were made Maids of Honour." Still, whatever the scale of Whig intentions, no one tried to deny that the domestic circle of the queen had been given a sharply political character (Peel, *Papers*, 402).

14. J. W. Croker, "The New Reign," *Quarterly Review* 59 (1837): 247.

15. All through Croker's gnashing anger runs the thought that the queen will disappear so far into the recesses of privacy that she will be a toy in the hands of her advisors. It is a terror of a space removed from the public arena, a space not regulated by Parliament or the press. So Croker warns that the Whigs have promulgated "a doctrine by which the nearest interests of the Sovereign, —the hourly attendance on her person, — the daily participation of her society, —and all the influences, both personal and political, of an intimate familiarity, might be irrevocably committed to the meanest, or the most mischievous, or the most mercenary hands, freed from any visible control, and exempt form all legal or even moral responsibility" (Croker, "Household," 261).

16. In his recent study of Victoria's reign, Richard Williams provides a succinct evaluation of the odd political contours of this incident. "The Tories, traditionally the upholders of royal prerogative were effectively prevented from taking office by an assertion of that prerogative and the Whigs, one of whose salient principles was the curtailment of prerogative, found themselves kept in power by it." See *The Contentious Crown: Public Discussion of the British Monarchy in the Reign of Queen Victoria* (Hants: Ashgate Publishing, 1997), 85.

17. J. W. Croker, Letter to Lord Hertford, May 29, 1839. *The Croker Papers*, ed. Louis J. Jennings (London: John Murray, 1885), 2:344.

18. Margaret Homans has shown how Victoria inherited a "paradigm of queenship" from Queen Caroline, a "queenly identification with vulnerable femininity." "The Powers of Powerlessness: the Courtships of Elizabeth Barrett and Queen Victoria," in *Feminist Measures: Soundings in Poetry and Theory*, ed. Lynn Keller and Christanne Miller (Ann Arbor: University of Michigan Press), 246. And between Caroline and Victoria, we suggest, there stands the additional vulnerable femininity of weakening male monarchs.

19. Homans argues persuasively that "the modern British monarch was first and foremost a woman." *Royal Representations*, 2.

20. Ian Newbould provides a detailed discussion of the events leading up to and down from this last royal dismissal of a ministry. *Whiggery and Reform: 1830–41* (Basingstoke: Macmillan, 1990), 152–59.

21. As it assumed published form, Croker's essay, with its bitterness and vehement accusation—it names Melbourne guilty of "enormous lying"—suggests the conversion of measured parliamentary rhetoric into polemical discharge. The press, in effect, could say what the politicians meant.

It is worth noticing that this view of 1839 stands in significant conflict with the position that Peel offered to Croker in July 5, 1837, when he wrote that "The theory of the Constitution is, that the King has no will, except in the choice of his Ministers—that he acts by their advice, that they are responsible, &c. But this, like a thousand other theories, is at variance with the fact. The personal character of the Sovereign, in this and all other Governments, has an immense practical effect." *Croker Papers*, 314.

22. Croker had written a vastly popular pamphlet on the royal marriage, *A Letter from the King to His People* (London: W. Turner, 1820).

23. Thomas Laqueur, "The Queen Caroline Affair: Politics as Art in the Reign of George IV," *Journal of Modern History* 54 (1982): 442.

24. Leonore Davidoff and Catherine Hall, *Family Fortunes: Men and Women of the English Middle Class, 1780–1850* (Chicago: University of Chicago Press, 1987), 155. Davidoff and Hall also demonstrate that "The reaction to the whole episode marks one of the first *public* moments at which one view of marriage and of sexuality was decisively rejected in favour of another. . . . The domestic had been imprinted on the monarchical" (152).

CHAPTER THREE

SARAH STICKNEY ELLIS: THE ARDENT WOMAN AND THE ABJECT WIFE

1. *The Home Life and Letters of Mrs. Ellis*, compiled by her nieces (London: J. Nisbet, 1893), 75.

2. Sarah Stickney Ellis, *The Young Ladies' Reader* (London: Grant and Griffith, 1845), 17.

3. Leonore Davidoff and Catherine Hall, *Family Fortunes: Men and Women of the English Middle Class, 1780–1850* (Chicago: University of Chicago Press, 1987), 182.

4. Catherine Hall, "The Early Formation of Victorian Domestic Ideology," in *White, Male and Middle Class: Explorations in Feminism and History* (New York: Routledge, 1992), 75–93.

5. Davidoff and Hall, *Family Fortunes: Men and Women of the English Middle Class, 1780–1850*.

6. See both Margaret Homans, *Royal Representations: Queen Victoria and British Culture, 1837–1876* (Chicago: University of Chicago Press, 1998), and Adrienne Munich, *Queen Victoria's Secrets* (New York: Cululmbia University Press, 1996).

7. Elizabeth Langland, *Nobody's Angels: Middle–Class Women and Domestic Ideology in Victorian Culture* (Ithaca: Cornell University Press, 1995).

8. Robin Gilmour, *The Victorian Period: The Intellectual and Cultural Context of English Literature, 1830–1890* (London: Longman, 1993).

9. Richard Sennett, *The Fall of Public Man* (Cambridge: Cambridge University Press, 1977).

10. Mary Poovey, *Making a Social Body: British Cultural Formation*, 1830–1864 (Chicago: University of Chicago Press, 1995).

11. Charles Dickens, *Barnaby Rudge* (1954; reprint, Oxford: Oxford University Press, 1989), ch. 55.

12. William Ellis, *Polynesian Researches during a Residence of nearly Eight Years in the Society and Sandwich Islands*, 2nd ed. (London: Fisher, Son and Jackson, 1831–32), 1:viii.

13. Christopher Herbert has provided strong interpretation of the double motives within Ellis's writing project. "Ellis," he notes, "bears witness to his ambiguously divided motives no later than his preface. Christian missionaries are not social scientists in search of 'accurate information,' he sternly tells his readers here, but rather are dedicated to counteracting 'delusive and sanguinary idolatries,' which are responsible for 'moral debasement and attendant misery' (PR 1: v). Barely a page later, a very different note is struck. Since all the 'usages of antiquity' have now, thanks to missionary influence, been overthrown in the Society Islands, Ellis says, there is a danger that all memory of the ancient system will very soon be lost, unless 'a variety of facts, connected with the former state of the Inhabitants, can be secured' at once, while the reliable informants are still alive. Thus one motive of this book, he says, is 'to furnish, as far as possible, an authentic record of these [ancient usages], and thus preserve them from oblivion.' " *Culture and Anomie: Ethnographic Imagination in the Nineteenth Century* (Chicago: University of Chicago Press, 1991), 168.

14. William Ellis, *History of Madagascar*, vol. 1 (London: Fisher, Son, 1838), 157.

15. Despite the islanders' perversion of domestic virtue, Ellis holds to the assumption that religious conversion can quickly bring the natives at least a simulacrum of English family life. In a sketch called "The House for Hidden Prayer," he tells of one Pohueta, a native chieftain, "an idolater, and a savage warrior" who had participated in the "rites of sacrifice in the idol temple," and who "when not engaged in war, athletic sports, or fishing . . . passed his days in that luxurious indolence which is so congenial to the untutored and savage, and prevails so extensively among semi-civilized, communities of men." But after the coming of the missionaries and the Christian awakening, Pohueta and his wife Teraimano give up their "lowly leaf-thatched hut in which they had been accustomed to sleep, on the earthen floor" in favor of a "neat and spacious house, with white-washed walls, glazed windows, and boarded floors," and an "extensive garden" beyond.

Nor is this all. Pohueta has built a second house, "a little native arbour or summerhouse": the floor was "covered with a native mat; near a window stood a small rustic table, beside it an equally rustic seat, and on a shelf, in one corner, lay a copy of the Scripture, and a hymn-book, in the native languages" ("House," 224). Pohueta explains that this is "a house for hidden prayer," and within Ellis's work the image serves as a rich epitome of that instinct which understands a coming into faith and a coming into a house as nearly identical acts of conversion. In *The Missionary; or Christian's New Year's* Gift, ed. William Ellis (London: Seeley and Sons, 1833), 223.

16. Reverend James Hough, "Immolation of Hindoo Widows," in ibid., 14.

17. Reverend J. Peggs, "The Festival of Juggernaut," in ibid., 194.

18. Sarah Stickney [Ellis], "The Young Hindoo," in ibid., 151.

19. Christopher Herbert notes that Polynesia and surrounding islands "exercised from the time of their rediscovery in the last third of the eighteenth century an especially

powerful influence on the European imagination and served as a theater for elaborating key themes of European thought" (*Culture and Anomie*, 156).

20. Sarah Stickney Ellis, *Pictures of Private Life*, 1st ser., 4th ed. (London: Smith, Elder, 1834), 312.

21. William Ellis, *The Christian Keepsake and Missionary Annual* (London: Fisher, Son, 1838), n.p.

22. Sarah Ellis, "Mrs. Fletcher, late Miss Jewsbury," in ibid., 32.

23. Sarah Ellis, "Mrs. Hemans," in ibid., 66.

24. The dignified William Ellis can appear ridiculous in his wife's letters. At one point she describes how he has had "his hair cut as short as possible, and what there is he strokes down as flat as he can make it, so that the other day, when he and I were talking grandly to two gentleman about imagination, I could scarcely help laughing to see him look so entirely opposed to anything of an imaginary nature. His manners, too, I am sorry to say, are far from improving" (*Home Life*, 114).

25. Sarah Stickney [Ellis], *The Poetry of Life* (Philadelphia: Carey, Lea and Blackwood, 1835), 13.

26. Sarah Stickney Ellis, *The Women of England: Social Duties and Domestic Habits* (Philadelphia: E. L. Carey and A. Hart, 1839), 19–25.

27. Sarah Ellis, *The Daughters of England, Their Position in Society, Character and Responsibilities* (London: Peter Jackson, 1842), 11.

28. Sarah Stickney Ellis, *The Wives of England, Their Relative* Duties, Domestic Influence, and Social Obligations (London: Fisher, Son, 1843), 17.

29. Judith Newton argues convincingly that "despite their class and gender collaboration, the writers of women's manuals, in their tendency to place men at the bottom of industrial capitalist and domestic ills and in their tendency to isolate women like themselves as social heroes, challenged the power relations of their world and in the process entertained a view of nineteenth-century society which middle-class men, by and large, did not share." "Making—and Remaking—History: Another Look at 'Patriarchy,'" in *Feminist Issues in Literary Scholarship*, ed. Shari Benstock (Bloomington: Indiana University Press, 1987), 130.

30. Elizabeth Langland has offered the most instructive account of the managerial responsibilities of the middle-class housewife. As opposed to a conventional picture of the homemaker as "passive, helpless, and dependent," Langland persuasively argues that this "ideology of domesticity was itself contested by the managerial function of the bourgeois housewife." *Nobody's Angels: Middle-Class Women and Domestic Ideology in Victorian Culture* (Ithaca: Cornell University Press, 1995), 21, 16.

31. Catherine Gallagher, *The Industrial Reformation of English Fiction, 1832–1867* (Chicago: University of Chicago Press, 1985), 119.

32. Gallagher has shown the strength of social paternalism in early Victorian life. Her work makes clear that the responsible paternalist was a mobile rhetorical figure, which might be applied either to the economic relations between employers and workers or to the domestic relationship between the husband or father and his household dependents. Ibid., 115–25.

33. Consider in this immediate context Newton's suggestion "that the creation of gender systems is a more reciprocal process than we have sometimes believed." "Making—and Remaking—History," 130.

34. On the complex relations between the family and the encompassing social world, see Gallagher's account of Ellis in relation to Arthur Helps: "Family and Society: Rhetoric of Reconciliation" in *The Industrial Reformation of English Fiction 1832–1867*, 113–26.

35. See Langland's chapter on "New Women in Old Guises," in *Nobody's Angels*, 222–49.

1. Charles Dickens, *The Life and Adventures of Martin Chuzzlewit* (1951; reprint, Oxford: Oxford University Press, 1989), ch. 51.

2. As Robert Lougy notes, Dickens's articulation of the "House of Chuzzlewit" leads him to "examine . . . the nature of 'human nature' itself and those conflicts, jealousies, and desires found within the family structure." See "Repressive and Expressive Forms: The Bodies of Comedy and Desire in *Martin Chuzzlewit*," *Dickens Studies Annual* 21 (1992): 49.

3. To C. C. Felton, January 2, 1844, in Charles Dickens, *Letters*, ed. Kathleen Tillotson (Oxford: Clarendon Press, 1977), 4:2.

4. Charles Dickens, *A Christmas Carol* (1954, reprint, Oxford: Oxford University Press, 1991), 24. The longing to be physically present where the text is being read appears in this remark to J. V. Staples: "I assure you that it would have given me heartfelt satisfaction to have been in your place when you read my little *Carol* to the Poor in your neighbourhood." April 3, 1844, *Letters*, 4:95.

5. "You know, as well as I, that I think *Chuzzlewit* in a hundred points immeasurably the best of my stories. That I feel my power now, more than I ever did. That I have a greater confidence in myself than I ever had. That I *know*, if I have health, I could sustain my place in the minds of thinking men, though fifty writers started up to-morrow. But how many readers do *not* think! How many take it upon trust from knaves and idiots, that one writes too fast, or runs a thing to death! How coldly did this very book go on for months, until it forced itself up in people's opinion, without forcing itself up in sale!" Dickens to Forster, November 2, 1843, *Letters*, 3:590.

6. To Thomas Powell, March 2, 1844, *Letters*, 4:61.

7. Some of the best recent readings of Dickens have emphasized the difficulties that beset the avowals of family happiness. See for example, Margaret Lane's argument that Dickens's "domestic ideal" is consistently challenged by "his domestic back-grounds cold, arid, comfortless." "Dickens on the Hearth," in *Dickens 1970: Centenary Essays*, ed. Michael Slater (London: Chapman and Hall, 1970), 154–55. Sylvia Manning addresses the unsettled condition of the family in her essay "Family in Dickens," in *Changing Images of the Family*, ed. Virginia Tufte and Barbara Myerhoff (New Haven: Yale University Press, 1979), 141–53. Kate Flint notes that "Instead of bland domesticity, we have the capricious variety of unpredictable tempers, the simmering possibilities for rebellion, the enjoyable voyeurism of looking into families where relatives are even more unreasonable and grotesque than our own. Not only does Dickens' fiction continually provide lively concrete examples which contradict the ideal articulated so easily in the narrative voice, not only do they call the possibility of realising these ideals somewhat into question, but they make us query whether the achievement

of marital felicity is all that we, in reading, desire." *Dickens* (Brighton: Harvester Press, 1986), 116.

8. Although he does not study the Pinches, Jon Sorgal's analysis of the latent male sibling rivalry that riddles the narrative of *Martin Chuzzlewit* calls attention to the density within the sibling plot. "The Parable of the Spoons and Ladles: Sibling and Crypto–Sibling Typology in *Martin Chuzzlewit," Dickens Studies Annual* 26 (1998): 51–71. Harry Stone insists on the importance of the brother-sister relation in particular, noting that in this novel and elsewhere, "happy wifehood is a vague status which comes late in the novel as a reward for loyal sisterhood." See "The Love Pattern in Dickens' Novels," in *Dickens the Craftsman: Strategies of Presentation*, ed. Robert B. Partlow Jr. (Carbondale: Southern Illinois Press, 1970), 10.

9. Charles Dickens, *The Posthumous Papers of the Pickwick Club* (1948; reprint, Oxford: Oxford University Press, 1989), ch. 57.

10. Charles Dickens, *Oliver Twist*, Oxford Illustrated Dickens (Oxford: Oxford University Press, 1991). ch. 32.

11. James Kincaid argues that "Sim's pose of fierceness is the result of domestic tyranny," and "the fact that he serves the gentlest of masters shows us finally how insidious the repression is." *Dickens and the Rhetoric of Laughter* (London: Clarendon Press, 1971), 127. Charles Dickens, *Barnaby Rudge*, Oxford Illustrated Dickens (Oxford: Oxford University Press, 1989), ch. 4.

12. Alexander Welsh argues persuasively that "if the problem that besets [Dickens] can be called the city, his answer can be named the hearth." We add that if the city presses from the outside, sexuality is its seditious confederate residing within. *The City of Dickens* (Cambridge, Mass.: Harvard University Press, 1986), 142.

13. Peter Ackroyd, *Dickens* (New York: Harper Collins, 1990), 419. Thompson was an older widower, and Sylvia Manning treats the episode in the context of Dickens's eroticization of encounters between older men and young women. See "Dickens, January, and May," *Dickensian* 71 (May 1975): 68.

14. And yet, as Welsh emphasizes, "the main affective relationship" is not between Ruth and John but between Ruth and Tom: "If anyone, it is really Tom who has discovered the sexual attraction of his sister." *The City of Dickens*, 150.

15. In writing of the connection between Tom and Ruth, Albert J. Guerard remarks that "The idealized relationship is one in which erotic attraction exists, and all the quieter joys of marriage, but with sexual intercourse impossible." *The Triumph of the Novel: Dickens, Dostoevsky, Faulkner* (New York: Oxford University Press, 1976), 75.

16. Speaking of *Dombey and Son*, but offering an insight more widely applicable, Audrey Jaffe writes that "What circulates is not a specific family structure, but a feeling that signifies 'family': an image of family in which conflict is absent and in which members are linked by the sharing of feeling, by in fact possessing the same feelings—feelings, not surprisingly, about family. For the novel, the *idea* of family, rather than any particular family structure, signifies; and since 'family' exists within each individual, it hardly matters what form it takes externally." Audrey Jaffe, *Vanishing Points: Dickens, Narrative, and the Subject of Omniscience* (Berkeley: University of California Press, 1991), 101.

17. Michael Slater, Introduction, to *The Christmas Books* (1971; reprint Harmondsworth: Penguin, 1984), 2:9–11. See also Robert L. Patten, " 'A Surprising Transformation': Dickens and the Hearth," in *Nature and the Victorian Imagination*, ed. U. C.

Knoepflmacher and G. B. Tennyson (Berkeley: University of California Press, 1977), 163–64.

18. As Slater indicates, Forster recorded that "its sale at the outset doubled that of both its predecessors." Introduction, 11.

19. Harry Stone points out that "the cricket plays much less of an interventionary role than its earlier counterparts," and there are fewer "intrusions of a supernatural force" in this Christmas tale. *Dickens and the Invisible World: Fairy Tales, Fantasy and Novel Making* (Bloomington: Indiana University Press, 1979), 131.

20. Charles Dickens, *The Cricket on the Hearth*, in *Christmas Books*, Oxford Illustrated Dickens (1954; reprint, Oxford: Oxford University Press, 1991), 176.

21. Welsh writes of Dickens's "fondness for portraying the heroine as both woman and child." *The City of Dickens*, 154.

22. For a study of this pattern see Sylvia Manning, "Dickens, January, and May," 67–75.

23. Charles Dickens, *David Copperfield*, Oxford Illusrated Dickens (Oxford: Oxford University Press, 1989), ch. 45.

24. "His style is spectacle," says Gillian Beer in writing of Dickens and the stage, and indeed it's clear that the will to theatricality meets the desire to reveal secrets. " 'Coming Wonders': Uses of Theatre in the Victorian Novel," in *English Drama: Forms and Development*, ed. Marie Axton and Raymond Williams (Cambridge: Cambridge University Press, 1977), 179.

25. In this connection consider Joseph Litvak's reading of *Nicholas Nickebly* and his discussion of "the disjunctive theatricality" in the novel, its "discontinuous theatricalities." *Caught in the Act: Theatricality in the Nineteenth-Century English Novel* (Berkeley: University of California Press, 1992), 116.

26. Compare Robert L. Patten's judgment that Dickens "wants to generate some uneasiness about the precise character of Dot's apparent deceit." " 'A Surprising Transformation,' " 165.

27. *Letters from Charles Dickens to Angela Burdett-Coutts, 1841–1865*, ed. Edgar Johnson (London: Jonathan Cape, 1953), 99.

CHAPTER FIVE

LOVE AFTER DEATH: THE DECEASED WIFE'S SISTER BILL

1. Charles Dickens, *The Cricket on the Hearth*, *Christmas Books*, Oxford Illustrated Dickens (Oxford: Oxford University Press, 1991), 196.

2. Steven Marcus has spoken of *The Battle of Life* as a "hopelessly dismal story." *Dickens from Pickwick to Dombey* (New York: W. W. Norton, 1965), 289.

3. Charles Dickens, *The Battle of Life, Christmas Books*, Oxford Illustrated Dickens (Oxford: Oxford University Press, 1991), 244.

4. Charles Dickens, *Martin Chuzzlewit*, Oxford Illustrated Dickens (Oxford: Oxford University Press, 1989), ch. 11.

5. Nancy Fix Anderson notes that the "specific motive was to guarantee the legitimacy and inheritance of the son of the seventh Duke of Beaufort, who had married his deceased wife's half-sister." "The 'Marriage with a Deceased Wife's Sister Bill' Controversy: Incest Anxiety and the Defense of Family Purity in Victorian England," *Journal of British Studies* 21 no. 2 (1982): 67.

6. See the perspicuous historical account offered by Jack Goody. *The Development of the Family and Marriage in Europe* (Cambridge: Cambridge University Press, 1983), 168–82.

7. Goody points out that the Table of Kindred and Affinity was not made formally legal until Lyndhurst's Act of 1835. Ibid., 175.

8. Cynthia Fraser Behrman provided a useful overview of the long parliamentary struggle in "The Annual Blister: A Sidelight on Victorian Social and Parliamentary History," *Victorian Studies* 11, no. 4 (June 1968): 483–502.

9. *First Report of the Commissioners Appointed to Inquire into the State and Operation of the Law of Marriage* (London: William Clowes and Sons, 1848; reprint, Shannon: Irish University Press, 1969), v.

10. Anderson argues that fear of incest, incited by the close relations among siblings, lay behind opposition to the bill. She quotes Macaulay's remark to his sister Hannah that "husbands and wives are not so happy and cannot be so happy as brothers and sisters." "The 'Marriage with a Deceased Wife's Sister Bill,' " 70.

11. Margaret Morganroth Gullette introduces another pressure, the aging of the population and the changed understanding of the course of life. As people lived longer, the possibility of second marriages began to circulate in the imaginative life of the culture. She sees the narratives emerging during the parliamentary debates as counterparts to nineteenth-century remarriage novels. "The Puzzling Case of the Deceased Wife's Sister: Nineteenth-Century England Deals with a Second-Chance Plot," *Representations* 31 (September 1990): 142–66.

12. The definitive account of this separation is found in Leonore Davidoff and Catherine Hall, *Family Fortunes: Men and Women of the English Middle Class, 1780–1850* (Chicago: University of Chicago Press, 1987).

13. See Anthony Wohl's important essay, "Sex and the Single Room: Incest among the Victorian Working Classes," *The Victorian Family: Structure and Stresses*, ed. Anthony Wohl (London: Croom Helm, 1978), 200.

14. Mary Poovey observes that the "Law Amendment Society, founded by Lord Brougham in 1844, had the express design of accelerating the rationalization of the entire legal system." *Uneven Developments: The Ideological Work of Gender in Mid-Victorian England* (Chicago: University of Chicago Press, 1988), 54.

15. Lord Wharncliffe, Speech in the House of Lords, May 14, 1841 (London: printed for the Marriage Law Reform Association), 1.

16. Abraham Hayward, *Remarks on the Law Regarding Marriage with the Sister of a Deceased Wife* (London: W. Benning, 1845), 22.

17. Richard Sennett, *The Fall of Public Man* (Cambridge: Cambridge University Press, 1977), 20.

18. William Campbell Sleigh, *Marriage with a Deceased Wife's Sister: Speech delivered at a public meeting of the inhabitants of Edinburgh held in Brighton Street Church on Wednesday, April 10, 1850* (Edinburgh: J. Wares, 1850), v.

19. Rev. E. B. Pusey, *A Letter on the Proposed Change in the Laws Prohibiting Marriages between Those Near of Kin* (Oxford: John Henry Parker, 1842), 17. Reprinted from the *British Magazine*, November, 1840.

20. Alexander Beresford Hope, *The Report of Her Majesty's Commission on the Laws of Marriage, Relative to Marriage with a Deceased Wife's Sister, Examined in a Letter to Sir Robert Harry Inglish, Bart. M.P.* (London: James Ridgway, 1850), 26.

21. "Marriage—Mr. Wortley's Bill," *Quarterly Review* 85 (1849): 171.

22. "Mr. Stuart Wortley's Marriage Bill," *North British Review* 12 (February 1850): 534.

23. Ibid., 537.

24. Berman follows "the intricate and ever-changing relationship between the Church and Parliament" as it developed later in the century. "The Annual Blister."

25. Compare Gullette, "The Puzzling Case of the Deceased Wife's Sister," 160–63.

26. Women were by no means universally opposed to the reform. A pamphlet of 1850 by a "woman of England" acknowledges the parliamentary petitions that women have signed in opposition to Wortley. But it goes on to argue that "the Ladies who signed these petitions were not allowed much time for consideration, and that in a great majority of instances they were sadly misled." Proclaiming that "these are the days in which even women dare to think for themselves," the author points out that thousands of women are now joining the reformist side in the battle of petitions. *The Women of England and Mr. Wortley's Marriages Bill: An Address to the Peers of the Realm* (London: Seeleys, 1850), 7, 11.

27. [Earl of Albemarle], *A Parent's Appeal to the Members of Both Houses of Parliament against Lord Bury's Bill for Legalizing Marriages with a Deceased Wife's Sister* (Tunbridge Wells: Henry S. Colbran, 1858), 6.

28. Gullette neatly observes that, "Those who say that the English could not produce anything comparable to, say, *Elective Affinities* or *Madame Bovary* have not read the pamphlets in the Deceased Wife's Sister controversy. Although the generic story lacks dialogue and narrative movement, nothing I know of in continental literature touches this sinister in-law plot imagined by Victorians intent on keeping matrimony pure." "The Puzzling Case of the Deceased Wife's Sister," 156.

29. Charles Dickens, *David Copperfield*, Oxford Illustrated Dickens (Oxford: Oxford University Press, 1989), ch. 59.

30. Charles Dickens, *Letters*, ed. Kathleen Tillotson (Oxford: Clarendon Press, 1977), May 8, 1843, 3:483.

31. Marcus has offered a close biographical reading of *The Battle of Life*, in which he argues that the sisters in the story "elaborate some fantasy about Dickens's relation to his wife's two sisters, Mary and Georgina." In writing the story, "Dickens is merely manipulating certain symbols and counters that refer to his personal life and one of the deeper disturbances in it; and he is dealing with the reawakened past merely by daydreaming about it, for even though he suffered severely in writing the story, it is no more than a day-dream." *Dickens from Pickwick to Dombey*, 289, 292.

32. Writing of Dickens, Alexander Welsh comments that "The point of transmuting sweethearts and wives into sisters and daughters as well as wives, was not necessarily to substitute one for the other female relation, but ideally to enjoy both, or all three relations within the enclosure of the hearth." *The City of Dickens* (Cambridge, Mass.: Harvard University Press, 1986), 155. Of *The Battle of Life*, Marcus writes that "Dickens is trying to have it all ways; he possesses all the sisters now, and everything they do has reference to him." *Dickens from Pickwick to Dombey*, 292.

33. Margaret Oliphant, *Miss Marjoribanks* (Harmondsworth: Penguin/Virago, 1989), 199.

CHAPTER SIX
THE TRANSVESTITE, THE BLOOMER, AND THE NIGHTINGALE

1. Eve Kosofsky Sedgwick observes the "breathtaking ellipsis with which *class* conflict is omitted." "Tennyson's *Princess*: One Bride for Seven Brothers," in *Critical Essays on Alfred Lord Tennyson*, ed. Herbert F. Tucker (New York: G. K. Hall, 1993), 130.

2. John Killham, *Tennyson and The Princess: Reflections of an Age* (London: Athlone Press, 1958), 86–119.

3. Caroline Norton, *English Laws for Women in the Nineteenth Century* (London: printed for private circulation, 1854), 2.

4. Christopher Ricks has secured the tie between *The Princess* and the queen, both in the general design of events and in small verbal details (for instance, the play with the word "victor"). "Thankful and calmative" is how he sees the poem because it lets its audience appreciate the difference between their real queen and the fictive princess. Where Ida flares and rages, Victoria entered her marriage gently and procreated promptly. "The Princess and the Queen," *Victorian Poetry* 25 (Autumn–Winter 1987): 135.

5. Alfred Tennyson, *The Princess*, in *Tennyson: A Selected Edition*, ed. Christopher Ricks (Burnt Mill: Longman, 1969), prologue, lines 217–19.

6. Sedgwick's phrase is apt. The poem is indeed a "passionate and confused myth of the sexes." "Tennyson's *Princess*: One Bride for Seven Brothers," 134.

7. Referring to Michael Hill's *The Religious Order* (1973), Elaine Showalter examines the pressure to organize religious communities for women throughout the 1840s. The first Anglican sisterhood was established in 1845, and during the next three decades more than forty such institutions were formed. See "Florence Nightingale's Feminist Complaint: Women, Religion, and *Suggestions for Thought*," *Signs* 6 (Spring 1981): 402.

8. *Alfred Lord Tennyson: A Memoir*, ed. Hallam Tennyson (London: Macmillan, 1899) 1:251.

9. On the poem's use of transvestism to introduce an androgynous ideal, see Rod Edmond *Affairs of the Hearth: Victorian Poetry and Domestic Narrative* (New York: Routledge, 1988), 94, 99. See also Marjorie Stone, "Gender Subversion and Genre Inversion: *The Princess* and *Aurora Leigh*," *Victorian Poetry* 25 (Spring 1987): 101–27.

10. And, as Edmond points out, Ida's assumption of the nursing role stands as a prelude to her marriage: "The return of feeling in Ida, begun by the child and sealed by her nursing the prince back to life, brings with it a return of the 'natural' order of the family." *Affairs of the Hearth*, 117.

11. "Bloomerism," *Bentley's Miscellany* 30 (1851): 642.

12. *Lancet* (September 1854): 281.

13. Quoted in *Punch* 21 (1851): 156.

14. Charles Dickens, "Sucking Pigs," *Household Words* 4 (November 8, 1852): 145.

15. "Husbands, Wives, Fathers, Mothers," *Blackwood's Magazine* 71 (January 1852): 84.

16. *Punch* 21 (1851): 189.

17. Sarah Stickney Ellis, *Women of England: Social Duties and Domestic Habits* (Philadelphia: E. L. Carey and A. Hart, 1939), 49.

18. Mary Poovey writes that "The image of the nurse had to be freed not only from the taint of its lower-class origins, but also from the contemporary specter of those 'strong-minded women' who aspired to be doctors. The two disreputable figures who flank the Nightingale nurse—the old monthly nurse and the lady doctor—were therefore inextricably bound up with—and, in part at least, constructed alongside of—the image of the nurse that the public embraced." *Uneven Developments: The Ideological Work of Gender in Mid-Victorian England* (Chicago: University of Chicago Press, 1988), 171.

19. *Notes on Nurses*, Florence Nightingale Archive, London.

20. Florence Nightingale, *Notes on Nursing: What It Is and What It Is Not* (London: Harrison, 1860).

21. Elizabeth Langland persuasively argues that, "Once women had succeeded at domestic accountancy and management, it is logical to conclude they felt emboldened and equipped to transfer their skills to the world outside the home." Langland follows Anne Summers in portraying "the nursing profession as a *fulfillment* of bourgeois managerial ideals." *Nobody's Angels: Middle-Class Women and Domestic Ideology in Victorian Culture* (Ithaca: Cornell University Press, 1995), 49.

22. See Poovey, *Uneven Developments*, 168. We might also note that Nightingale saw herself in such sacrificial, Christlike terms. In the famous "Cassandra" portion of *Suggestions for Thought*, Nightingale prophesizes "at last there shall arise a woman, who will resume, in her own soul, all the sufferings of her race, and that woman will be The Saviour of her race." *Suggestions for Thought to the Searchers after Truth among the Artizans of England* (London: George E. Eyre and William Spottiswoode, 1860), 3:403. On this point, see also Donald R. Allen, "Florence Nightingale: Toward a Psychohistorical Interpretation," *Journal of Interdisciplinary History* 6 (Summer 1975): 33–36, and Elaine Showalter, "Florence Nightingale's Feminist Complaint: Women, Religion, and *Suggestions for Thought*," *Signs* 6 (Spring 1981): 402.

23. Florence Nightingale, *Letters from the Crimea, 1854–56*, ed. Sue M. Goldie (New York: Mandolin, 1997), 144.

24. Nightingale had rejected marriage as a possible destiny precisely because she saw the incompatibility between her public ambitions and private desires. She decides not to marry Richard Monckton Milnes because, although "I could be satisfied to spend a life with him combining our different powers in some great object," she recognizes "I could not satisfy this nature by spending a life with him in making society and arranging domestic things." Quoted in Margaret Goldsmith, *Florence Nightingale: The Woman and the Legend* (London: Hodder and Stoughton, 1937), 71.

25. Anna Jameson, *The Relative Position of Mothers and Governesses* (London: Spottiswoode and Shaw, 1848), 7.

26. Frederick Denison Maurice, *Queen's College, London: Its Objects and Methods* (London: Francis and John Rivington, 1848), 12.

27. Anna Jameson, *Sisters of Charity: Catholic and Protestant, Abroad and at Home* (London: Longmans, 1855), 10.

28. Frederick Denison Maurice, *Lectures for Ladies on Practical Subjects*, 3rd ed. (Cambridge: Macmillan, 1857), 10.

29. Martha Vicinus describes the development of the nursing vocation in the first decades after Nightingale's apotheosis. See the chapter on "Reformed Hospital Nursing: Discipline and Cleanliness," in *Independent Women: Work and Community for Single Women: 1850–1920* (London: Virago, 1985), 85–120.

30. Poovey, *Uneven Developments*, 168–70, 187–89. Vicinus has also written of the working of military imagery within the nursing project. In her account of the early history of professional nursing, Vicinus notes that "The second generation shifted the emphasis away from military metaphors to maternal ones while simultaneously strengthening the control of women over women." *Independent Women: Work and Community for Single Women: 1850–1920*, 88.

31. Harriet Martineau, "Miss Nightingale's *Notes on Nursing*," *Quarterly Review* 107 (April 1860): 403.

32. It was also, of course, the decade of the debacle of the Crimea. But the unruly military confusion of that war heightened the will toward administrative efficiency. Nightingale was only one of the many who came home from the war with zealous plans to reform the army.

CHAPTER SEVEN
ON THE PARAPETS OF PRIVACY: WALLS OF WEALTH AND DISPOSSESSION

1. Florence Nightingale, *Notes on Nursing for the Labouring Classes* (London: Harrison, 1860), 15.

2. Charles Dickens, *Our Mutual Friend*, Oxford Illustrated Dickens (Oxford: Oxford University Press, 1992), bk. 1, ch. 5.

3. Charles Dickens, *Dombey and Son*, Oxford Illustrated Dickens (Oxford: Oxford University Press, 1989), ch. 3.

4. Henry Mayhew, *London Labour and the London Poor*, vol. 1 (London: Griffin, Bohn, 1861), 43.

5. George Godwin, *London Shadows: A Glance at the Homes of the Thousands* (London: G. Routledge, 1854), 10.

6. Thomas Beames, *Rookeries of London: Past, Present, and Prospective* (London: T. Bosworth, 1852), 2–3.

7. John Burnett, *A Social History of Housing, 1815–1985*, 2nd ed. (London: Methuen, 1986), 67.

8. *Quarterly Review* 82 (December 1847): 144.

9. Quoted in *The Housing Question in London*, London County Council (1900), 2.

10. W. J. Fox, Parliamentary Debates, *Hansard*, April 8, 1851, col. 1274.

11. Martin Daunton, "Housing," in *The Cambridge Social History of Britain*, ed. F.M.L. Thompson, vol. 2 (Cambridge: Cambridge University Press, 1990), 202.

12. Quoted in J. Mordaunt Crook, "Metropolitan Improvements: John Nash and the Picturesque," in *London: World City, 1800–1840*, ed. Celina Fox (New Haven: Yale University Press), 90.

13. Charles Dickens, in Michael T. Bass, *Street Music in the Metropolis: Correspondence and Observations on the Existing Law, and Proposed Amendments* (London: John Murray, 1864), 41. On the subject of street music in London, see John Picker, "Sound Proof: Victorian Professionals Make the Case against Street Music" (University of Virginia, unpublished paper).

14. See Pamela Gilbert " 'Scarcely to Be Described': Urban Extremes as Real Spaces and Mythic Places in the 1854 Cholera Epidemic" (University of Florida, Unpublished paper).

15. See F.M.L. Thompson, "The Rise of Suburbia," In *The Victorian City: A Reader in British Urban History, 1820–1914*, ed. R. J. Morris (London: Longman, 1993), 179.

CHAPTER EIGHT
ROBERT KERR: THE GENTLEMAN'S HOUSE AND THE ONE-ROOM SOLUTION

1. George Gissing, *In the Year of the Jubilee* (London: Lawrence and Bullen, 1895), 410.

2. Charles Dickens, *Dombey and Son*, Oxford Illustrated Dickens (Oxford: Oxford University Press, 1989), ch. 44.

3. Memorandum, correspondence series, 1861, K23, King's College London Archives.

4. F.J.C. Hearnshaw, *The Centenary History of King's College London, 1828–1928* (London: George C. Harrap, 1929), 260.

5. By the end of the decade Kerr was grumbling over the terms of payment. In a letter to the secretary of the College Council he writes that he would "feel very much obliged if you would kindly take some opportunity of directing the attention of the Council to the singular inadequacy of the remuneration of my professorship—that of the Arts of Construction. Not only is the share of fees appropriated to it quite incommensurate with the importance of the subject (namely Civil Engineering and Architecture) in the curriculum of the Applied Sciences Department, but I believe it will be found that such share is so far beneath the standard allowance to other professors as to render comparison surprising." Correspondence series, 1869, K31, King's College London Archives.

6. Mark Girouard puts it well: "Whenever a discussion was held, a deputation mounted, or a correspondence embarked on he was certain to be in the foreground." *The Victorian Country House* (New Haven: Yale University Press, 1979), 263.

7. During one turbulent debate over the merits of a voluntary examination for members of the Royal Institute of British Architects, Kerr brought an unfocused discussion to an end by soaring into administrative blandness, moving that "That the Council be instructed to proceed with the preparation of a curriculum and bye-laws, and be recommended to appoint a committee to this end, and to report to a general meeting." Robert Kerr, Special General Meeting, January 14, 1861, *RIBA Proceedings*, 1st ser. (1860–61): n.p.

In an excess of institutional enthusiasm, he proposed the appointment of a "special Literary Committee," which might "secure a good supply of papers to be read during each session," but the idea seems to have been more public-spirited than others could bear, and the proposal was respectfully declined. Meeting of December 2, 1867, RIBA Council Minutes, 317, RIBA Archive, London.

8. See Girouard's discussion of the match between Kerr and the *Times*. *The Victorian Country House*, 263–64.

9. Stanley Morison, *The History of the Times*, vol. 2 (London, 1935–52), 47.

10. Robert Kerr, *The Gentleman's House*, 3rd ed. (London: John Murray, 1871), 1.

11. Mark Girouard, *Life in the English House* (New Haven: Yale University Press, 1978), and *The Victorian Country House*. In the latter book Girouard writes that the many people within the country house "were carefully stratified and subdivided; there were territories reserved for each stratum and territories common to one or more; each territory was subdivided according to the activities that went on it; this analysis of activities became more and more exact, and more and more activities were given a separate room" (28).

12. See Girouard, *Life in the English Country House*.

13. Robert Kerr, *A Small Country House*, 2nd ed. (London: John Murray, 1874), 55.

14. The "metonymic association of odor and the lower classes" is well discussed in Elizabeth Langland, *Nobody's Angels: Middle-Class Women and Domestic Ideology in Victorian Culture*. (Ithaca: Cornell University Press, 1995).

15. "London Life among The Million: Tenemented Dwellings of the Better Class," *Builder* 22 (January 2, 1864): 13.

16. Robert Kerr, paper delivered on December 3, 1866. *RIBA Proceedings* (1866–67): 37–47.

17. John Nelson Tarn has offered a valuable chronicle of the philanthropic housing movement in *Five Per Cent Philanthropy: An Account of Housing in Urban Areas between 1840 and 1914* (Cambridge: Cambridge University Press, 1973).

18. Although Kerr had no firm statistical basis for his judgment, one member of his audience would eventually make a detailed empirical study of philanthropic housing. Nearly a decade later, Charles Gatliff, secretary of the Metropolitan Association, presented to the Statistical Society an account of the number of houses constructed by the agencies working in London and the number of people accommodated in those buildings. The accompanying chart (see p. 240) is Gatliff's table as published in his pamphlet *On Improved Dwellings and Their Beneficial Effect on Health and Morals* (London: Edward Stanford, 1875); originally published in the *Journal of the Statistical Society*, March 1875.

19. Tarn notes that the "Exhibition cottages established a standard of accommodation which Roberts and the Society [for Improving the Conditions of the Labouring Classes] thought should constitute a norm." *Five Per Cent Philanthropy*, 21.

20. See ibid.

21. "Discussion of Professor Kerr's Paper—'On the Problem of Providing Dwellings for the Poor,' " *RIBA Proceedings* (1866–67): 48.

22. See Daunton's discussion of housing and "social definition." Daunton remarks that a "society based on achievement required strict rules to legitimate social relationships," rules that can determine the provision of housing. "Housing," in *The Cambridge Social History of Britain*, ed. F.M.L. Thompson, vol. 2 (Cambridge: Cambridge University Press, 1990), 212–13.

23. Anthony Wohl has shown how the figure of the crowded single room belonged to a strain of sexual dread: the terror of incest among the working classes. Wohl notes that "Incest represented in its most debased form the horror of the realities of family life in overcrowded rooms." "Sex and the Single Room: Incest among the Victorian Working Classes," in *The Victorian Family: Structure and Stresses*, ed. Anthony S. Wohl (London: Croom Helm, 1978), 211.

The Provision of Philanthropic Housing, 1830–1875, Charles Gatliff*

	Families Accommodated	Individuals	Capital Expended
Metropolitan Association for Improving the Dwellings of the Industrious Classes	1,060	5,206	189,028
Society for Improving the Conditions of the Labouring Classes	341	1,657	36,407
St. George's Hanover Square, Parochial Association for Improving the Dwellings of the Industrious Classes	67	240	6,000
Marylebone Association for Improving the Dwellings of the Industrious Classes	572	2,860	28,203
Strand Buildings Company	38	200	5,000
Central Dwellings Improvement Company	180	800	10,823
London Labourer's Dwellings Society	383	1,915	50,294
Trustees for Peabody's Gift to the London Poor	954	3,815	380,284
Improved Industrial Dwellings Company	1,452	7,260	274,773
Baroness Burdett Coutts	189	694	24,000
C. J. Freake, Esq.	108	700	10,000
William Gibbs, Esq.	175	660	36,500
Corporation of the City of London	180	849	54,000
Countess of Ducie, J. Ruskin, Esq., and others	312	1,560	17,467
Right Hon. Russell Gurney, MP	10	44	2,400
W. E. Hilliard, Esq.	108	540	—
G. Newson, Esq.	93	465	—
Mr. M. Allen	126	630	18,860
Sir Sydney Waterlow, Bart., MP	95	475	12,500
W. H. Hall, Esq.	35	140	5,689
Miss Harrison	61	230	9,085
Miss J. Ogle	100	500	10,000
G. Cutt, Esq.	80	400	—
J. H. Bedford, Golden Lane, Old Street	—	—	—
Brewers' Company	24	120	6,495
Duchy of Cornwall	50	250	11,451
Jewish and East London Model Lodging House Associations	29	145	7,800
C. Gatliff, Esq.	16	80	2,300
Total	6,838	32,435	1,209,359

*(See note 18, p. 239.)

24. In fact, over the next several decades Kerr's single-room vision was in large measure achieved—not through any deliberate will or conscious public policy, merely through the working of grinding poverty. Wohl, for instance, notes that a government survey of 1887 showed that "fifty percent of all dock-workers and forty-six percent of all costermongers were living with their families in only one room." "Sex and the Single Room," 204.

25. Henry Roberts, letter received January 30, 1867, Royal Institute of British Architects Archive, London.

26. Henry Roberts, *The Dwellings of the Labouring Classes* (London: Society for Improving the Condition of the Labouring Classes, 1850), a paper first read to the Royal Institute of British Architects, January 21, 1850.

27. Gareth Stedman Jones, *Outcast London: A Study in the Relationships between the Classes in Victorian Society* (Oxford: Clarendon Press, 1971).

CHAPTER NINE

THE EMPIRE OF DIVORCE: SINGLE WOMEN, THE BILL OF 1857, AND REVOLT IN INDIA

1. Dinah Mulock Craik, *A Woman's Thoughts about Women* (London: Hurst and Blackett, 1858), 331.

2. J. Hain Friswell, *The Gentle Life: Essays in Aid of the Formation of Character*, 2 vols. (London: Sampson Low, Son, and Marston, 1864), 1:129.

3. *The Letters of Queen Victoria*, ed. Arthur Christopher Benson and Viscount Escher, 3 vols. (New York: Longmans, Green, 1907), 3:557, 556.

4. "Proposed National Memorial to His Royal Highness the Prince Consort," Minutes of a Public Meeting Held at Mansion House, January 14, 1862, British Library MS. BM10805 C22, London.

5. Margaret Oliphant, "The Domestic Life of the Queen," in *The Life and Times of Queen Victoria*, ed. Robert Wilson, 2 vols. (London: Cassell, 1900), 1:112.

6. David Cannadine, "The Context, Performance and Meaning of Ritual: The British Monarchy and the 'Invention of Tradition,' c. 1820–1977," in *The Invention of Tradition*, ed. Eric Hobsbawm and Terence Ranger (Cambridge: Cambridge University Press, 1983), 119.

7. Dinah Mulock Craik, *Mistress and Maid*, 2 vols. (London: Hurst and Blackett, 1863), 1:104–5.

8. Dora Greenwell, "Our Single Women," *North British Review* 36 (February 1862): 73.

9. Anthony Trollope, *Can You Forgive Her?* (London: J. M. Dent, 1994), 604.

10. Michael Anderson, "The Social Position of Spinsters in Mid-Victorian Britain," *Journal of Family History* 9, no. 4 (Winter 1984): 387. See also Anderson's detailed study of the statistical record in "The Social Implications of Demographic Change," in *Cambridge Social History of Britain*, ed. F.M.L. Thompson (Cambridge: Cambridge University Press, 1990), 2:1–70.

11. The essay "Why Are Women Redundant?" by W. R. Greg has been taken as the locus classicus of the debate over female superfluity. No doubt Greg's opinions, and his rhetoric, deserve to be acknowledged, but it is important to recognize that the singleness of women had been made a question from the time of the 1851 census. Greg,

in effect, is consolidating the anxious thought of a decade. *National Review* 14 (April 1862): 434–60.

12. Throughout our next phase of interpretation, we rely on the foundational work of Mary Poovey, whose discussion of divorce in *Uneven Developments: The Ideological Work of Gender in Mid-Victorian England* (Chicago: University of Chicago Press, 1988) sets the terms for all further analysis; the carefully documented reconstructions of Mary Lyndon Shanley in *Feminism, Marriage and the Law in Victorian England, 1850–1895* (Princeton: Princeton University Press, 1989); and the richly detailed history of Lawrence Stone. See *Road to Divorce: England 1530–1987* (Oxford: Clarendon Press, 1990) and *Broken Lives: Separation and Divorce in England, 1660–1857* (Oxford: Oxford University Press, 1993).

13. Poovey remarks that "The one anomaly that legislators were by and large unwilling to rectify or even consider . . . was the sexual double standard." *Uneven Developments*, 60.

14. See Thaïs E. Morgan's discussion of the disparity between the number of divorce suits filed and the sensational treatment in the press. "Afterword: Victorian Scandals, Victorian Strategies," in *Victorian Scandals: Representations of Gender and Class*, ed. Kristine Ottesen Garrigan (Athens: Ohio University Press, 1992), 293–94.

15. Anthony Trollope, *The Small House at Allington* (1980; reprint, Oxford: Oxford University Press, 1985), 158, 160.

16. William Gladstone, "The Bill for Divorce," *Quarterly Review* 102, no. 203 (July 1857): 284.

17. Consider Poovey's remark that "in acknowledging the fact of marital unhappiness [the debates] inevitably exposed the limitations of the domestic ideal." *Uneven Developments*, 52.

18. Lord John Manners was not alone in complaining of the "hurried consideration bestowed upon the bill" and blaming the government, which "called upon the House to sit, at the end of August, from noon to midnight to consider a question of such vast importance" (*Hansard*, August 17, 1857, col. 1720).

19. Rev. E. B. Pusey, *A Letter on the Proposed Change in the Laws Prohibiting Marriages between Those Near of Kin* (Oxford: John Henry Parker, 1842), 17 (reprinted from the *British Magazine*, November 1840). For the historical reconstruction of post-1857 divorce patterns, see O. R. McGregor, *Divorce in England* (London: Heinemann, 1957), and the revisionary analysis of Gail L. Savage, " 'Intended Only for the Husband': Gender, Class, and the Provision for Divorce in England, 1858–1868," in Garrigan, *Victorian Scandals: Representations of Gender and Class*, 11–42.

20. Consider here Morgan's suggestion that "Rather than a cycle of revolt and repression, the itinerary of scandal seems to move from protest, to dissemination, and then to assimilation of dissenting opinions and deviant behaviors, making these, in turn, the next 'norm' to be broken." "Afterword," 311.

21. "An Old Bachelor," *Divorce: A Sketch* (London: A. W. Bennett, 1859).

22. Thus as the debate reached its end, Mr. Spooner commented that, "With regard to the Bill itself, he must once for all declare that it completely failed in one great act of justice, namely, in not giving the injured and innocent wife as full, easy and complete a remedy as was offered to the injured and innocent husband." *Hansard*, August 25, 1857, col. 2087.

23. "Husbands, Wives, Fathers, Mothers," *Blackwood's Magazine* 71 (January 1852): 74.

24. "Widow-Burning—Major Ludlow," *Quarterly Review* 89 (September 1851): 263, 262.

25. Poovey, *Uneven Developments*, 62–70.

26. Joseph Noel Paton, *In Memoriam*, private collection.

27. Charles Dickens to Angela Burdett-Coutts, *The Letters of Charles Dickens*, vol. 8, ed. Graham Storey and Kathleen Tillotson (Oxford: Clarendon Press, 1995), 459.

28. Charles Dickens and Wilkie Collins, "The Perils of Certain English Prisoners," *Household Words*, December 7, 1857 (extra Christmas issue), 10.

29. R. M. Coopland, *A Lady's Escape from Gwalior and Life in the Fort of Agra during the Mutinies of 1857* (London: Smith, Elder, 1959).

CHAPTER TEN
BIGAMY AND MODERNITY: THE CASE OF MARY ELIZABETH BRADDON

1. Although most of the examples sort into the class of ephemeral productions contrived by eager authors and canny publishers, it is worth remembering that a novel that escapes her notice, the self-consciously magisterial *Romola*, also belongs to the same strange efflorescence. Jeanne Fahnestock, "Bigamy: The Rise and Fall of a Convention," *Nineteenth-Century Fiction* 36 (June 1981): 47–71.

2. Geraldine Jewsbury, *Athenaeum* (December 3, 1864): 743–44, as quoted in Fahnestock, "Bigamy," 57.

3. Mary E. Braddon, *Lady Audley's Secret* (1987; reprint, Oxford: Oxford University Press, 1992), 85.

4. See Fahnestock, "Bigamy," 66; and David Skilton, introduction to *Lady Audley's Secret*.

5. Mary E. Braddon, *Aurora Floyd* (New York: Lovell, Coryell, 1885), 350.

6. Mrs. Henry Wood, *East Lynne* (Phoenix Mill: Alan Sutton, 1993), 675.

7. Two prominent critiques were by Margaret Oliphant, "Sensation Novels," *Blackwood's* 91 (1862): 464–84; and H. L. Mansel, "Sensation Novels," *Quarterly Review* 133 (1863): 481–514.

8. See D. A. Miller's recovery of the *body* of sensationalism, *The Novel and the Police* (Berkeley: University of California Press, 1988), 146–91.

9. Winifred Hughes argues that the sensation novel exposes the inherent corruption lurking within the feminine ideal; thus it is important to see the extent to which Lady Audley *exemplifies* (rather than merely impersonates) the Victorian ideal. The mask merges with the fact. *The Maniac in the Cellar: Sensation Novels of the 1860s* (Princeton: Princeton University Press, 1980), 124. Anthea Trodd claims that Lady Audley "is an ambitious careerist who has adopted the most promising career pattern available to her, that of the angel of the house." *Domestic Crime in the Victorian Novel* (London: Macmillan, 1989), 116.

10. Strong studies that discuss performative aspects of this fiction include Martha Vicinus, " 'Helpless and Unfriended': Nineteenth-Century Domestic Melodrama," *New Literary History* 13 (Autumn 1981): 127–43; Joseph Litvak, *Caught in the Act: Theatricality in the Nineteenth-Century English Novel* (Berkeley: University of California Press, 1992), 141–45; Lyn Pykett, *The "Improper" Feminine: The Women's Sensation Novel and The New Woman Writing* (London: Routledge, 1992), 93; Elizabeth Tilley, "Gender and Role-Playing in *Lady Audley's Secret*," in *Exhibited by Candle-*

light: *Sources and Developments in the Gothic Tradition*, ed. Valeria Tinkler-Villani and Peter Davidson (Amsterdam: Rodopi, 1995), 197–204.

11. Compare Ann Cvetkovich's observation that, "Rather than relegating terror to the exotic fringes of society, the sensation novel exploits the disparity between apparently stable families and marriages and the horrifying secrets and extremes of passion that disrupt them." *Mixed Feelings: Feminism, Mass Culture, and Victorian Sensationalism* (New Brunswick: Rutgers University Press, 1992), 45.

12. See Pykett, *The "Improper" Feminine*, 97–102. Pamela Gilbert demonstrates how in sensation fictions a female audience was seduced into identification with the male position through the impersonations of the female protagonist. *Disease, Desire, and the Body in Victorian Women's Popular Novels* (Cambridge: Cambridge University Press, 1997), 77. Focusing on a rather different aspect of the "cultural moment," Jonathan Loesberg describes the instability of class identity and the possibilities for reform as provocations that sensation literature exploits. See "The Ideology of Narrative Form in Sensation Fiction," *Representations* 13 (Winter 1986): 115–38. In "What Is 'Sensational' about the 'Sensation Novel'?," *Nineteenth-Century Fiction* 37 (1982): 1–28, Patrick Brantlinger reminds us of the *continuity* between sensation and other forms of fiction, and points to the prominence of the detective and the newly energized aura of mystery. In this regard, see also John Kucich, *The Power of Lies: Transgression in Victorian Fiction* (Ithaca: Cornell University Press, 1994), 75–118.

13. Natalie Schroeder has shown how Braddon allows her characters to exploit female sexuality in order to usurp masculine power. See "Feminine Sensationalism, Eroticism, and Self-Assertion: Mary Elizabeth Braddon and Ouida," *Tulsa Studies in Women's Literature* 7(1988): 87–103. Litvak writes that "She represents not femaleness itself, but rather the confusion of stereotypically female traits . . . with a certain phallic aggressivity." *Caught in the Act*, 142.

14. Thomas Boyle emphasizes the contemporaneity of the plot in his reading of Lady Audley. See *Black Swine in the Sewers of Hampstead: Beneath the Surface of Victorian Sensationalism* (New York: Viking, 1989), 145–58.

15. On this point, see Elaine Showalter's fine essay, "Family Secrets and Domestic Subversion: Rebellion in the Novels of the 1860s," in *The Victorian Family: Structure and Stresses*, ed. Anthony S. Wohl (London: Croom Helm, 1978), 101–16.

16. William Cohen, *Sex Scandal: The Private Parts of Victorian Fiction* (Durham: Duke University Press, 1996), 6.

17. Among others who have discussed the relevance of journalistic spectacle to sensation fiction, see Fahnestock, "Bigamy"; Jenny Bourne Taylor, *In the Secret Theatre of Home: Wilkie Collins, Sensation Narrative and Nineteenth Century Psychology* (London: Routledge, 1988); Anthea Trodd, *Domestic Crime and the Victorian Novel*; and Patrick Brantlinger, *The Reading Lesson: The Threat of Mass Literacy in Nineteenth-Century British Fiction* (Bloomington: Indiana University Press, 1998), 147–50. Nicholas Rance observes that "A sensation novelist might have maintained that stories in the morning newspaper had the advantage over Gothic sensationalism in being more sensational as well as being true." *Wilkie Collins and Other Sensation Novelists: Walking the Moral Hospital* (Cranbury, N.J.: Fairleigh Dickenson University Press, 1991), 123.

18. Litvak argues that "The novel in fact demonizes a theatricality conceived as essentially female—embodying it in the villainous Lady Audley—and idealizes a narrative conceived as essentially male—associating it with the heroic efforts of the detective-like Robert Audley." *Caught in the Act*, 141. Compare Cvetkovich's view that even as Lady Audley may "satisfy female readers' fantasies of rebellion and affective expression," she is "also the product of a masculine fantasy about women's hidden powers." *Mixed Feelings*, 48.

19. Ann Cvetkovich discusses professionalism and the novel in *Mixed Feelings*, 56–60; see also Kucich, *The Power of Lies*: 106–8.

20. Elaine Showalter, "Desperate Remedies: Sensation Novels of the 1860s," *Victorian Newsletter*, no. 49 (Spring 1976): 4.

21. Notice how slowly madness matures into a diagnostic category. Through the early stages of the novel, it had been little more than casual folk wisdom. When in the guise of the poor governess Lucy Graham, the soon to be Lady Audley hesitates before accepting Sir Michael, we read that her employers would have considered it "something more than madness" for her to refuse. Later, the narrator muses conspicuously on the provocations of dreary daily life, with its "unflinching regularity," which "knows no stoppage or cessation": "Who has not felt, in the first madness of sorrow, an unreasoning rage against the mute propriety of chairs and tables, . . . the unbending obstinacy of the outward apparatus of existence?" There follows the ominous surmise: "Madhouses are large and only too numerous; yet surely it is strange they are not larger, when we think of how many helpless wretches must beat their brains against this hopeless persistency of the orderly outward world, as compared with the storm and tempest, the riot and confusion within" (*Lady Audley*, 205). Finally, when Dr. Mosgrave makes his ponderously serious appearance at Audley Court, his first reaction to Robert's story is to doubt that Lady Audley is mad, and this simply because "there is no evidence of madness in anything that she has done. She ran away from home, because her home was not a pleasant one, and she left it in the hope of finding a better. There is no madness in that. She committed the crime of bigamy, because by that crime she obtained fortune and position. There is no madness there" (*Lady Audley*, 377). Only when Robert yields to the demand to tell everything, including his suspicion of Lady Audley's murder of her first husband, and when the doctor examines the culprit for himself does he at last settle on the fateful term: "There is latent insanity!" (*Lady Audley*, 379). The perpetual slippage in the concept of madness, its use as a casual descriptive epithet or as a general figure for human frustration, indicates what an unsharpened tool it has been. Yet at a moment of narrative crisis that corresponds closely to a social instability—What is one to do with the free woman unrestrained by the weight of convention?—madness is refined for its punitive labor. Having marked Lady Audley as insane, the doctor sets in motion the brutal professional sanction that leads to her confinement in a madhouse on the Continent.

22. In this connection consider Alexander Welsh's elegant formulation, stimulated by his reading of *Lady Audley's Secret*: "The process of covering and uncovering, uncovering and covering, stands in the imagination for crime and punishment." Welsh situates Braddon's sensationalism within the culture of blackmail produced by a complex information revolution. *George Eliot and Blackmail* (Cambridge, Mass.: Harvard University Press, 1985), 24.

23. Margaret Oliphant, *Salem Chapel* (London: Virago, 1986), 6.

EPILOGUE
BETWEEN MANUAL AND SPECTACLE

1. James Fitzjames Stephen, "Luxury," *Cornhill* 2 (1860): 350.

2. Charles Dickens, *Our Mutual Friend*, Oxford Illustrated Dickens (Oxford: Oxford University Press, 1992), bk. 1, ch. 11.

3. Charles Dickens, *Barnaby Rudge*, Oxford Illustrated Dickens (Oxford: Oxford University Press, 1989), ch. 55.

INDEX